TACKLING TORTURE

Prevention in Practice

Malcolm D. Evans

BRISTOL
UNIVERSITY
PRESS

First published in Great Britain in 2023 by

Bristol University Press
University of Bristol
1-9 Old Park Hill
Bristol
BS2 8BB
UK
t: +44 (0)117 374 6645
e: bup-info@bristol.ac.uk

Details of international sales and distribution partners are available at bristoluniversitypress.co.uk

© Bristol University Press 2023

British Library Cataloguing in Publication Data
A catalogue record for this book is available from the British Library

ISBN 978-1-5292-2568-6 hardcover
ISBN 978-1-5292-2569-3 paperback
ISBN 978-1-5292-2570-9 ePub
ISBN 978-1-5292-2571-6 ePdf

Cover design: Liam Roberts
Front cover image: Malcolm D. Evans

Contents

Acknowledgements

At the end of every UN Subcommittee on Prevention of Torture session, I used to apologise to all those whose vital contributions to our work I had failed to recognise, and once I again resort to that strategy. It would take another volume to list all those to whom I wish to extend my most grateful thanks for all that they have done that permits me to write this book – and there would still be omissions.

At the risk of offending so many, a few nevertheless demand mention, and they will know why: Silvia Casale, Claudine Haenni, Patrice Gillibert, Jens Modvig, Rod Morgan, Joao Nataf.

And also to Bristol University Press, who believed that this book would be written even when I did not.

To Debs Harrison, whose genius produced the sculpture reproduced on the front cover which inspired me to keep on trying to write this book when I could not.

To my cousin Hilary White, who taught me how to write a book like this.

To Nick and Dawn, for that fishing weekend.

And to Alison, Olivia, Isobel and Amelia, obviously: as this book is about what I was doing when I should have been doing more – much more – with you all at home.

Introduction

This book is about the prohibition and the prevention of torture. In 1948, Article 5 of the Universal Declaration of Human Rights proclaimed that '[n]o one shall be subjected to torture or to cruel, inhuman or degrading treatment or punishment'.[1] This is repeated word for word in Article 7 of the International Covenant on Civil and Political Rights, which entered into force in 1976 and legally binds 173 of the countries of the world.[2] The prohibition on torture is repeated or reflected in identical or similar terms in each of the three great legally binding regional human rights conventions covering Europe,[3] the Americas[4] and Africa.[5] Torture is also prohibited by the 2012 ASEAN Human Rights Declaration[6] and the 2020 Cairo Declaration of the Organization of Islamic Cooperation on Human Rights.[7]

In some way or another, virtually every country has acknowledged that torture is to be forbidden. Indeed, it is now accepted that *all* states, irrespective of whether they have formally agreed to the prohibition or not, are bound by international law to refrain from torture. In 2012 the International Court of Justice in The Hague affirmed that 'the prohibition of torture is part of customary international law, and it has become a peremptory norm (*jus cogens*)'.[8] This means that it is a rule from which no derogation is permitted and that it takes priority over any other conflicting legal obligation.

In times of war, torture is prohibited by the Geneva Conventions, and it is a war crime and a crime against humanity falling within the jurisdiction of the International Criminal Court (Cryer, 2020, pp 297–311). All states which are bound by the 1984 UN Convention against Torture are required to make torture a crime under their domestic law.[9] For the avoidance of doubt, Article 2(2) of the UN Convention also confirms that '[n]o exceptional circumstances whatsoever, whether a state of war or a threat of war, internal political instability or any other public emergency, may be invoked as a justification for torture'.

It is not necessary to list the very many other treaties, declarations, court judgments and much else besides which confirm that torture is absolutely prohibited as a matter of international law in all countries, always. Indeed, there are few practices – if any – which are so comprehensively outlawed, and with there being no space whatsoever for justifications, exceptions or excuses. As Sir Nigel Rodley, the former UN Special Rapporteur on Torture, once put it, when it comes to the prohibition of torture, 'Absolute means Absolute' (Rodley, 2006). Except that it is not. It really all depends on what one means by a prohibition. As a matter of law, the prohibition of torture is indeed absolute. In practice, however, in many countries there is barely a prohibition at all, and torture and ill-treatment continue to be meted out, largely with impunity, daily. This is no great secret: it is well known, well documented and for the most part largely ignored, if sometimes lamented.

The first international human rights instruments addressed torture and ill-treatment in the language of 'freedom from' – that no-one should be subjected to torture, cruel, inhuman or degrading treatment. However, this 'freedom from' was not initially seen as being a 'right' of the individual as such; rather – and in accordance with the dominant view of international law being the 'law between states' – it was seen as something which *states* should ensure was the case as regards those who were subject to their jurisdiction and control. As a result, 'freedom from' torture subtly changes into a 'prohibition' on states torturing people, as in the human rights prohibitions referred to earlier. This shifts the focus away from *ensuring* that people are not tortured and towards determining whether the state has breached its obligations not to torture, or whether it responds appropriately to allegations that it has. To use the more formal contemporary language, the question morphs into whether the state is in breach of its 'substantive' or 'procedural' obligations that flow from the prohibition of the right in question. All this is very important and in its own way helps prevent torture and ill-treatment from occurring. But is this enough to ensure that 'no-one' is tortured?

In his seminal work that helped lay the foundations of the modern era of international human rights protection, Sir Hersch Lauterpacht (Lauterpacht, 2013 [1945], p 47) observed that

> we can trace two strains in modern international law. One has been concerned with the relations between States as such: with the law of treaties, with the jurisdictional immunities of diplomatic representatives and of foreign states generally, with acquisition of territory, and with the rules governing the conduct of war. The other has used international law to promote and protect, through international co-operation and institutions, the interests and the welfare of the individual.

This distinguishes between the role that international law plays in setting out the law between states, and the role that international law can play in setting up systems and structures through which states can work to promote and protect 'the interests and the welfare of individuals'. In some ways, the history of human rights protection through the mechanisms of international law has been the history of how these two strains of thought interact with each other: how states have sought to promote and protect themselves as they seek to promote and protect the interests and welfare of individuals.

Lauterpacht also observed that 'no system of protection of the rights of man can be satisfactory if the international machinery is called upon to act only after a violation of the law has occurred or is about to occur' (Lauterpacht, 2013 [1945], p 173). This is a truth which has long been known – that prevention is better than cure. At the very outset of the 'modern' human rights era, then, Lauterpacht argued that international mechanisms are needed which not only address violations but seek to ensure that violations do not occur in the first place. This hardly sounds radical – yet in practice it has proven difficult and controversial.

Sir Nigel Rodley also once said that 'in the case of torture prevention is not better than cure. Prevention is protection by another name' (Rodley, 2009, p 29). By this, I think he meant that the cure for torture lay in protection, and prevention was a form of protection. But while it is certainly true that prevention and protection should not be seen as alternatives or as being at odds with each other, the tools of human rights protection developed by the international community, and particularly those of the United Nations, are generally quite weak (see the various chapters in Mégret and Alston, 2020). As a result, it is unsurprising that these systems of 'international protection' are by themselves completely insufficient to prevent torture from occurring, and it is perfectly obvious that they have not done so. Torture appears to be as widespread today as it ever has been, as the reports now surfacing from the war in Ukraine make all too obvious. The threat of personal accountability or state responsibility may deter some torturers and some torturing states some of the time, but by themselves they will never achieve all that might be achieved to reduce the prevalence of torture. Nevertheless, while we may never live in a world in which *no-one* is ever subjected to torture, we *can* live in a world in which far fewer people are.

In November 2009, I became a member of the United Nations Subcommittee for Prevention of Torture (known as the SPT), and from February 2011 until December 2020, when my time on the SPT came to an end, I was its Chair. The SPT was established in 2006 following the coming into force of the 'Optional Protocol to the United Nations Convention against Torture' (known as the OPCAT).[10] The OPCAT – yet another international treaty concerning torture – currently binds over 90 states – approaching half of all the countries in the world. This meant that I was at the helm of arguably the most powerful legal tool that has yet been established by the international community to try to 'tackle torture' at the global level. But was it? Did it? Could it?

The purposes of this book are twofold. The first is to give a frank account of what the SPT has been able to achieve over the first 15 years or so of its existence. This also involves being honest about what the SPT has *not* been able to achieve too, and – more importantly – the reasons for this. The second purpose, and perhaps the more significant, is to seek to expose some of the myths – some of which are more accurately described as lies – which permit torture to continue to flourish, despite the plethora of prohibitions.

The primary focus of the first part of this book is the OPCAT and the SPT, why they came about, and how they seek to prevent torture and ill-treatment. To do this, though, it is necessary first to consider what is meant by 'torture'. Although the word is frequently used, for good or ill it has a very specific meaning in international law, and this is not always generally understood. While not pretending to be an exhaustive examination of what is a difficult and highly contested question (Başoğlu, 2017), the first chapter sets out the contours of the definition of torture in international law, and its relationship to 'inhuman and degrading treatment or punishment'. This allows us to have a better understanding of what torture, legally speaking, really is – and therefore what it is that the OPCAT and the SPT are intended to prevent.

Much of the orthodoxy concerning the definition and understanding of 'what is torture' will be challenged at various points throughout this book. Chapter 2 does so by looking in more detail at the various 'thresholds' that have been used to differentiate between torture, between inhuman and between degrading treatment, illustrating that while this might at times be necessary, this is both difficult, invidious and in some ways an inherently flawed exercise. Moreover, this reliance on 'thresholds' does not contribute as much as one might expect to the very thing which the prohibition is intended to achieve, which is that no-one should be subjected to torture or inhuman or degrading treatment. Indeed, engaging in these fine-grained, ever-shifting and ultimately inconclusive debates shifts attention away from the need to prevent violations from occurring and runs the risk of downplaying the significance of ill-treatment which does not cross the higher thresholds of seriousness, despite them all being absolutely prohibited. For all these reasons, it is important to seek to prevent prohibited ill-treatment from occurring, rather than overly focusing on how precisely to categorise ill-treatment that already has occurred.

It is important to recognise that it is not a matter of 'either/or'. From the very beginning of what might be called the 'torture prevention movement' in the international legal sphere, the idea has been to 'complement' the prohibition of torture through 'means of a preventive nature' rather than to supplant it. However, this has always been a touch disingenuous: there was, and remains, a need to look beyond the more traditional tools used by the international community to 'police' the prohibition on torture, and in many ways the focus on 'prevention' is exactly that. It is less of a 'complement' to the tools of prohibition as offering an alternative means of bringing it about. This may seem a distinction without difference – but in practice it is important. Paradoxically, at least in the international sphere, 'prevention' still tends to be seen as a secondary means of achieving 'prevention', the primary means being the effects of an international accountability paradigm which, for most cases most of the time, scarcely exists and rarely works.

Against this background, Chapters 3 and 4 present the OPCAT, how it came into being and what is so different about its work. They show how the OPCAT and the SPT are meant to 'fit' alongside other means of tackling torture established by the international community. They also highlight the many hesitations and concerns felt by states in setting up such a system, and the constraints which were placed on it as a result. Although these were accepted as the 'necessary price to pay' to get the system off the ground, one of the reasons that system has been unable to properly 'fly' has been the extent to which its wings were clipped from the outset. To say it was designed to fail would be quite wrong – and, indeed, it has not failed. But it is not so wide of the mark to say that it was designed to appear to be more effective than it was ever thought likely to be. Chapter 4 looks in some detail at the SPT's mandate and begins the process of exploring how through its work its mandate has been developed and come to be understood using practical examples and experiences, an approach which is then used throughout the rest of the book.

Undertaking visits to places of detention sits at the heart of the OPCAT, and Chapter 5 looks at how the SPT has interpreted and applied its visiting mandate in practice, highlighting the practical problems that it faces when seeking to do so. Some problems, such as the hostility of states from time to time, are to be expected. Others may be less so. Overall, being a part of the UN human rights system brings with it many benefits, but it is also a source of many constraints that hamper its practical effectiveness – though arguably no more than is true for most independent human rights mechanisms working under the aegis of what is, at the end of the day, a state-centric organisation in which the interests and prerogatives of states are, ultimately, paramount. This theme is returned to in the concluding chapter, where it is argued that, ultimately, the benefits of working as part of the UN system overwhelmingly outweigh the frustrations and irritations that are encountered along the way.

But in a sense these constraints are a useful discipline, as they mirror the day-to-day experiences of those seeking to advance the protection of human rights at the country, or as the international lawyer rather condescendingly would say, at the domestic level. It is particularly important for the SPT to be alive to this, since a central element of the OPCAT system is that every state party must establish a 'National Preventive Mechanism' (NPM), which are explored in Chapter 6. These are mechanisms set up by each state and which operate and work with the state's national authorities to prevent torture. Without doubt, this is the most innovative element of the OPCAT, and helping establish and support NPMs is the SPT's most important role.

Having now completed the task of considering what is meant by torture and ill-treatment, highlighting the importance of prevention, presenting the OPCAT, the SPT, NPMs and outlining their work and mandate, the first part of the book is concluded. The second part turns to what the work of the SPT has revealed – or, more accurately, what it has revealed to me. Others will have different stories and accounts and will doubtless draw different conclusions. These are mine, and they pretend to be no other.

Part II considers some of the less predictable barriers to effective torture prevention. Some of these have already been touched on in the earlier chapters which looked at the more 'mechanical' reasons why torture prevention under the OPCAT system is not as effective as it might be. Yet there are far deeper issues at play. If the first part of the book draws on my 'operational' experience of working with the SPT, the chapters in this second part unashamedly represent my personal reflections drawn from my experience of having visited with the SPT many places of detention, and many different types of places of detention, in most parts of the world. The situations I encountered were all so very different – and yet in essence so very much the same: they were largely broken systems breaking people.

This is hardly a new insight, and much good work is being done, nationally and internationally, to help fix broken systems, including through domestic legal reform, enhanced training of police and custodial staff, improvements to detention facilities, better provision of health care for those in detention and very much more besides. It remains striking how little this seems to achieve over time, and sustainable gains are often at best incremental. Yet embedding incremental improvements is certainly not to be decried – after all, it is how all lasting change is achieved – and this may be all that can be achieved in practice at a given place, at a given time.

It may seem difficult to accept that when it comes to the prevention of torture and ill-treatment, incrementalism is good enough: the prohibition on torture is not incremental, it is absolute. But the incremental enhancement of prevention is designed to reduce the incidents of torture over time – not to excuse or justify the existence of torture or ill-treatment now. And as the SPT has said, there is no logical limit to what measures might have a preventive effect.[11] It is, or should be, an ever-upwards rachet. The trick is to aim high – for the best that can be achieved in terms of prevention in a particular place at a particular time. But a failure to reach the highest standards of prevention does not, and cannot, justify torture or ill-treatment. It means that more should be done to prevent it. So why is it that torture is still not being tackled as effectively as it should be? The chapters that follow offer some suggestions.

Chapter 7 sets the scene, providing a first-hand account of the reality of undertaking preventive visits to places of detention within the OPCAT system, what they feel like and what they can (and do) achieve. For many, this is what the preventive system established by OPCAT is all about. So does it deliver? Does it really 'tackle torture'? And if not, what can be done to ensure that it does? Some of the answers to these questions are probably predictable – and involve better resourcing and changes in how the SPT goes about doing what it does. This are all very important. But there is much more to it than that.

Chapter 8 is entitled 'Accepting the Unacceptable'. There are many serious problems which are not even considered to be problems at all; it's 'just the way things are'. As a result, completely unacceptable forms of ill-treatment are allowed to pass not only unchallenged but even unnoticed by those who are responsible for them. The currently fashionable expression 'hidden in plain sight' might seem to sum this up: that we do not notice what is going on right in front of us. Except that, at times, we can see it very well indeed and, in truth, it is not 'hidden' at all – it is just accepted as acceptable when obviously it is not.

There is a very close connection between 'accepting the unacceptable' and 'excusing the inexcusable', which is considered in Chapter 9. It highlights how even when something is known to be wrong – or accepted to be unacceptable – it may just not be considered to be all that wrong, or not wrong enough to merit notice, attention or comment. As a result, excuses are offered which try to justify what those offering them really do know is inexcusable – but there is nothing quite like a plausible justification to make one feel better about not doing anything about it.

The classic and most stark example is the extent to which some continue to try to excuse the continued use of torture and ill-treatment itself. We all know how in the wake of the 9/11 destruction of the Twin Towers in New York the 'war on terror' prompted a long debate probing whether torture could in fact be justified if it was used in the interests of seeking to save innocent lives (see, for example, Greenberg, 2006; Levinson, 2006; Waldron, 2010). I well remember feeling quite sick when, during a BBC radio discussion in which I was participating, rational, measured argument was being made concerning whether it was proportionate to insert a *sterilised* needle under a person's finger nails for such purposes. I doubt whether the needles had or had not been sterilised would have been uppermost in the victim's mind at the time – but I suspect it was important to the proposer of the torture: it might appear as some form of 'mitigation' or add an air of 'moderation', and thus of 'humanity' to the unfortunate 'necessity'. Think your way through this act for a moment. To me, this increased, rather than diminished, the enormity of what was being proposed. It speaks of a real understanding of what is being done, in a cold and controlled, calculated and calibrated fashion. This is the epitome of cruelty; and while not all pain is cruel, all cruelty is a form of pain. And as will shortly be seen, these are hallmarks of torture, which requires purpose and intent. What we see here is purpose and intent coupled with exculpatory argument, a classic example of trying to excuse the inexcusable.

There are other ways of seeking to excuse the inexcusable, such as it being just too difficult to do otherwise, or that it is someone else's fault, problem or responsibility. I recall visiting a detention facility in which a nasty brawl was taking place yet none of the security staff were intervening. I was told that detention facility staff were not responsible as the detainees involved had been detained under police powers and not a court order. Officers of two different units of the police were present on site, but they said that those involved were detained based on powers exercised by yet another arm of the policing forces that was not currently present, and so the brawl continued while everyone watched. Perhaps it was entertaining. There is a difference between a reason and an excuse – and sometimes there are genuine reasons why problems remain unaddressed. But far too often, ill-treatment is allowed to continue simply because no-one really wants to deal with it or feels the need to deal with it. There are problems which are seen and recognised but are, in effect, ignored or side-lined.

Sometimes, even when problems are being addressed, the means adopted are hopelessly inadequate, cannot realistically be done or even if done would never make much of a difference anyway. Such responses are considered in Chapter 10, which is about 'prescribing the inappropriate'. To foreshadow what will be said later, human rights bodies are particularly prone to this. They have their 'playbook' – things they usually recommend – and when they see a problem, they simply trot out the usual prescription. This is terribly attractive, since human rights bodies are under constant scrutiny by states – and I am afraid to say, academics and others – to be models of consistency in a world which is not. And to recommend one thing to one state and something else to another in respect of a roughly similar situation is seen as a form of prejudice or partisanship, and certainly not consonant with the universality of human rights and of independence and impartiality. In consequence, treaty bodies often end up making utterances that are either devoid of context, content or both. Rarely will such recommendations make much of a difference, and some are pitched at so high a level of generality that it is almost impossible to know what they really mean or what their recipients are really meant to do to achieve them. That is just not helpful – and making such recommendations, arguably, is not really preventive.

In a sense, this is the key to understanding the overall approach of the SPT to the concept of prevention and – simple and obvious though it may sound – this has arguably been one of its principal contributions to thinking about how to tackle torture. Difficult situations may call for unusual solutions, and numerous examples will be given later. It is very important to retain sufficient flexibility to be able to come up with solutions which may actually *work* – which may actually *prevent* – even if this goes beyond, or outside of, the established repertoire. It was for this reason that the SPT during my time as Chair did not go down the route of setting out formal statements of standards or guidelines, instead limiting itself to offering a series of reflections concerning how prevention might be approached in a number of important contexts or in relation to particularly vulnerable groups, before deciding that even this ran the risk of becoming overly directive and prescriptive. The absolute nature of the prohibition on torture and ill-treatment ought to merit an open mind as to what might best prevent. Indeed, it should demand no less. Yet this is not always so.

This line of thinking is taken up in Chapter 11, entitled 'Working with Fictions'. In some ways, this is the most challenging part of this book as it asks us to look honestly at many of the 'solutions' that are offered to states and which all too often reflect the way we might like things to be, rather than the way we know they really are. Indeed, perhaps 'fictions' is too euphemistic: what we are talking about is pretending that things are not what they are, because it is difficult for us to accept the truth. In some ways, it is the human rights' defender's equivalent of 'excusing the inexcusable'.

To give an example to which we shall return, it is undoubtedly correct to say that the risk of torture and ill-treatment is lessened if a detainee can have immediate access to an independent lawyer, has a medical examination and is swiftly brought before a judicial authority who can determine whether continued detention is justified or whether the person must be released from custody. These three preventive safeguards are well established and routinely insisted upon. Yet they can be worthless: if the independent lawyers just give bad advice, or fail to turn up or to pay attention, for example. We assume that lawyers will act in their clients' best interests. Many do. Others do not. As a safeguard, it can be something of a lottery. The same is true of medical professionals and judges. Just because we want these professionals to be the bastions of probity that they ought to be does not mean that they are. Of course, there are always poor examples – but the truth is that this is not as exceptional as we might wish it to be, and there are deep-seated structural reasons why such professionals in some countries either cannot, will not or do not act with the integrity that the theory of human rights protection assumes. In such circumstances the 'solutions' are not 'solutions' and all that is achieved is a false reassurance, since these preventive safeguards are not that preventive at all.

Where does this take us? Chapter 12 takes stock of what all these reflections might mean for the better future of prevention of torture and ill-treatment. Much can be done through existing systems and structures. Indeed, those systems and structures probably have all that is necessary to enable this to happen. The real question is how to release that potential. Some of the answers lie in rather mundane but nevertheless important changes in the ways things are done. This is largely the stuff of Part I of this book. But any such changes at least need to reflect on the observations made in Part II, which, as has been said, seeks to go beyond the 'mechanical' and asks some difficult questions about why it is that torture remains so prevalent and why the ways in which we are trying to address torture seem to be deficient. It is for this reason that Part I is entitled 'The Solutions' and Part II 'The Problems'. The various 'solutions' described in Part I have largely been devised with little consideration of the problems highlighted in Part II. Yet these are very real problems indeed, and until they are acknowledged as such and the 'solutions' advanced take proper account of them, torture and ill-treatment will continue to be tackled less effectively than they could be.

This book is inevitably and irredeemably informed by my personal experiences as a member and as the Chair of the SPT, but it is also informed by my work as an academic international lawyer who has looked at matters concerning torture prevention for over 30 years. It does not purport to be an academic study. It does try to be an honest and personal reflection on what I have learnt from both academic study and the practical experience of undertaking preventive visits to places of detention and working within the UN human rights system.

★★★

I am conscious that this Introduction commenced in a rather down-beat fashion and has continued in a similar vein. When I became a member of the SPT in 2009, I doubt I would have thought that likely. As will be seen in Chapter 3, for over ten years I was an active participant in the campaigns to bring the OPCAT into being, and my enthusiasm for what it is and what can be achieved through the OPCAT to help prevent torture and ill-treatment in places of detention has neither wilted nor wavered. I consider myself as passionately committed to the cause of prevention, and of the OPCAT and its system of prevention built around the SPT and the NPMs, as I have ever been. If I were not, I would not have written this book. It is not written to criticise or to condemn. Quite the opposite. It may at times appear to be little more than a litany of criticism, but if it is, then it is written to encourage yet further self-reflection, development, improvement and change. The prevention of torture is just too important to become trapped in the 'this is the way we do it' syndrome when there are other, better ways of doing things. The SPT has probably been the most innovative of the UN treaty bodies, and several times already it has reinvented its ways of working in the light of its experience and of changing circumstances. It will surely do so again, and my only hope for this book is that it might assist in that process.

And although there is room for criticism, there is far more to celebrate. Because of the OPCAT system there is now much greater knowledge and awareness of what goes on inside many places of detention, in many countries, than has ever been the case before. The establishment of NPMs has resulted in independent oversight of places of detention being put in place in countries where previously none had existed at all. In other countries, independent oversight has been extended to include places previously excluded from its reach: in the UK, for example, it was because of the OPCAT that police custody first became subject to independent inspection.

The concept of detention has itself been explored and expanded. Do those held by the armed forces of a state in detention facilities overseas fall within the oversight mandate of the national NPM and SPT? Answer: Yes. Can it include persons in state-regulated social care institutions who fall within the OPCAT definition of detention, even if those institutions are privately owned and operated? Answer: Yes.[12] During the COVID-19 pandemic, the question arose of whether quarantine facilities were places of detention for OPCAT purposes. Answer: Yes.[13] What about migrants picked up at sea and held for prolonged periods on board vessels, rather than being taken ashore? Answer: Yes.[14] There is a new voice at the table, able to draw attention to the many and varied settings in which individuals can be rendered vulnerable to the power of authority and at risk of ill-treatment as a result. This is no mean thing. It is a great achievement, the importance of which is not to be underestimated or trivialised.

What *is* needed is for that greater knowledge and awareness to be converted into more effective preventive action. Prohibiting torture will not, by itself, stop people from being tortured and ill-treated. Making it easier to prosecute and to hold to account those responsible for torture is unquestionably an imperative, an essential response to torture and a means of securing justice for victims of torture. But there is little evidence to suggest that the deterrent effect of punishment alone will be sufficient to prevent torture and ill-treatment from occurring. If 'no-one shall be subjected to torture' is to mean what it says, then torture must not only be prohibited and those responsible prosecuted, but it must also be prevented to the extent that it is possible to do so. Currently this is not the case. The OPCAT and the OPCAT system of prevention is the most ambitious attempt yet made to change this, and this is my version of its story.

A note on notes

As will become apparent, much of the work of the SPT, and particularly its work relating to visits, is confidential. Even when a state gives its permission for a report on it to be made public, there remains much that must remain so. To preserve that confidentiality, it has been necessary to avoid naming names – of countries, places and people. This also means that it is impossible to cite sources for much of what I recount, as to do so would identify the countries concerned, and to do so in the limited number of cases where that is might be possible could raise issues of a different nature, including the safety of some potential sources. As a result, Part II of this book, which is almost wholly derived from such materials, is largely devoid of references to sources or other written materials. As it is largely a personal account, the reader must take it or leave it as it is.

Part I is rather different but since this is not intended to be an academic work references have been largely limited to citations and quotations, with just a small number of references to more general literature on a particular point or topic where it seems helpful. I am not citing materials to support my arguments, as I am not offering any. I am setting out my thoughts, observations and beliefs – and as I am the sole source of these, citing materials to bolster them is neither necessary nor, indeed, appropriate: I take full responsibility for what I think, as well as for what I write.

Notes

1 Universal Declaration of Human Rights, UNGA Res 217A (III) (adopted 10 December 1948).
2 International Covenant on Civil and Political Rights (adopted 16 December 1966, entered into force 23 March 1976), 999 UNTS 171. By way of confirmation, Article 7 adds to this a second sentence: 'In particular, no one shall be subjected without his free consent to medical or scientific experimentation.'
3 European Convention for the Protection of Human Rights and Fundamental Freedoms (ECHR) (adopted 4 November 1950, entered into force 3 September 1953), ETS no 5, Article 3.
4 American Convention on Human Rights (adopted 22 November 1969, entered into force 16 July 1978), Treaty no B-32, OAS Treaty Series no 36, Article 5(2).
5 African Charter on Human and Peoples' Rights (adopted by the Organisation of African Unity [OAU] Assembly on 27 June 1981, OAU Doc CAB/LEG/67/3 rev 5), entered into force 21 October 1986, Article 5.
6 ASEAN Human Rights Declaration, adopted 18 November 2012, Article 14.
7 The Cairo Declaration of the Organization of Islamic Cooperation on Human Rights, 2020, Article 4 (b), which provides that '[n]o person shall be subjected to physical or psychological torture or to cruel, inhuman or degrading treatment or punishment' (available from: https://www.oic-oci.org/upload/pages/conventions/en/CDHRI_2 021_ENG.pdf). A similarly worded provision was found in the otherwise very different earlier Cairo Declaration on Human Rights in Islam, adopted 5 August 1990, UN GAOR, World Conference on Human Rights, 4th Session, Agenda Item 5, U.N. Doc. A/CONF.157/PC/62/Add.18 (1993), Article 20.
8 *Questions Relating to the Obligation to Prosecute or Extradite* (*Belgium* v *Senegal*), Judgment, ICJ Reports, 2012, p 155, para 99.
9 Convention against Torture and Other Cruel, Inhuman or Degrading Treatment or Punishment (adopted 10 December 1984, entered into force 26 June 1987), 1465 UNTS 85.
10 Optional Protocol to the Convention against Torture and Other Cruel, Inhuman or Degrading Treatment or Punishment (adopted 18 December 2002, in force 22 June 2006), 2375 UNTS 237.
11 'The approach of the Subcommittee on Prevention of Torture to the concept of prevention of torture and other cruel, inhuman or degrading treatment or punishment under the

Optional Protocol to the Convention against Torture and Other Cruel, Inhuman or Degrading Treatment or Punishment', CAT/OP/12/6 (2010), para 3.

12 See 'Compilation of Advice Provided by the Subcommittee in Response to Requests from National Preventive Mechanisms: I. "The Scope of Article 4 of the OPCAT"', paras 1–3 in CAT/OP/C/57/4, annex.

13 See 'Advice Provided by the Subcommittee to the National Preventive Mechanism of the United Kingdom of Great Britain and Northern Ireland regarding Compulsory Quarantine for Coronavirus (COVID-19 Virus)', 31 March 2020, CAT/OP/9.

14 This inexorably follows from decisions such as that of the European Court of Human Rights in *Medvedyev and Others* v *France* [GC], no 3394/03, ECHR 2010, in which those detained at sea by a French warship fell within the jurisdiction of the Court and is an uncontroversial proposition, though one which monitoring mechanisms often overlook and which is admittedly complex to operationalise.

PART I

The Solution

1

What Is Torture?

Introduction

When a critic says that listening to a musical performance or watching a film or a play was for them a form of 'torture', they do not mean to suggest that they have been tortured. While they might be suggesting that they found the experience excruciating, they do not mean to suggest that they really were in pain. They mean that they thought the performance was very poor, and that they did not enjoy it at all. Though some might object to such experiences being described in this way, believing that it trivialises the reality of torture, the use of the word in such a context is effective because it conveys the depth of the critic's response to their experience. The reader is left in no doubt about what the critic thinks: they know that the critic thinks they have been exposed to something terrible, artistically speaking. The reader, like the critic, does not believe that torture has really taken place – but they do know what they mean. But when we are talking about torture – real torture – *do* we really know what that means?

For many, the abiding image of torture remains that of some medieval castle chamber in which terrible torments are inflicted on the human body by strange and fearful looking instruments or contraptions in a careful, calibrated and calculated fashion to elicit information, a confession or simply to impose the will of the torturer (or, more likely, the will of those responsible for ordering the torture) on the terrified victim in some way. That terror was mental as well as physical – instruments of torture were shown to the victims in advance of their use, and there was no doubting what might be in store for those taken away to be tortured (see generally Langbein, 1977; Peters, 1996). There is, perhaps, some comfort in that image since it seems remote from the realities of the modern world. It encourages us to believe that such things do not really take place today – that torture belongs in the past and, if it does take place today, that at least it is not 'like that'.

While the places in which torture is inflicted and the tools and techniques of physical and mental torture employed may indeed be different, remove the medieval setting and in many ways very little else really has, in truth, changed (Modvig and Quiroga, 2020). Yet when we do see and hear of torture today, it is often projected as something that happens in remote and unfamiliar locations and settings – places that we do not know or of which we have no experience. Or it is something that happens in films or dramas that we know are not really true – *James Bond* films and series such as *Homeland, Deutschland 83, 86* and *89*, for example – an impression confirmed by the remarkable capacity of the characters who have been tortured to appear fully recovered in next to no time at all. If torture cannot be kept remote in time, it can at least be kept at a distance in other ways: as something that happens somewhere else, and not to 'people like us', or it is something that is not committed by 'people like us', and its consequences are fleeting. But none of this is true (Alleg, 1958; Rejali, 2007; Corbain, 2012).

Legally speaking, it is surprisingly difficult to answer the question 'what is torture?' And this is troubling. Determining that a person has been tortured or that someone is responsible for torturing another is an extremely serious matter. As has been said, torture is one of the relatively few things which international law prohibits absolutely, with no exceptions and no defences. As Article 2(2) and 2(3) of the 1984 UN Convention against Torture puts it, when making torture a crime within their national law states must ensure that

   (2) No exceptional circumstance whatsoever, whether a state of war or a threat of war, internal political instability or any other public emergency, may be invoked as a justification of torture.

   (3) An order from a superior officer or a public authority may not be invoked as a justification of torture.[1]

Moreover, according to Article 4(2), those found criminally responsible for torture must be punished 'by appropriate penalties which take into account their grave nature'.

But what is it that is to be subject to so draconian a regime? It would seem to be very important that what torture 'is' should be as clear as possible. Yet the entire question of 'what is torture?' is mired with difficulties, partly resulting from the conflation of human rights law and criminal law (Rodley, 2002; Ginbar, 2017).

Most human rights treaties, such as the International Covenant on Civil and Political Rights, the European Convention on Human Rights, the American Convention on Human Rights, the African Charter on Human and Peoples' Rights, and others, do not actually *define* torture at all. Along with inhuman and degrading treatment or punishment, they simply prohibit it. The 1984 UN Convention against Torture, however, is very different and does the opposite. It does not expressly prohibit torture, but it does define it, since the Convention requires states to make torture a criminal offence under their domestic law. It also requires that states investigate and consider bringing criminal charges against anyone who is suspected of having committed torture, no matter where in the world that torture might have taken place, if they are within their jurisdiction – the exercise of 'universal jurisdiction'.[2] In doing so, the 1984 Convention takes its place alongside numerous other conventions which seek to criminalise activities the international community wishes to eradicate in the same way (Kittichaisaree, 2018).

Human rights law is primarily focused on determining whether a state has acted in breach of its obligations to those who are subject to its jurisdiction or control (that is, in a general sense, subject to its power). Criminal law is primarily focused on holding individuals to account for undertaking actions which carry a criminal liability. States cannot be held criminally liable. Individuals can. Although both states and individuals can be responsible for acts of torture, only individuals can be held criminally liable and be subjected to criminal punishment. While in popular parlance there may be such things as 'criminal states' which undertake 'criminal acts', there are no such concepts in international law. As will be seen shortly, this has – for the best of intentions – caused considerable conceptual confusion and has had unfortunate practical consequences.

In a nutshell, the prohibition of torture and ill-treatment in international human rights law, which is directed at the actions of the state, has come to be understood in terms of the definition of a criminal law offence which is intended to determine whether an individual is to be held criminally liable. These are two very different things. The freedom of expression, as a matter of human rights law, is not 'defined' in accordance with any criminal, or indeed civil, standard of domestic legal liability. The freedom of religion as a human right is not understood in terms of what amounts to an offence under domestic law, nor is privacy, family life or most other human rights obligations.

The entire point of human rights law is that what states do, or permit to be done, should be subject to challenge and scrutiny. And if such challenge and scrutiny is conducted in the light of what that law permits, then it would be a nonsense. It is, in fact, quite unusual for an international human rights treaty to set out the details of a criminal law offence, since one of the very purposes of international human rights law is to question the appropriateness of domestic law from a human rights perspective. Surely human rights standards ought to have a degree of aspiration about them, if they are to be an effective source of questioning and challenge?

The problem has arisen because unlike most other human rights obligations, the UN Convention against Torture requires states to make torture a criminal offence within their domestic jurisdictions and it provides a definition that is to be used for that purpose.[3] That definition will be looked at shortly. Before doing so, however, it is important to stress that while that definition might be appropriate as a definition of a criminal offence for which individuals may be subject to criminal punishment, this does not mean that it is necessarily an appropriate way of approaching a human rights standard that is meant to be a touchstone against which the behaviour of states can be measured. Things are prohibited when they are recognised as not being right, and one way of doing so is to criminalise such conduct. But there may be many things which we believe to be 'not right' and which do not (yet) amount to a criminal offence, just as there things which are criminal offences that we do not think should be, either in detail or at all. To understand the scope of the human rights obligation not to torture or ill–treat a person in terms of a criminal law definition, albeit a definition which is internationally recognised, seems limiting and restrictive and potentially hampers the broadening of our understanding of what torture might be by imposing a definitional 'straightjacket' around it.

Just because international law sets out a definition of a crime of torture that is to be used by states when they make torture a crime within their domestic legal systems does not mean that torture must be understood in terms of that definition for all other legal purposes. Indeed, it is not. The definition of torture set out in the Rome Statute, establishing the jurisdiction of the International Criminal Court, is different from that found in the UN Convention against Torture.[4] This is because it is serving a different purpose – defining torture as an element of a war crime or crime against humanity for the purposes of exercising international criminal jurisdiction over individuals where additional requirements need to be met which are not relevant to domestic criminal prosecutions. In other words, the approach taken to the 'definition' of torture can and should reflect the context and purpose for which it is being defined. Torture for the purposes of international human rights protection does not have to be understood in the same way as it is understood for the purposes of defining an offence in domestic criminal law, and it is not at all obvious why it should be. The purposes are very different.

At the very least, we might say that the definition of torture found in Article 1 of the 1984 United Nations Convention against Torture is 'a floor, not a ceiling' – and there is nothing to stop human rights law pitching higher. Indeed, it should be. But the definition in the UN Convention is now routinely endorsed by international courts and human rights bodies around the world, and, as a result, it is taken as providing the definition of torture which the texts of most other human rights treaties have refrained from providing. As a result, for good or ill, the almost inevitable starting point for determining 'what is torture' for the purposes of international human rights law is now found in Article 1 of the UN Convention against Torture.

The definition of torture in international law

Because the Convention against Torture requires states to make torture a criminal offence under their domestic laws no matter where it is committed, it needs to set out what, exactly, it considers torture to be. Otherwise, individuals might find themselves liable before the courts of another country for the crime of torture when what they have done might not have been considered to amount to an act of torture in the country where the act took place. As a result, Article 1 provides that

> [f]or the purposes of this Convention, the term 'torture' means any act by which severe pain or suffering, whether physical or mental, is intentionally inflicted on a person for such purposes as obtaining from him or a third person information or a confession, punishing him for an act he or a third person has committed or is suspected of having committed, or intimidating or coercing him or a third person, or for any reason based on discrimination of any kind, when such pain or suffering is inflicted by or at the instigation of or with the consent or acquiescence of a public official or other person acting in an official capacity. It does not include pain or suffering arising only from, inherent in or incidental to lawful sanctions.[5]

Breaking this down, the Convention defines torture as requiring (a) the infliction of 'severe pain or suffering'; (b) that such pain is inflicted intentionally; (c) that such pain is inflicted for a purpose; and (d) that the person inflicting that pain, or responsible for the infliction of that pain, was 'a public official or other person acting in an official capacity'.

While there are numerous uncertainties and controversies concerning the interpretation of the various elements of this definition, it conjures up an instantly recognisable vision of what torture is. It reflects the traditional and archetypal – some might say stereotypical – image of torture, of a torturer and of a torture victim. It involves the infliction of pain, by a person in a position of officially sanctioned authority, done so deliberately and for a specific purpose. It is not a random act of violence or cruelty. According to the Convention, torture does not happen inadvertently, or by chance.

Each of the four principal definitional 'elements' of torture – 'pain', 'officially sanctioned authority', 'intent' and 'purpose' – can raise difficult definitional issues, but none more so than the question of 'pain' (Scarry, 1985). Torture and pain seem synonymous – but to what extent is that true, or perhaps more accurately, what is the relationship between torture and pain? This is a question which continues – in my view quite wrongly – to dominate discussions about 'what is torture?'. I am conscious that the remainder of this chapter runs the risk of falling into that 'trap' too – although its purpose is to argue the dominant approach to the relevance of 'pain' in international human rights law has been largely misguided.

When a person who is being held and questioned by policing or security services is tethered and beaten with batons or lashed with electrical cords; when electrodes are attached to the body and powerful currents run through it; when a head is forcibly held under water to the point of drowning or plastic bags forced over a person's head to the point of suffocation – these are no accidents, and it takes no great powers of legal analysis to know that the victim is being tortured. Faced with the examples of torture just given, the question which just about nobody would ever think to ask is 'but was it painful enough?' These, I might add, are just some of the examples of torture that the UN Subcommittee on Prevention of Torture (SPT) has encountered in its work over the years, and the SPT certainly never asked itself this question when considering whether to describe such treatment as 'torture'. Perhaps this was because we just assumed that its effect on the victim was sufficiently painful, but I do not really think that that was the reason. I think we did not ask ourselves that question because we considered it to be completely unnecessary: the very doing of such things to a person meant that they were acts of torture – how could they not? And precisely *how* painful they were for the victim was just not important at all. These are all things which we simply *knew* should not be done and that, in consequence, the victims were being subjected to torture.

In truth, when we say that we just 'know', intuitively, that something amounts to torture, there is probably something of a conflation of two different things taking place: it is not that the existence of pain is necessarily irrelevant, but we can confidently assume that pain of a requisite intensity has been inflicted simply because of the nature of the act – it *has* to have been; how could it not? But I am equally sure that if, for some extraordinary reason, the victim did not actually feel any physical pain, it would not have mattered in the slightest. It might be correctly pointed out that pain is not only physical but also mental (Pérez-Sales, 2017; 2020) and the mental pain of being subjected to such ordeals would itself justify such acts as being described as torture, but this would not go to the heart of the matter. There are some things which just *are* acts of torture (Rodley and Pollard, 2009, pp 95–7) – and the things described earlier were examples of that.

But according to the definition of torture in the UN Convention, pain or suffering alone is insufficient. Article 1 insists that torture not only involves the infliction of pain (physical or mental), but of *severe* pain or suffering. As a result, a great deal of time and attention has been devoted to determining 'how much' pain or suffering is required before someone can be said to have been tortured. Famously – infamously – in the early years of the US 'war against terror' guidance was issued concerning 'enhanced' interrogation techniques. In these so-called 'Torture Memos' it was suggested that the interrogation methods employed by the United States at its detention centre at Guantanamo Bay and elsewhere did not amount to torture. This was because, while certainly causing pain, the level of pain involved did not cross the 'threshold' of severity, which, it concluded, 'must be of an intensity akin to that which accompanies serious physical injury such as death or organ failure'.[6] The best that could be offered in terms of a rationale for this appears to have been the suggestion that this reflected the threshold of 'severity' at which a medical emergency might trigger a compensation payment, the relevance of which is beyond baffling and verges on the obscene.

Even the medieval torturer did not seek to claim that a person had not been tortured because the severity of the pain or suffering inflicted had been insufficient.[7] Being subjected to torture was a process in which the level of pain inflicted was often carefully calculated to reflect the strength of the evidence against the victim – the greater the evidence, the greater the degree of pain that might be inflicted to extract a confession, which was usually the purpose of the exercise. It did not 'become' torture only when a certain threshold of pain had been crossed. The pain was the product of the process, and it was the process, not the pain, that constituted torture. Be that as it may – there is no getting away from the fact that, according to the UN Convention against Torture, intentionally inflicted pain and suffering alone is 'not enough' to constitute torture.

Paradoxically, perhaps tragically, this continued fixation with the severity of pain and suffering is, at least in part, a product of human rights law itself. As has been seen in the Introduction, the most common modern form of the prohibition on torture, as found in Article 5 of the Universal Declaration of Human Rights and repeated as Article 3 of the European Convention on Human Rights, provides that 'no one shall be subjected to torture, cruel or inhuman or degrading treatment or punishment'. One of the first legal considerations of what this means was given by the European Commission on Human Rights in 1969 in a case brought against Greece, known as the *Greek* case. Rather than seeing Article 3 of the European Convention on Human Rights as a single, general and absolute prohibition of torture, inhuman and degrading treatment or punishment in all its potential forms, the European Commission chose to see it as comprising a number of separate elements, each of which was equally prohibited but each of which referred to something different. The Commission said that

[i]t is plain that there may be treatment to which all these descriptions apply, for all torture must be inhuman and degrading treatment, and all inhuman treatment also degrading. The notion of inhuman treatment covers at least such treatment as deliberately causes severe suffering, mental or physical, which in the particular situation is unjustifiable. The word 'torture' is often used to describe inhuman treatment which

has a purpose such as the obtaining of information or confessions, or the infliction of punishment, and it is generally an aggravated form of inhuman or degrading treatment. Treatment or punishment of an individual may be said to be degrading if it grossly humiliates him before others or drives him to act against his will or conscience.[8]

This statement has long been the cause of some considerable embarrassment, since it seems to suggest that torture or inhuman treatment might in some circumstances be justifiable. Nevertheless, the basic approach to the prohibition of torture set out in the *Greek* case became widely accepted not only for the purposes of the European Convention on Human Rights but for human rights law generally. It involves differentiating torture from other forms of treatment and punishment which are 'inhuman' and from those which are 'degrading'. Though equally prohibited, these three words are seen as referring to separate concepts and to be qualitatively different things which stand in a relationship to each other within the overall prohibition. There are three different things (possibly six, if 'treatment' is differentiated from 'punishment', as it probably should be) bundled up in this single prohibition, rather than a single prohibition: it is 'three in one', not 'one in three'. But is this correct? And if it is, what is it that differentiates them? And how do these different elements relate to each other?

Though it seems to fly in the face of 60 years' worth of jurisprudence, endless Resolutions, Declarations, Conventions and other forms of legal pronouncements and associated paraphernalia too numerous to cite to say so, I have long believed this entire approach to the prohibition of torture and ill-treatment to be fundamentally misconceived (Evans, 2002), and it is now increasingly accepted that pain and suffering alone cannot be the determinant of the distinction (Nowak et al, 2019, p 45). At the same time, it must be accepted that the genie cannot be put back into the bottle – too much has happened to embed that misguided approach in law and practice. But had a different approach been followed, at the very least we might have been spared the excruciating US Torture Memos seeking to defend the indefensible in the way that they did and claiming that the tortures they were inflicting were not 'quite' severe enough to be called torture and as a result were 'only' inhuman or degrading.[9] To which, from a human rights perspective, should anyone really be expected to respond – 'Oh, all right, that makes it better'?

Pain and suffering and the prohibition of inhuman or degrading treatment or punishment

But what of 'inhuman or degrading treatment or punishment'? While this too is prohibited absolutely under human rights law, the UN Convention against

Torture addresses it very differently. It does not require states to criminalise such treatment, but in Article 16 it requires that they undertake to prevent

> other acts of cruel, inhuman or degrading treatment or punishment which do not amount to torture as defined in article 1, when such acts are committed by or at the instigation of or with the consent or acquiescence of a public official or other person acting in an official capacity.

This has the practical result of cementing in law a distinction between torture on the one hand and inhuman or degrading treatment on the other, since very different legal consequences flow from this distinction under the Convention and international law more generally. However, the UN Convention does not really say what the difference between them is. All it says is that inhuman or degrading treatment or punishment comprise 'other acts' which are of such a nature but which do not fall within the definition of torture set out in Article 1. This is not particularly illuminating and is more akin to a general description. Given that Article 16 repeats the requirement found in Article 1 that such 'other acts' must have been undertaken on the basis of some form of official authority, these 'other acts' must either be 'less severe' than acts of torture, or they must lack the purpose needed for them to be acts of torture, or they must be unintentional. Unless they differ in at least one of these respects, such 'other acts' would themselves be acts of torture for the purposes of the Convention as they would be fulfilling all the criteria set out in Article 1.

In practice, it has been widely assumed that what distinguishes torture from inhuman and degrading treatment is that torture requires that the level of pain and suffering must be 'severe', whereas this is not a requirement of inhuman and degrading treatment; that is to say, inhuman and degrading treatment refers to cases of ill-treatment which fall short of the severity required for them to be acts of torture. It is this form of thinking which results in the arguments found in the US Torture Memos: the argument that while the proposed interrogation methods might well be inhuman or degrading, they were not sufficiently close to the top of the 'scales of suffering' to turn them into acts of torture. But why should there be such a focus on the intensity of pain and suffering at all? Why isn't the deliberate infliction of pain and suffering by a public official during the course of an interrogation, or for similar purposes, enough?

To understand the origins of all this, it its necessary to return to the *Greek* case. Dates are significant here. The case against Greece had been brought by a group of other European states, including Sweden and the Netherlands, and the report of the European Commission on Human Rights which set out its approach to the prohibition of torture quoted in the previous section was issued in 1969. Shortly afterwards, in the early 1970s and influenced by Amnesty International and others, the UN was pressed to take a stand against torture. This resulted in the adoption in 1975 of the UN Declaration on the Protection of All Persons from Being Subjected to Torture and Other Cruel, Inhuman or Degrading Treatment or Punishment.[10] Article 1 of that Declaration included a definition of torture which provided that:

1. For the purpose of this Declaration, torture means any act by which severe pain or suffering, whether physical or mental, is intentionally inflicted by or at the instigation of a public official on a person for such purposes as obtaining from him or a third person information or confession, punishing him for an act he has committed or is suspected of having committed, or intimidating him or other persons. It does not include pain or suffering arising only from, inherent in or incidental to, lawful sanctions to the extent consistent with the Standard Minimum Rules for the Treatment of Prisoners.
2. Torture constitutes an aggravated and deliberate form of cruel, inhuman or degrading treatment or punishment.

It was this definition which then formed the basis for the definition of torture which is now found in Article 1 of the 1984 UN Convention.

Sweden and the Netherlands played a leading role in drafting both the Declaration and the Convention (Danelius and Berger, 1988). Unsurprisingly, then, the draft texts they proposed drew heavily on the report of the European Commission in the *Greek* case, which had been given in response to the case they had brought and in which they had provided extensive argument. In this way, the idea that torture stands at the 'apex' of the architecture of the human rights prohibition of torture, inhuman or degrading treatment or punishment and that it is an 'aggravated' form of inhuman and degrading treatment became embedded in those instruments (Nowak et al, 2019, p 43) and has become generally accepted as the orthodoxy. Except that this is not what the *Greek* case says.

All those years ago, what the Commission actually said in the *Greek* case was that '[t]he notion of inhuman treatment covers at least such treatment as deliberately causes severe suffering'. In other words, 'inhuman treatment' *is* severe treatment. It is true that it went on to say that torture 'is generally an aggravated form of inhuman or degrading treatment' – but what is the source of that 'aggravation'? The Commission said that '[t]he word "torture" is often used to describe inhuman treatment which has a purpose such as the obtaining of information or confessions, or the infliction of punishment'. In other words, it said that while torture might indeed involve inflicting a level of pain or suffering that is *even greater than* that which is to be considered 'inhuman', this is *not* what causes the infliction of such pain to become an act of torture.

What causes inhuman treatment to become torture is its being deliberately applied for a particular purpose, such as to extract information, to force a confession or to punish. In short, to inflict severe pain or suffering on another is an inhuman thing to do – and this is absolutely prohibited. To set out to inflict severe pain or suffering, to plan, to prepare and to execute the infliction of such pain or suffering in a cold and calculating manner to fulfil a specific purpose is what makes the infliction of such pain an act of torture. It was *not* because of the relative severity of the pain or suffering that was being inflicted. Clearly, it must be severe 'enough' to be inhuman, but once it had crossed that threshold nothing else was required for it to be an act of torture. Contrary to widely held assumptions, it is not the severity of the treatment but the context in which that treatment was is meted out that distinguishes torture from inhuman treatment. If it is intentionally done by those acting on the basis of official authority for the purposes described, it is torture, and the *precise* magnitude of pain has (or should have) nothing to do with it.

The deliberate infliction of pain and suffering on detainees at Guantanamo Bay, in detention centres in Syria, in China, in Russia and anywhere and everywhere else where this happens is indeed what it is routinely called in the popular press and in the popular imagination – torture. What else can it be called? Torture is a means of achieving an outcome. It is a technique. It is the deliberate infliction of pain for a purpose, by those in positions of power upon those over whom they can exercise their power. It always has been. And when the state gives a person that power, or allows them to exercise such power, then the state is violating the rights of the victims.[11] It is not that difficult to grasp, and it is breath-taking that somehow this seems to have become lost sight of in the midst of a global campaign to combat torture. It may be that the reason was always simple enough – it provides a way of pretending that what is being done, while bad, is not 'very bad': it may be wrong, but at least we are not torturing people. Except that we are.

Avoiding the stigma of torture?

The very word 'torture' stirs up deep-seated fears, of both pain and of vulnerability. It conjures up the ultimate image of powerlessness, as torture exposes its victims to the uncontrolled force of the forces of power. This may be why states and national authorities are so concerned when they are accused of engaging in acts of torture and are so anxious to avoid it or deny it. In all my time on the SPT, I cannot recall a single occasion when after we had told the government representatives at the end of a visit that we had found evidence that torture was routine or widespread that they accepted this was so, irrespective of the evidence. They might accept that some officers may have been acting unlawfully and that this should be investigated, that there was a need for more training and so on. They might even accept that, in some places, the forces of law and order were out of control. But there was never any acceptance anywhere that torture was just a routine part of the way in which the state went about things. It was always a criticism to avoid, deflect or seek to excuse – in marked contrast to the general willingness of national authorities to accept that much else concerning the treatment of detainees was inhuman or degrading. I vividly remember one minister telling me, following my rather lengthy recitation of the terrible state of the detention and justice systems in the country concerned: "That's a fair assessment, I'm not going to quarrel with that." Evidence of systematic torture does not elicit so candid a reaction.

To be a state that tortures is to be a state that abuses its power to a degree which calls into question its own legitimacy, in the eyes of its citizens as well as the eyes of others. Can a state which is prepared to authorise the torture of its citizens, or indeed anyone else's, really be a state that can be trusted not to abuse its powers in many other ways besides? Can you really be comfortable – and free from fear – if you know that your government can and does authorise the purposive infliction of severe pain on those subject to its power to achieve its ends? States and national authorities may be willing to admit to many things, but they are rarely willing to admit to torture, and arguing that what has taken place is not sufficiently serious to amount to torture is one of the ways they seek to avoid doing so. This why the 1978 judgment of the European Court of Human Rights in its first major and 'seminal' decision concerning 'what is torture' in the case of *Ireland* v *UK* was and remains so shocking.

The case, brought by the Republic of Ireland against the UK, concerned the use of five notorious 'interrogation techniques' by UK security forces in Northern Ireland. The European Court, borrowing the description of the European Commission, described these as:

(a) wall-standing: forcing the detainees to remain for periods of some hours in a 'stress position', described by those who underwent it as being 'spread eagled against the wall, with their fingers put high above the head against the wall, the legs spread apart and the feet back, causing them to stand on their toes with the weight of the body mainly on the fingers';

(b) hooding: putting a black or navy coloured bag over the detainees' heads and, at least initially, keeping it there all the time except during interrogation;

(c) subjection to noise: pending their interrogations, holding the detainees in a room where there was a continuous loud and hissing noise;

(d) deprivation of sleep: pending their interrogations, depriving the detainees of sleep;

(e) deprivation of food and drink: subjecting the detainees to a reduced diet during their stay at the centre and pending interrogations.[12]

The European Commission on Human Rights issued a report in which it said that 'the combined use of the five techniques in the cases before it constituted a practice of inhuman treatment and of torture in breach of Article 3'.[13]

In the eyes of the Commission, then, this was torture. In accordance with the procedures in place under the European Convention at that time, the case was referred to the European Court of Human Rights. The UK sought to avoid a finding against it by the Court, but unusually it did not do so by contesting the finding of the Commission that the use of the interrogation techniques meant that it had been subjecting the detainees to torture. Instead, it argued that since it had now renounced the use of these techniques the Court need not consider the matter: it was all in the past.[14] The Court rejected this argument and decided to consider for itself whether the use of the five techniques amounted to torture. Remarkably, it chose to reverse the Commission's finding on this key question, even though that finding was not contested by the UK, and decided that they did not.

The Court emphasised that torture carried with it a 'special stigma', and in this it was undoubtedly correct. Where it was undoubtedly wrong was to equate that stigma with the precise degree of pain and suffering brought about by the application of these pain-infliction techniques. The Court said: '[I]t was the intention that the Commission, with its distinction between "torture" and "inhuman or degrading treatment", should by the first of these terms attach a special stigma to deliberate inhuman treatment causing very serious and cruel suffering.'[15] This *could* mean that torture is inhuman treatment − understood as treatment which causes very serious and cruel suffering − which is deliberately inflicted. But this is not what the Court meant. The Court was clear that, in its view, 'this distinction derives principally from a difference in the intensity of the suffering inflicted'.[16] As a result, it decided that the application of the five techniques − which the UK government had itself accepted amounted to torture − was not, in fact, torture after all. Rather, it thought that

[a]lthough the five techniques, as applied in combination, undoubtedly amounted to inhuman and degrading treatment, although their object was the extraction of confessions, the naming of others and/ or information and although they were used systematically, they did

not occasion suffering of the particular intensity and cruelty implied by the word torture as so understood.

So, there we have it. It is not enough for a state to ill-treat people in a way which is inhuman and degrading – which, as the Court itself acknowledged, means that the state inflicts upon them severe pain and suffering. It is not enough that this is done deliberately to 'extract' (the Court's word, not mine) something from the victim: the techniques of extraction involved must surpass this if they are to be acts of torture – they must have a particular 'intensity' and 'cruelty' as well, without which they are 'merely' inhuman, or degrading.

There is no doubt at all that it meant what it said. The Court went out of its way to say it, when it really did not have to say anything about this at all. But it was insistent:

> [T]he responsibilities assigned to it within the framework of the system under the Convention extend to pronouncing on the non-contested allegations of violation of Article 3. The Court's judgments in fact serve not only to decide those cases brought before the Court but, more generally, to elucidate, safeguard and develop the rules instituted by the Convention, thereby contributing to the observance by the States of the engagements undertaken by them as Contracting Parties.[17]

This case presented the European Court of Human Rights with its first opportunity to say what it considered torture under Article 3 of the ECHR to be, and it set the bar high. To re-iterate: the deliberate infliction of pain and suffering during an interrogation was not enough. The pain and suffering it brought about had to be of a 'particular intensity and cruelty'. In this instance, it seems, the Court thought that the techniques were just not painful enough, or sufficiently intense or sufficiently cruel, to amount to torture. The medieval inquisitor carefully measuring out the degrees of their tortures would be as amazed to find that they might not actually be inflicting torture at all as the latter-day human rights advocate should be aghast. There *is* a special stigma to subjecting a person to torture, and the Court's judgment, in effect, allowed it to be avoided.

Repentance

In the light of this, it is perhaps unsurprising – if depressing – that it was not until 1996 that the European Court of Human Rights first found a state to have committed an act of torture, in the case of *Aksoy* v *Turkey*. It should not have been a difficult case to decide. The victim had been subjected to 'Palestinian hanging', that is, 'he was stripped naked, with his arms tied together behind his back, and suspended by his arms'. The Court thought that

> this treatment could only have been deliberately inflicted; indeed, a certain amount of preparation and exertion would have been required to carry it out. It would appear to have been administered with the aim of obtaining admissions or information from the applicant. In addition to the severe pain which it must have caused at the time, the medical evidence shows that it led to a paralysis of both arms which lasted for some time … this treatment was of such a serious and cruel nature that it can only be described as torture.[18]

It would be difficult to disagree.

Similarly, the following year, in *Aydın* v *Turkey*, the Court found that a 17-year-old girl had been tortured, having been

> blindfolded, beaten, stripped, placed inside a tyre and sprayed with high-pressure water, and raped … on the basis of suspicion of collaboration by herself or members of her family with members of the PKK, the purpose being to gain information and/or to deter her family and other villagers from becoming implicated in terrorist activities.[19]

These judgments paved the way for others in which the particular cruelty and intensity of the pain and suffering brought about by acts that had been purposefully inflicted meant that they were considered to amount to torture. But it was still necessary for them to cross the high threshold of additional cruelty or intensity set by the Court in *Ireland* v *UK*. In 1999, the Court finally addressed this when, in the case of *Selmouni* v *France*, it said:

> [C]ertain acts which were classified in the past as 'inhuman and degrading treatment' as opposed to 'torture' could be classified differently in future. It takes the view that the increasingly high standard being required in the area of the protection of human rights and fundamental liberties correspondingly and inevitably requires greater firmness in assessing breaches of the fundamental values of democratic societies.[20]

In other words, if the Court were to hear the *Ireland* v *UK* case again it would come to a different conclusion – which suggests that the Commission and the UK had been right all along and the application of the 'five techniques' was indeed the application of techniques of torture. To put it another way, the Court finally accepted that the threshold of 'intensity' required to achieve the 'special stigma' necessary for inhuman or degrading treatment to be elevated into an act of torture was not as high as it had originally thought. Nevertheless, there is still a need for some degree of 'additionality'. The Court was quite clear about this. It first established that the treatment was 'inhuman' and took account of its purpose when doing so. It thought it was.[21] It then went on to consider whether, on the facts of the case, this inhuman treatment was 'severe enough' to amount to torture and concluded that it did.[22] As such, *Selmouni* took a classic 'severity of suffering' approach. Being 'inhuman', it seems, was still not enough.

What the Court's judgment in *Selmouni* did was to 'narrow the gap' between the purposive application of inhuman treatment which *does not* amount to torture, and purposive application of inhuman treatment which *does*. But why does there need to be a gap at all? And if there is still a need for 'something extra', what is it? Must that 'something extra' relate to the degree of pain and suffering, or could it relate to something else, such as the purposive infliction of pain and suffering by those acting on the basis of, or with the connivance of, those exercising public authority? While the nature of difficulties in determining what is torture for the purposes of international law may have changed, the difficulty itself remains.

Notes

[1] This does not prevent superior orders being a 'mitigation' when it comes to sentencing, but that still must take account of the grave nature of the offence.

[2] United Nations Convention against Torture (UNCAT), Article 5. For example, in 2012 the International Court of Justice decided that Senegal was in breach of the UN Convention because it had not taken such action in respect of the former President of Chad, Hissène Habré, who had been living in Dakar since the early 1990s, once it became a party to the UNCAT in 1999. See *Questions Relating to the Obligation to Prosecute or Extradite (Belgium v Senegal)*, Judgment, ICJ Reports, 2012, p 155.

[3] Another which does this, and which was modelled on the Convention against Torture, is the Convention for the Protection of All Persons from Enforced Disappearance (adopted 20 December 2006, entered into force 23 December 2010), 2716 UNTS 3.

[4] For example, the Rome Statute of the International Criminal Court (adopted 17 July 1998, entered into force 1 July 2002), 2187 UNTS 3, Article 7(2)(e) defines torture for the purposes of a crime against humanity as being 'the intentional infliction of severe pain or suffering, whether physical or mental, upon a person in the custody or under the control of the accused; except that torture shall not include pain or suffering arising only from, inherent in or incidental to, lawful sanction'. The 'Elements of Crimes' adds that it must have taken place within the context of a widespread or systematic attack directed against a civilian population, and that the perpetrator knew or intended this. No specific purpose other than this is required. See Cryer, 2020, pp 301–6.

[5] UNCAT, Article 1(1).

[6] See Memorandum for Alberto R. Gonzales, Counsel to the President, Re Standards of Conduct for Interrogation under 18 USC SS2340-2340A (Jay Bybee, Assistant Attorney General), 1 August 2002, in Danner, 2004, appendix 1, pp 119–20 and p 155.

[7] For example, in Inquisitorial Courts, the process was often carefully calibrated to ensure that the 'amount' of pain applied was commensurate with the weight of the evidence (or

suspicions) against them. Extreme severity would be reserved for extreme cases – at least in theory.

[8] *The Greek case*, Application no 3321/67, *Denmark* v *Greece*, Application no 3322/67, *Norway* v *Greece*, Application no 3323/67–*Sweden* v *Greece*, Application no 3344/67–*Netherlands* v *Greece*, Report of the European Commission of Human Rights, 5 November 1969, (1969) 12 *ECHRYb* 186.

[9] Although it is worth pointing out that the US drafters at least thought it necessary to attempt to justify themselves in terms of the law, no matter how lamentable was their attempt – very many others around the world, then and now, do not even think it worth bothering to try.

[10] UN Declaration on the Protection of All Persons from Being Subjected to Torture and Other Cruel, Inhuman or Degrading Treatment or Punishment, UNGA Res 3452 (XXX), adopted 9 December 1975. For the background, see Rodley and Pollard, 2009, pp 18–36.

[11] For the concept of powerlessness as a factor in the identification of torture, see the Report of the UN Special Rapporteur on Torture, Manfred Nowak, in UN Doc E/CN.4/2006/6, and see generally Nowak, 2018.

[12] *Ireland* v *the United Kingdom*, 18 January 1978, Series A no 25, para 96.

[13] This finding of the Commission is recorded in detail in the Court's later judgment, *Ireland* v *the United Kingdom*, para 147.

[14] Corbain, 2012 argues persuasively that this was, in fact, extremely unlikely.

[15] *Ireland* v *the United Kingdom*, para 167.

[16] *Ireland* v *the United Kingdom*, para 167. It supported this by pointing to Article 1 of the 1975 UN Declaration against Torture, which describes torture as an 'aggravated and deliberate' form of inhuman treatment.

[17] *Ireland* v *the United Kingdom*, para 154.

[18] *Aksoy* v *Turkey*, 18 December 1996, 'Reports of Judgments and Decisions', 1996-VI, para 64.

[19] *Aydın* v *Turkey*, 25 September 1997, 'Reports of Judgments and Decisions', 1997-VI, para 40 (reporting and endorsing the findings of fact made previously by the European Commission on Human Rights in this case).

[20] *Selmouni* v *France* [GC], no 25803/94, ECHR 1999-V, para 101.

[21] *Selmouni* v *France* [GC], no 25803/94, ECHR 1999-V, para 99.

[22] *Selmouni* v *France* [GC], no. 25803/94, ECHR 1999-V, paras 100–5.

2

Why Prevention?

Introduction

In the seminal case of *Selmouni* v *France*, the European Court of Human Rights established that Mr Selmouni had been

> repeatedly punched, kicked, and hit with objects ... forced to kneel down in front of a young woman to whom an officer had said "Look, you're going to hear somebody sing"; having a police officer show him his penis, saying "Here, suck this", before urinating over him; being threatened with a blowlamp and then with a syringe; etc[1]

This was done to induce him to confess to a crime. Is this torture? The purpose was clear enough. But was what was done to him sufficiently 'severe' even to be 'inhuman', let alone being sufficiently 'more severe' to be capable of being torture? Indeed, might it 'only' have been 'degrading'? Or was it none of the above? Some things are just not serious *enough*. Not every incidence of pain or suffering, not every use of unlawful violence or every degrading act can be absolutely prohibited in this way. How does one tell which is which?

Following the *Selmouni* case, it was as if the floodgates finally were opened and a torrent of findings of torture by the European Court have followed. A common theme in virtually all these cases is the need to demonstrate that the treatment which has been inflicted on the victim is sufficiently grave to carry with it the 'special stigma' that torture signifies.[2] While in some of the cases already considered it may seem self-evident that torture has taken place − and there are many others[3] − this may not be true in all cases, and some fine-grade distinctions still must be made to decide whether a particular example of inhuman treatment is 'sufficiently inhuman' to be called an act of 'torture'. Perhaps this is inevitable in a court of law, where so much turns on the precise nature of the finding that is made and the arguments presented are focused on this very question.

Nevertheless, there can be something almost voyeuristic about the obsession with the severity of suffering that characterises, or underpins, much of the discussion about the distinction between inhuman treatment and torture, and the very descriptions found in some of the cases seem to be intended to highlight – or downplay – the severity of what has occurred. With rare exceptions – the *Ireland* v *UK* case considered in the previous chapter being an example – findings that physical ill-treatment is 'inhuman' for the purposes of human rights law can be made relatively swiftly and easily: it is only when it is necessary to demonstrate that an additional 'line' has been crossed that fuller and sometimes quite graphic descriptions of ill-treatment are set out in considerable detail. If the Court has 'concluded' that what has occurred does not amount to torture, then a short, fairly factual recitation in quite bland language often tends to suffice, whereas a finding of torture merits a more fulsome exploration.[4]

Whether intended or not, this can have the effect of diminishing the significance of a finding that 'inhuman' treatment has taken place. Inhuman treatment is what the word says it is – inhuman – and it is important that it is recognised for what it is. There is an almost inescapable tendency to want to use the word 'torture' to describe the worst that we see – just like the critic with whom we opened Chapter 1 might want to describe as torture the worst performances that they hear: after all, there is a 'special stigma'. But when the word 'torture' is reserved for such cases it can result in those 'other' cases, cases in which the pain and suffering inflicted is not thought to be 'quite so severe', not being called out for what they really is – torture. Torture does not *always* have to take the form of the most severe and painful physical or mental suffering that a person might receive at the hands of the state. Equally, shocking behaviours do not always have to be labelled as torture for their magnitude to be recognised.

If this a criticism, it is one which I too must accept. While working with the UN Subcommittee on Prevention of Torture (SPT) I often felt the same need to justify my use of the word 'torture' by stressing the enormity of what I had seen, and I am sure my colleagues did so too. Perhaps this did have the effect of lessening the impact of our findings concerning 'other' forms of ill-treatment – by which we meant treatment which is 'inhuman and degrading'. This was not intended. We probably meant to highlight just how terrible had been the treatment which we were describing as torture. And it is difficult to do this without conveying the impression that ill-treatment which is not being called out as torture is, somehow, less terrible, less noteworthy and, perhaps, less serious – whereas in truth what one wants to say is that both are terribly serious in their different ways. It is not a hierarchy. But we are all hierarchically minded, and if it is difficult to fight against this impulse in general, it is certainly difficult to fight against it when encountering the forms of ill-treatment that detainees can be subjected to. We want to highlight the worst we see. But it is vital that this is done in a way that does not reduce the focus on everything else that we see which is equally wrong.

And therein lies the point. Some things *are* worse than others – and some forms of torture and inhuman treatment (let us call it by its name for once, not by its somewhat euphemistic and relativising shorthand 'ill-treatment') do *not* result in as great a degree of pain or suffering as others. But it is not (or should not be) a relative exercise. If torture is wrong, then all cases of torture are wrong, irrespective of how 'painful' they might be. The real question is whether pain or suffering of a sufficient degree was purposively and intentionally inflicted. Once that has happened, the precise degree of pain and suffering that was purposively and intentionally inflicted should not be the benchmark.

It is important to remember this when we turn in the next section to the 'thresholds' between torture and ill-treatment that loom so large in many key legal decisions. Some of these decisions might seem questionable if approached on the basis of the 'severity of suffering' ('was it really that awful when compared with "x"?'), but they make much more sense if the question asked is 'was such treatment of those over whom the authorities exercised power sufficiently serious to be properly described as inhuman?', since, if so, that is sufficient for it to amount to torture when intentionally and purposively inflicted. Otherwise, those so-called 'thresholds' for distinguishing between torture and 'other forms' of ill-treatment appear almost impossible to make sense of. Indeed, they may be impossible to make sense of.

The thresholds

We need to keep reminding ourselves that the prohibition of torture, inhuman and degrading treatment or punishment is an absolute prohibition. It does not admit of any exceptions, under any circumstance. Even in situations which threaten the life of the nation, torture is prohibited. You cannot torture terrorists or those suspected of terrorism, even if you think it might help prevent an act of terrorism from taking place.[5] Osama bin Laden could not lawfully have been tortured or treated in an inhuman or degrading way on 9/10 in the hope that it might have prevented 9/11.

However, there has always been a certain degree of relativity involved when determining whether what has taken place falls within the scope of the prohibition at all, as well as 'which' of the prohibitions it falls foul of. As the European Commission put it back in the *Greek* case, as the Court repeated in *Ireland v UK*, and as virtually every relevant case before the European Court of Human Rights has endorsed ever since, ill-treatment must attain a minimum level of severity if it is to fall within the scope of Article 3 ... The assessment of this minimum is, in the nature of things, relative; it depends on all the circumstances of the case, such as the duration of the treatment, its physical or mental effects and, in some cases, the sex, age and state of health of the victim, etc.[6]

In other words, there must always be a certain level of severity, and there is a 'minimum' threshold of seriousness that must be crossed. While this is true of the 'entry' threshold – the question of whether there has been ill-treatment sufficient to trigger the prohibition at all – it is also true of the 'thresholds' between the various 'forms' of ill-treatment which that prohibition contains. To that extent, the prohibition is rather less 'absolute' than it seems. It absolutely prohibits what falls within its scope. But how is this to be determined, particularly since our understandings of what might cross that threshold can, and does, change over time? It is helpful to consider an example in some detail to help illustrate this.

The case of *Costello-Roberts v UK* was decided by the European Court in 1993 and related to an incident which occurred in 1985. It concerned a seven-year-old boy who was 'punished in accordance with the disciplinary rules in force within the school in which he was a boarder. This amounted to being "slippered" three times on his buttocks through his shorts with a rubber-soled gym shoe by the headmaster in private.'[7] The Court thought that this did not meet the threshold of severity necessary to bring Article 3 into play: in other words, it was not severe enough to be degrading, irrespective of what the boy (and the boy's family) might have thought.[8] In reaching that conclusion the Court drew on its decision in *Tyrer v UK*, a judgment given by the Court some 15 years earlier in 1978 and which concerned the beating in 1972 by the police of a 15-year-old boy three times on his bare buttocks with a specially designed birch rod in execution of a judicial sentence passed by a court on the Isle of Man, and in conformity with the law then in force.

In the *Tyrer* case, the Court accepted that all judicial punishment is, in a sense, humiliating and therefore degrading and so, unless all judicial punishment were to be prohibited – which would 'be absurd' – 'some further criterion must be read into the text'.[9] This has to be correct – and finds reflection in the wording of the definition of torture in Article 1 of the UN Convention against Torture, which says that '[i]t does not include pain or suffering arising only from, inherent in or incidental to lawful sanction'. Although the reach of this is controversial and much debated, the underlying point – usually more relevant to 'inhuman or to 'degrading' treatment than to torture as torture is rarely judicially sanctioned[10] – is doubtless correct. However, the problem that it raises is, once again, that of 'thresholds': what is above or below, what is in and what is out. In the *Tyrer* case, the Court concluded that

> [t]he very nature of judicial corporal punishment is that it involves one human being inflicting physical violence on another human being. Furthermore, it is institutionalised violence that is in the present case violence permitted by the law, ordered by the judicial authorities of the State and carried out by the police authorities of the State .... Thus, although the applicant did not suffer any severe or long-lasting physical effects, his punishment – whereby he was treated as an object in the power of the authorities – constituted an assault on precisely that which it is one of the main purposes of Article 3) to protect, namely a person's dignity and physical integrity. Neither can it be excluded that the punishment may have had adverse psychological effects.[11]

This is a very powerful passage, condemning the judicial use of corporal punishment as violating the prohibition on torture, inhuman and degrading treatment or punishment because of its 'very nature'. But which of these three was it? The Court, like the Commission, was clear that this was not a case of torture, and it concluded that the 'circumstances of the applicant's punishment were such as to make it "degrading" within the meaning of Article 3 (art. 3)'.[12] But why was this not a case of 'inhuman' treatment or punishment, rather than being 'degrading'? Because the Court thought it wasn't. The Court said that it 'does not consider on the facts of the case that that level was attained and it therefore concurs with the Commission that the penalty imposed on Mr. Tyrer was not "inhuman punishment" within the meaning of Article 3 (art. 3)'.[13] The Court did not elaborate in any detail on which particular facts these were.

One judge thought otherwise, believing that it was not sufficiently serious even to justify being considered as 'degrading'. Sir Gerald Fitzmaurice took the view that the birching fell below the necessary threshold altogether, since while it might be undesirable to inflict corporal punishment on children and juveniles, it was not necessarily degrading to do so, whereas its infliction on adults might be.[14] His reasoning expressly referred to his early childhood experiences at school, observing that corporal punishment might be considered by the boy himself as preferable to probable alternative punishments such as being kept in on a fine summer's evening to copy out 500 lines or learn several pages of Shakespeare or Virgil by heart, or be denied leave of absence on a holiday occasion'.[15]

Such were not the views of the young boy at the centre of the *Costello-Roberts* case, but the Court still thought that

> [t]he circumstances of the applicant's punishment may be distinguished from those of Mr Tyrer's which was found to be degrading within the

meaning of Article 3 (art. 3). Mr Costello-Roberts was a young boy punished in accordance with the disciplinary rules in force within the school in which he was a boarder. This amounted to being slippered three times on his buttocks through his shorts with a rubber-soled gym shoe by the headmaster in private ... Mr Tyrer, on the other hand, was a young man sentenced in the local juvenile court to three strokes of the birch on the bare posterior. His punishment was administered some three weeks later in a police station where he was held by two policemen whilst a third administered the punishment, pieces of the birch breaking at the first stroke.[16]

This time, several judges disagreed, thinking the Court was being too stringent. They thought that the slippering had amounted to degrading treatment because

> the ritualised character of the corporal punishment is striking. After a three-day gap, the headmaster of the school 'whacked' a lonely and insecure 7-year-old boy. A spanking on the spur of the moment might have been permissible, but in our view, the official and formalised nature of the punishment meted out, without adequate consent of the mother, was degrading to the applicant and violated Article 3.[17]

But why would a headmaster, a person in authority, 'whacking' a young child on the spur of the moment not be degrading too? How 'ritualised' must corporal punishment be for it to be degrading?

These are old and well-known cases which have been pored over many times, and it may seem strange that I should spend so much time rehearsing them yet again, but there is a reason. The very fact that they are old cases dealing with a familiar issue, the prohibition of corporal punishment which is now generally (though not entirely) accepted as uncontroversial, is important. It shows there is nothing new in the problems presented by the 'gradations' found in the prohibition of torture, inhuman or degrading treatment or punishment. We may be startled at the idea that something which today seems as barbaric as the judicial beating of juveniles as in the *Tyrer* case – and the relevant legislation referring to the 'whipping' of younger children – could ever have been thought as being anything less than inhuman, and we may recoil from the suggestion that such beatings might lie outside the prohibited degrees of conduct on the grounds that those beaten were not yet adults. We may be equally shocked at the idea that the very judges who thought that the young Costello-Roberts had been subjected to degrading treatment also thought that this might not have been the case had it been meted out on the spur of the moment in a fit of anger. But none of this should really surprise us at all.

These cases were difficult because they called into question the legitimacy of long-established practices and assumptions about what was and what was not acceptable. Once it has been decided that such treatment falls within the scope of the prohibition – that the threshold has been crossed – its unacceptability may suddenly appear obvious, but that may not be the case until it has been. For example, it was not until the case of *Aydın* v *Turkey* in 1996[18] that the Court first acknowledged that rape could be a form of torture (McGlynn, 2009). How extraordinary that sounds today. How could it ever have been thought not to be? As will be seen in later chapters, the SPT has encountered many practices which are considered acceptable and so fall outside the scope of the prohibition or are not considered sufficiently 'serious' to amount to torture but which doubtless in time will come to be considered as unacceptable or as barbaric as judicial corporal punishment is in the UK today. However, it must also be remembered that judicial corporal punishment is still practised in numerous countries around the world, and there is not yet a global consensus among states concerning its barbarity. Decisions must be made, and thresholds set, and these older cases remind us that this may be a long, difficult and incremental process. Torture and ill-treatment may be prohibited absolutely, but our understanding of what this means in practice develops incrementally.

The danger of thresholds

Whenever the authorities of a state treat a person in a manner which we consider to be outrageous, there is an all too understandable desire to want to see such treatment described as torture, even when this may not be obviously so. For example, in 2001 a G8 summit was held in Genoa during which a series of demonstrations by anti-globalisation protestors was met with a violent response from the police. In one incident, the police stormed a school building in which there was a 62-year-old male protester and

> when the police arrived he sat down against the wall beside a group of persons with his arms in the air ... He was mainly struck on the head, arms and legs, whereby the blows caused multiples fractures: fractures of the right ulna, the right styloid, the right fibula and several ribs. ... The aforementioned injuries left him with a permanent weakness in his right arm and leg.[19]

Indisputably (and it was not disputed), this was inhuman treatment – but was it torture, legally speaking?

There was no doubt that the violence was intentional and premeditated, severe in its nature and severe in its consequences. A whole host of other, shockingly aggravating factors were set out by the Court, which also attached 'particular importance to the gratuitous nature of the violence committed against a detained applicant'.[20] It is difficult to read the judgment without being left with the impression that the Court could find not a single reason to explain the behaviour of the police, which appeared to be outrageous in almost every conceivable way. As a result, it may be entirely understandable that the Court concluded that what had happened amounted to torture. Moreover, this is what the applicant asked the Court to do and it was this that the Italian government was contesting. To do anything other than conclude that the applicant had been tortured would, in effect, mean that the Court was siding with the state, whose authorities had, by common consent, acted appallingly. But was the Court right to do so?

This was a very difficult decision. We have seen that it is not really the relative 'severity' of the ill-treatment which is the hallmark of an act of torture but its *purpose*. In this case, however, the Court seems to suggest that it is the *lack* of any real purpose which made it appropriate to describe what had happened as torture. It was 'gratuitous' – a frenzy of unnecessary violence resulting in serious injury meted out by security forces on unresisting protesters, and all the worse again for its being intended and premeditated. But this runs the risk of putting us back on a lawyerly merry-go-round, and a dangerous one at that. How can the random purposeless of violence be a hallmark of torture if it must also be for a premeditated purpose? It is difficult to see how the premeditated nature of the violence could be 'aggravated' by its randomness, converting what would otherwise have been 'inhuman' treatment into 'torture'. This turns everything on its head – but it is entirely understandable since what occurred was truly outrageous.

Whether that outrage ought to have led to this being described as torture is another matter. But the case certainly highlights the pressure and desire to describe as torture the worst that we see and actions of which we strongly disapprove, just as we strive to avoid describing as torture – or ill-treatment – those things which we might approve of. However, there is little point in an absolute prohibition which only attaches to things that we want to prohibit absolutely, since this is open to constant change. The focus on thresholds can not only be difficult, but it can also be damaging. Moreover, inhuman treatment and degrading treatment is also absolutely prohibited too and we must not fall into the trap of thinking that something is 'not so bad' because it is 'only' inhuman. It is this which can result in the 'grey zone' in which torture and ill-treatment can flourish.

The never-ending question

Be that as it may, thresholds must be thought about since only if they are crossed does it become possible to say whether a violation of the prohibition of torture or ill-treatment has occurred. Moreover, thresholds raise questions which will never go away and cannot really be finally answered. The sad truth is that the ways in which people can mistreat each other are almost limitless. In principle, almost *anything* can have within it the potential to be inhuman or degrading, and almost anything can be used for the purposes of torture. The decisions of courts and international human rights bodies now provide an enormous number of examples of situations in which those thresholds of severity have been crossed.

As we saw in both Chapter 1 and at the start of this chapter, some forms of ill-treatment appear so obviously wrong that the very need to consider their severity in a particular case seems not only unnecessary, but almost improper. As the European Court put it in *Zhyzitskyy v Ukraine*, 'subjecting a person to electric shocks is a particularly serious form of ill-treatment capable of provoking severe pain and cruel suffering and therefore falling to be treated as torture, even if it does not result in any long-term health damage. ...'[21]

As a result, some forms of ill-treatment will *always* cross that threshold and will *always* be absolutely prohibited: they are, by their very nature, inhuman and degrading, and their use may amount to torture – if state officials take you away and rape you; if they tie you up and beat you; if they lock you up without food or water and deprive you of sleep, or other essentials of life for prolonged periods – and so much else besides – we really do not need any great discussion to know that this is 'inhuman' treatment. If you are stripped naked, paraded in front of others and urinated on by police officers (as in the *Selmouni* case) – can this ever *not* be inhuman or degrading? The point is quite simple: in cases such as these, we 'just know' (or we ought to know).

In many other situations, however, we don't 'just know', and there is a need for some context and further detail before we can know. What might be an inhuman or degrading way of treating one person might not be an inhuman or degrading way of treating another – as the European Court has rightly said: 'Police behaviour towards minors may be incompatible with the requirements of Article 3 of the Convention simply because they are minors, whereas it might be deemed acceptable in the case of adults.'[22] A prison regime that might be acceptable for a younger adult detainee might not be suitable for a much older prisoner in frail health: dietary, nutrition or health care needs may vary, and so on. In addition, things which we might not normally think of as being particularly severe may be so as far as the person involved is concerned. For example, it may be inhuman or degrading to require some detainees to shave off their beards, but this would not be true of all, and in such cases 'it may well suffice that the victim is humiliated in his own eyes, even if not in the eyes of others' for treatment to be considered degrading.[23]

The difficulties posed by the interconnectedness of such circumstances are well illustrated in the case of *Bouyid v Belgium*, decided by the Grand Chamber of the European Court in 2015. The case concerned an allegation that police officers had slapped two young men in the face while they were at a police station, and that such treatment was degrading. A Chamber of the Court had previously dismissed this, on the grounds that

> [e]ven supposing that the slapping took place … it was an isolated slap inflicted thoughtlessly by a police officer who was exasperated by the applicants' disrespectful or provocative conduct, without seeking to make them confess. Moreover, there was apparently an atmosphere of tension between the members of the applicants' family and police officers in their neighbourhood. In those circumstances, even though one of the applicants was only 17 at the time and whilst it is comprehensible that, if the events really took place as the applicants described, they must have felt deep resentment, the Court cannot ignore the fact that these were one-off occurrences in a situation of nervous tension and without any serious or long-term effect. It takes the view that acts of this type, though unacceptable, cannot be regarded as generating a sufficient degree of humiliation or debasement for a breach of Article 3 of the Convention to be established. In other words, in any event, the above-mentioned threshold of severity has not been reached in the present case.[24]

There is a resonance here with the separate opinions in the much earlier *Costello-Roberts* case, that the 'unpremeditated' might be less unacceptable than the deliberate, and it is also notable that the Chamber thought the slap was not intended to 'make them confess'. But when the case was referred to the Grand Chamber, it thought differently. The Grand Chamber said that 'even one unpremeditated slap devoid of any serious or long-term effect on the person receiving it may be perceived as humiliating by that person'.[25] Taking account of the overall context in which that slap had been given – by the police, in a police station, to (in one case) a minor, and other factors – the Court concluded that the slap *had* amounted to degrading treatment. However, it also thought that '[g]iven that the applicants referred only to minor bodily injuries and did not demonstrate that they had undergone serious physical or mental suffering, the treatment in question cannot be described as inhuman or, *a fortiori*, torture'.[26]

In other words, the Grand Chamber thought that although the slap was 'degrading', it was not sufficiently serious to be anything more than that. Of course, in other circumstances slapping *can* be torture: think of a person, tied to a chair, being slapped around the face as questions are asked of them. Does the level of pain matter? Or the number of slaps? Perhaps meaningful distinctions can be made on these grounds, but is that really the point? The Court is surely right – intuitively, on the facts of the case: the young men were treated in a degrading manner, it should never have happened and there was no excusing it. However, it is also clear that whether a slap is torture, whether it is inhuman, whether it is degrading or whether it is 'just a slap' needs to be examined and discussed – when as in the case of *Zhyzitskyy* v *Ukraine* a police officer subjects a detainee to electric shocks, it does not need discussion, it simply needs to be called what it is: torture.

The obligation to prevent torture

Why is this long discussion of thresholds relevant to the question posed by the title of this chapter, which is 'Why Prevention'? The answer is simple. The Introduction to this book showed that the human rights 'promise' that no-one should be subjected to torture or ill-treatment has increasingly been seen as being met by finding that a state has breached that obligation, and by an obligation that those individuals who torture, or who are responsible for torture, are held to account. When a judicial or quasi-judicial determination is being made about whether there has been a breach of an obligation then it may be necessary to determine whether what has taken place amounts to torture or whether it is 'inhuman or degrading'. This question *must* be answered because other things may turn on it, such as whether a foreign court has jurisdiction, or whether evidence is admissible, or whether the particular crime with which a person has been charged has been committed. I have argued that the way in which this has so often been approached – by focusing on the degree of pain and the severity of suffering which such acts cause – is not the right way to determine what is torture and what is not. But it is also clearly true that some thresholds must exist and the crossing of them must have consequences. The questions are where they are, and what they are – and these change over time. There is no avoiding this; indeed, it is a necessary part of the process of applying and developing the law.

But how does this help ensure that 'no-one' shall be subjected to torture or ill-treatment? It does so in part by contributing to our understanding of what torture and ill-treatment may be, but the endless (and inevitably endless) discussion of thresholds does little to 'ensure' that torture or ill-treatment does not occur. It contributes to 'defining' what individuals are to be free from, but it does not contribute to achieving this. The debates concerning thresholds can cause something to become 'torture' or 'ill-treatment'; they can also mean that something is understood as not amounting to 'torture' or 'ill-treatment'; they can clarify and classify, but what they cannot do is 'ensure' that a person is *not* tortured or subjected to ill-treatment (other than, perhaps, defining the potential violation away). And this is where prevention comes in.

As well as being under an obligation not to commit acts of torture, states are also under an obligation to try to *prevent* acts of torture from taking place. For the overwhelming majority of states, the clearest source of this obligation is the 1984 UN Convention against Torture itself. In many ways, this Convention is all about prevention, its preamble saying that the purpose of the Convention is to 'make *more effective* the struggle against torture. ...'[27] To that end, and in what are some of its most important provisions, Article 2 of the Convention provides that '[e]ach State Party shall take effective legislative, administrative, judicial or other measures *to prevent* acts of torture in any territory under its jurisdiction'. This, for the first time, meant that there was a clear, unambiguous treaty-based obligation within the UN framework related directly to the prevention of torture.[28]

Article 16(1) then goes on to confirm that this also extends to the prevention of inhuman or degrading treatment too.[29]

The existence of an obligation to take steps to prevent torture is also well established outside of the UN Convention framework. As long ago as 1988, in the *Velásquez Rodríguez* case, the Inter-American Court stressed that states have a legal duty to take reasonable steps to prevent human rights violations.[30] Early on in its work, the International Criminal Tribunal for the Former Yugoslavia said that

[s]tates are obliged not only to prohibit and punish torture, but also to forestall its occurrence: it is insufficient merely to intervene after the infliction of torture, when the physical or moral integrity of human beings has already been irremediably harmed. Consequently, States are bound to put in place all those measures that may pre-empt the perpetration of torture.[31]

In the *Bosnia Genocide* case in 2007, the International Court of Justice drew attention to the obligation to prevent torture in Article 2 of the United Nations Convention against Torture (UNCAT), highlighting that '[t]he content of the duty to prevent varies from one instrument to another, according to the wording of the relevant provisions, and depending on the nature of the acts to be prevented'.[32]

The following year, in 2008, the Committee against Torture issued its General Comment no 2, which set out in detail its approach to the preventive obligation in Article 2 of the Convention, highlighting that the duty to prevent is 'wide-ranging' and that the content of that duty is not static, since 'the Committee's understanding of and recommendations in respect of effective measures are in a process of continual evolution' and so are 'not limited to those measures contained in the subsequent articles 3 to 16'.[33]

Reflecting and building on these comments, in 2010 the SPT issued what currently remains one of its most important and foundational documents, 'The Approach of the SPT to the Concept of Prevention of Torture, and Other Cruel, Inhuman or Degrading Treatment or Punishment under the OPCAT'.[34] This contains ten 'Guiding Principles' which reflect its experience during its early years and are prefaced by an introduction which sets out the underlying philosophy of its work. The SPT says that

> it is not possible to devise a comprehensive statement of what the obligation to prevent torture and ill-treatment entails *in abstracto*. It is of course both possible and important to determine the extent to which a State has complied with its formal legal commitments as set out in international instruments and which have a preventive impact but whilst this is necessary it will rarely be sufficient to fulfil the preventive obligation: it is as much the *practice* as it is the *content* of a State's legislative, administrative, judicial or other measures which lies at the heart of the preventive endeavour. Moreover, there is more to the prevention of torture and ill-treatment than compliance with legal commitments. In this sense, the prevention of torture and ill-treatment embraces – or should embrace – as many as possible of those things which in a given situation can contribute towards the lessening of the likelihood or risk of torture or ill-treatment occurring. Such an approach requires not only that there be compliance with relevant international obligations and standards in both form and substance but that attention is also paid to the whole range of other factors which bear upon the experience and treatment of persons deprived of their liberty and which by their very nature will be context specific.

This has remained the SPT's credo ever since and is, in my view, one of its most important contributions to thinking about prevention. Prevention is not about (or only about) standard-setting or compliance; it is not (only) about determining liability or breach. It is certainly not about classifying the nature of breaches or about determining the most appropriate legal labels. It is about identifying what can make a difference and then doing it – whatever that might be. As such, the SPT's concept of prevention is less based in law and is more focused on the situation as it is: it is not textually or theoretically driven but rooted in the realities which have to be confronted. Too much international human rights law and international human rights 'protection' engages with worlds of their own imagining rather than the situations they are meant to be addressing. The remainder of this book looks at how the SPT has attempted to do otherwise.

Notes

[1] *Selmouni v France* [GC], no 25803/94, ECHR 1999-V, paras 82 and 103.

[2] Simply by way of example, see the case of *Petrosyan v Azerbaijan*, no 32427/16, 4 November 2021, para 68. Yet this was a case in which it was simply impossible to determine this. The case was brought by a man, the corpse of whose son was returned to him, decapitated, badly decomposed yet showing signs of severe ill-treatment. The Court concluded that

there had been – that there had to have been – a violation of Article 3, without even trying to differentiate between its various elements.

3   For reasons of space, consistency and ease of comparability, the examples discussed in this chapter, and generally throughout this book, are limited to those of the European Court of Human Rights. Similar questions arise in the work under the other regional and global human rights systems, for which see Mute, 2020 (Africa); Rodríguez-Pinzón, 2020 (Inter-American); and Heyns et al, 2020 (UN Human Rights Committee).

4   It is true that, in part, the reasons for this may be evidential, and this is particularly so where facts are contested. Nevertheless, the underlying point that there is more to this than the presentation and evaluation of evidence stands: *how* that presentation and evaluation is projected matters.

5   This is the so-called 'ticking bomb' scenario, much discussed as an abstract matter but rarely encountered in the manner in which it is discussed in practice. For an overview, see Farrell, 2020. For possibly the most definitive and compelling account see Ginbar, 2008.

6   *Ireland v the United Kingdom*, 18 January 1978, Series A no 25, para 162, quoting the European Commission in the *Greek* case.

7   *Costello-Roberts v the United Kingdom* 25 March 1993, Series A no 247-C, para 31.

8   *Costello-Roberts v the United Kingdom*, para 31.

9   *Tyrer v the United Kingdom*, 25 April 1978, Series A no 26, para 30.

10   It has, however, been argued that it could – and even should – be. See Dershowitz, 2002.

11   *Tyrer v the United Kingdom*, para 33.

12   *Tyrer v the United Kingdom*, para 33.

13   *Tyrer v the United Kingdom*, para 29.

14   *Tyrer v the United Kingdom*, Separate Opinion of Judge Fitzmaurice, para 11.

15   *Tyrer v the United Kingdom*, Separate Opinion of Judge Fitzmaurice, para 12.

16   *Costello-Roberts v the United Kingdom*, para 31.

17   *Costello-Roberts v the United Kingdom*, Joint Partly Dissenting Opinion of Judges Ryssdal, Thór Vilhjálmsson, Matscher and Wildhaber.

18   *Aydın v Turkey*, 25 September 1997, 'Reports of Judgments and Decisions', 1997-VI.

19   *Cestaro v Italy*, no 6884/11, 7 April 2015, paras 34–5.

20   *Cestaro v Italy*, para 174.

21   *Zhyzitskyy v Ukraine*, no 57980/11, 19 February 2015, para 43.

22   *Bouyid v Belgium* [GC], no 23380/09, ECHR 2015, para 110. It might be noted that this is the opposite of the argument advanced in *Tyrer v UK*, where it was suggested that it was less degrading to cane a juvenile than it was an adult.

23   *Bouyid v Belgium* [GC], para 87 and see also para 105.

24   *Bouyid v Belgium*, no 23380/09, 21 November 2013, para 51.

25   *Bouyid v Belgium* [GC], para 105.

26   *Bouyid v Belgium* [GC], para 112.

27   UNCAT, preamble, para 6 (emphasis added).

28   It should be noted that the obligation is not 'to prevent' acts of torture from occurring, but to take measures which are of a preventive nature. Evidence that torture has occurred does not therefore necessarily give rise to a breach of Article 2(1). But a breach of Article 2(1) may occur in the absence of evidence of torture having happened, if there has been a failure to take steps which are of a preventive nature. The Committee against Torture has set out its understanding of Article 2 in the UN Committee against Torture, General Comment no 2, Implementation of Article 2 by States Parties, UN Doc CAT/C/GC/2 (24 January 2008). On this, see Nowak et al, 2019, pp 72–96.

29   Article 16(1) provides that '[e]ach State Party shall undertake to prevent in any territory under its jurisdiction other acts of cruel, inhuman or degrading treatment or punishment which do not amount to torture as defined in article I, when such acts are committed by

or at the instigation of or with the consent or acquiescence of a public official or other person acting in an official capacity. In particular, the obligations contained in articles 10, 11, 12 and 13 shall apply with the substitution for references to torture of references to other forms of cruel, inhuman or degrading treatment or punishment.'

[30] *Velásquez Rodríguez* v *Honduras*, Merits, Judgment of 29 July 1988, Series C no 4, para 174.

[31] ICTFY, *The Prosecutor* v *Anton Furundzija*, Case no IT-95-17/1-T, Judgment of 10 December 1998, para 148.

[32] 'Application of the Convention on the Prevention and Punishment of the Crime of Genocide (*Bosnia and Herzegovina* v *Serbia and Montenegro*)', Merits, Judgment of 26 February 2007, para 429.

[33] UN Committee against Torture, General Comment no 2, Implementation of Article 2 by States Parties, UN Doc CAT/C/GC/2 (24 January 2008), paras 3–4. The breadth of prevention is shown by its saying that preventive measures include, for example, activities such as the training and education of law enforcement personnel.

[34] 'The Approach of the Subcommittee on Prevention of Torture to the Concept of Prevention of Torture and Other Cruel, Inhuman or Degrading Treatment or Punishment under the Optional Protocol to the Convention against Torture and Other Cruel, Inhuman or Degrading Treatment or Punishment' (n 11 above).

3

Establishing the Optional Protocol to the United Nations Convention against Torture

Introduction

No-one ever accuses the United Nations of drafting and adopting international human rights treaties quickly, and the Optional Protocol to the United Nations Convention against Torture (OPCAT) was no exception. When what is proposed is as radical an idea as was the OPCAT, the only surprise is that it was ultimately adopted at all. Seen in that light, the roughly 25 years that it took from inception to completion – from 1977 until 2002 – seems almost expeditious. In some ways, what is so radical about the OPCAT is its very simplicity. At its heart lies the idea that any place where a person might be detained, by or with the approval of the public authorities, should be able to be visited without notice by an independent body to try to ensure that those who are being detained are not subjected to torture or ill-treatment. It is as simple as that. And yet achieving this was far from simple, and making such a system work in practice remains far more complicated than it needs to be.

During my years on the UN Subcommittee on Prevention of Torture (SPT) I learnt that many things can be as simple or as complicated as you wish them to be. Complexity can be a state of mind and a matter of choice. As an academic (or perhaps as an academic lawyer) I am naturally drawn to complexity: our stock-in trade is to discern distinctions and difficulties which may not always exist and to expound upon them in ways that often confuse or confound rather than clarify – the reification of obfuscation, so to speak. As Chair of the SPT, I rapidly found myself drawn in a very different direction, trying to make things which I knew to be rather complicated to achieve seem as simple as possible. The importance of what we were doing demanded this. There is a huge amount that can be done to help prevent torture and ill-treatment, but the truth is that those with operational or political responsibility often do not want to do it.

It is all too easy for the 'I will not' to be camouflaged as the 'I cannot', and the more difficult and demanding the prevention of torture and ill-treatment appears to be, the easier that becomes. There are many genuine complexities which need to be overcome, but all too often these complexities are used as convenient excuses by those who are unwilling to overcome them and, if they try at all, they are more than happy to fail. As a result, I came to see my role as being to make things as simple as possible. No matter how difficult the situation, there are always some things that can be done to improve matters, even if the result is still a very long way from what it should, or even could, be. It is about making the seemingly impossible appear possible and achievable. There are problems enough without having to add to them unnecessarily. And some things really can be as simple as they seem.

This chapter looks at the OPCAT, its background, how it came into being and how it contributes to the prevention of torture.[1] The story needs to be told here, not only because it is important but also because it illustrates what has just been said. The original idea seemed simple enough but it became increasingly bogged down by problems both real and imaginary. Compromise and innovative thinking cut through this to produce the OPCAT that we have today. I am the first to accept that the OPCAT is in many ways a complex and difficult international human rights treaty to implement, but I also believe that approaching those complexities through a lens of simplicity and by focusing on the heart of what the OPCAT is all about has helped make what many considered an implausible fantasy a preventive reality.

The background

The inspiration for the OPCAT lies in the work of the International Committee of the Red Cross (ICRC). Although it does much else besides, at its core the ICRC is empowered by the 1949 Geneva Conventions and its later Protocols to visit those detained during armed conflicts, both prisoners of war and civilian internees, with a view to ensuring they are treated humanely. Its work is confidential, and the ICRC is strictly independent and works on the basis of neutrality. In the mid-1970s, Jean-Jacques Gautier, a Swiss banker from Geneva, the home of the ICRC, asked himself the following question – if it is possible for the ICRC to send delegates to visit places of detention in times of war or armed conflict in order to offer humanitarian assistance, would it also be possible for an independent and neutral body to visit places of detention during times of peace to try to ensure that no-one is tortured or ill-treated? (Gautier, 1980). The OPCAT, ultimately, answers that question; and the answer is yes, it is.

Being initially modelled on the work of the ICRC had important consequences. It suggested that the approach of such a body should be humanitarian in nature, seeking to ensure that those individuals who were at risk were protected from torture and ill-treatment. It suggested that such work should be confidential: indeed, this was considered essential if states were to be persuaded to allow representatives of an independent body into their places of detention. And although it was not really thought about in great detail, it suggested that while the visiting system was international in nature, it would work through a broad network of people who might also be based at a more local level, as is the case with the ICRC. Above all else, however, it suggested that such a scheme was possible. But there were also downsides too.

Some of the idea's critics thought that the establishment of a new system of this nature might undermine the work of the ICRC, since states might think that the ICRC might no longer be needed, or that it might be excluded from visiting places of detention which fell within the remit of the new system in order to avoid duplication between them. At a formal level, this concern was quite easy to deal with, and the OPCAT, Article 32, provides that 'the present Protocol shall not affect the obligations of States Parties to the four Geneva Conventions of 12 August 1949 and the Additional Protocols thereto of 8 June 1977'. But saying that something does not affect the obligations of the state does not really address the potential problems of overlap and duplication in practice,[2] and in truth this has unfortunately resulted in some difficulties.

For example, I certainly recall an occasion when the SPT and the ICRC, unbeknown to the other, turned out to be visiting the same facility at the same time, much to the confusion of the prison staff, and probably the detainees too. The confidentiality of the work of the SPT and ICRC can stand in the way of what others might consider helpful information sharing on even such fundamental and seemingly easy to resolve matters. It certainly stands in the way of coordinated responses to problems which both have observed and which both wish to raise.

It would be quite wrong to suggest that this has ever been a major problem in practice, but it certainly has been an issue from time to time. This is the sort of largely theoretical problem which could have derailed the adoption of the OPCAT from the very outset, and it is true that while it supported the OPCAT, not all in the ICRC were enthusiastic about it for that very reason. However, a relatively simple solution which did not really seek to address the more 'operational' questions proved sufficient to quell concerns. The SPT and the ICRC have fostered greater general awareness of each other's work, and, in most situations most of the time, that has proved to be more than sufficient to avoid any serious difficulties arising.

Other critics took exception to the suggestion that the work of the new visiting body would be confidential. While this might be a necessary price to pay to allow the ICRC to visit detainees in times of war and armed conflict, was confidentiality really necessary in order to gain access to detainees in times of peace? After all, many countries already permit independent inspectors and monitors into prisons without their reports being confidential. Once again, the confidential nature of SPT reports could call that into question – and this is a problem that has arisen in practice. But more fundamentally, how does confidentiality square with the premise of so much human rights work, which is based on ideas of transparency and accountability; of 'shining a light' on what is taking place in some of the darkest corners of the state and on revealing and placing under public scrutiny their hidden secrets? Was confidentially just too high a price to pay for access? It really all depends on how you look at it: for Gautier, the essence of the idea was that 'instead of a state being found guilty of a violation, stress will be laid on prevention' (Gautier, 1980, p 35). Others have suggested that this meant 'we save the state's face, in return for which we hope to get more effective action than would be achieved by exposure' (Rodley, 2009, p 29).

These comments reflect different approaches to what human rights protection is about, and how it is to be achieved. Stripped back to basics, the impulse underlying Gautier's idea was, ultimately, humanitarian in nature. It was about doing what could be done to try to alleviate or reduce the risk of suffering. This, of course, is what human rights protections are also meant to achieve. But the standard techniques of human rights protection only do this indirectly. They are primarily geared towards testing compliance, holding states, or perpetrators, to account for breaches of their obligations and achieving remedies for victims. Naturally, this is not a binary divide, an either/or. Both support (or should support) each other, and, in many ways, they do indeed boil down to the same thing. When the SPT, and similar bodies, visit places of detention, they are, in practice, investigating and inquiring as they go about their preventive work, even if they are not formally undertaking an 'investigation' or an 'inquiry' as such. The claim that they are not doing so is, perhaps, one of the OPCAT system's 'little white lies'. While it might not be investigating a particular allegation or inquiring about a particular concern, it is evaluating the protections against torture and ill-treatment, and what is this if it is not an investigation or inquiry into the prevention of torture in a given place, at a given time? A rose by any other name …

But there is one, irreducible, inescapable and vital difference. Effective prevention can often mean guarding your tongue, biting your lip, and holding back on what you might want to say (or how you might want to say it) in the hope of achieving a more effective outcome than would be achieved through exposure and denunciation. You are not making a formal finding of compliance or non-compliance based on what you have found. You are making a judgement about what is most likely to prevent torture and ill-treatment, in this place, now. Sometimes this may well require denunciation and public condemnation and the OPCAT system does permit this under its formal process for issuing 'public statements',[3] although it is interesting that only recently has this for the first time occurred. This will be returned to in chapter 5. It is also true that the SPT has gone further than perhaps some thought was possible, given its obligations of confidentiality, when issuing public press statements at the end of its visits: these can certainly give a flavour of its overall impressions, if not the details of its findings and its thinking.[4] But the bottom line is that sometimes 'saving the state's face' may indeed be necessary if you are to prevent a person from being tortured or ill-treated. And denunciation and exposure can sometimes achieve absolutely nothing worthwhile and can be counterproductive or down-right dangerous for those at risk of harm. The desire publicly to denounce can be overwhelming. Yet discretion can indeed be the better part of valour, and the most difficult part of prevention can be resisting the urge to denounce, even when every ounce of you is crying out to do so.[5] But who is prevention *for*? In truth, this book in some ways is a form of public denunciation of some of the things which as a member of the SPT I just could not denounce at the time in public and in relation to a particular state.

The road to a result

Gautier's idea, first advanced in 1977, came at an important time. The UN Declaration against Torture had been adopted in 1975 and the process that would result in the adoption of the 1984 UN Convention against Torture was about to begin. Several leading international bodies – including the ICRC and the International Commission of Jurists – gave their backing, and to help advance his plan Gautier formed the 'Swiss Committee against Torture' (Haenni, 1997).

The original thought was that the UN Convention against Torture might itself include provisions setting up a system allowing for international experts to visit places of detention in the states which became a party to it. However, it quickly became apparent that many states had hesitations about this, and that seeking to include such a scheme would make it even more difficult to agree upon the text of the new Convention than it already was, as well as making it less likely that any resulting Convention would be widely signed and ratified. It soon became clear that preventive visiting was just too ambitious and controversial an idea to be included in the main text of the new Convention itself.

As an alternative, it was therefore suggested that there could be an 'Optional Protocol' to the Convention against Torture that would set up such a system. This would be a separate legal treaty which could be signed and ratified by those states which not only were willing to be a party to the Convention against Torture but who were also prepared to accept the additional obligation concerning the visiting system as well. This was the approach that had been used when the 1966 International Covenant on

Civil and Political Rights (ICCPR) was negotiated to facilitate the creation of a system under which individuals could bring 'communications' – that is, complaints – against states before the UN Human Rights Committee, the expert body established under the ICCPR which had just come into force.[6]

Putting such mechanisms in an Optional Protocol makes them available to those who are willing to be bound by them but keeps them at 'arm's length' from those who do not want to be and, perhaps more importantly, from those who do not want to be seen to be endorsing the idea at all. To that end, a draft of a possible Optional Protocol to the Convention against Torture was prepared which would have established such a system of preventive visits to places of detention. However, soundings among states suggested that even *discussing* the idea of such a thing might complicate the process of agreeing the text of the new Convention itself, as some states were concerned that this might lead to their being criticised for not supporting the proposal.

Ultimately, a draft of an Optional Protocol was tabled, by Costa Rica, in March 1980,[7] but this was on the strict understanding that it would not be discussed until after the Convention on Torture itself had been adopted. It was, in effect, putting down a 'marker' for future discussions at a UN level at some unspecified point in the future. But that was not the *only* reason for tabling the proposal: even if it were not possible to make progress at the global level through the UN, it *might* be possible to make progress elsewhere once the proposal was in the official domain, and so it proved.

Soon after, in 1981, the inability to advance the proposal for the establishment of an international system of prevention at the UN was used as a springboard for transferring the project to the regional level, and to the Council of Europe – the institutional home of the European Convention on Human Rights. Today, the Council of Europe has 46 member states, including all of Europe (except for Belarus), and until its expulsion following its invasion of Ukraine in 2022, it also included Russia. In 1981, it was a very different organisation, composed of only 20 states, predominantly in Western Europe together with Greece, Malta and Turkey.

In a decision somewhat tinged with pomposity, self-importance and (misplaced) self-satisfaction, the Parliamentary Assembly of the Council of Europe decided that 'the countries of Europe might set an example and institute such a system among themselves in the framework of the Council of Europe, without waiting for the proposal to be implemented at the world level'.[8] To be fair, once this had been agreed upon in 1983, work proceeded swiftly, and in 1987, a little over three years later, the European Convention for the Prevention of Torture and Inhuman or Degrading Treatment or Punishment (ECPT) was adopted (Evans and Morgan, 1998, pp 106–41). The system it established, though different in many points of detail, reflected the essence of Gautier's proposal. The ECPT entered into force in 1989,[9] and the international body of experts it created – the European Committee for the Prevention of Torture, known as the CPT – conducted its first 'preventive visit' to a place of detention in 1990.

The idea of preventive visiting to places of detention in times of peace by an international expert body had become a reality, but only on a relatively small scale. What could not possibly have been predicted at the time when the Council of Europe agreed to set up such a system was how swiftly its reach would grow. When the CPT undertook that first visit, to Austria, in 1990, only eight of what by then had become the 23 member states of the Council of Europe were parties to the ECPT. By the end of the year, that number had grown dramatically, to 20 out of the then 25 member states.

The entry into force of the ECPT also coincided with the dramatic transformation of the Council of Europe itself. In November 1989, the fall of the Berlin Wall precipitated the collapse of communist governmental control in Central and Eastern Europe, and there was a reciprocal desire for them to join the 'democratic club' which the Council of Europe represented. The very origins of the Council of Europe were rooted in a desire to strengthen democracy by guaranteeing human rights, and so as they became members it was expected that the newly admitted states would become parties to the Council's major human rights treaties, which included the ECPT. And they did.

By 2006, all the then 47 member states of the Council of Europe were parties to the ECPT – approaching 25 per cent of all countries in the world, and at its height, before the departure of Russia, it embraced populations totalling over 820 million people. This certainly had not been foreseen when the Convention was drafted, and a system originally intended to operate principally among the 'mature' democracies of Western Europe and as an example to the rest of the world was swiftly transposed to many others with histories of egregious human rights abuses and at best fledgling systems of human rights protection. The ECPT has now been in force for over 30 years, and the CPT has carried out over 500 preventive visits to all states within the Council of Europe, including visits to overseas territories where the ECPT is also applicable.[10] Some countries have been visited very often indeed.[11] Moreover, the overwhelming majority – indeed, nearly all – of its otherwise confidential reports have been made public with the consent of the state concerned.[12] It is a now a well-respected fixture in the architecture of human rights protection within Europe. But what of the rest of the world?

The accidental OPCAT

My own involvement with torture prevention commenced around the time when the ECPT had just entered into force and the work of the CPT was just beginning. It was all rather accidental. Having just started work as a lecturer in law at the University of Bristol, in an era when young academics still had the time to read things purely out of interest, I chanced upon an article by

Antonio Cassese in the *American Journal of International Law* (Cassese, 1989). Professor Cassese had recently been elected as Chair of the CPT, and his article explained what the Convention was all about.[13] For reasons which I can no longer remember, I decided to learn more about the Convention. Having spent a little time doing so, I thought about writing about it and jotted down some thoughts, which, though I can still remember them, are best forgotten.

Shortly afterwards, I happened to hear a radio interview with Rod Morgan, then recently appointed as Professor of Criminology at Bristol, in which he also spoke of the Convention, as he had been asked to advise it on how best to conduct visits to places of detention. Even now, I smile to think about this. How entirely typical of the international community and the international legal and diplomatic process this was: to spend a great deal of time, energy and angst on negotiating an international treaty and setting up an international visiting mechanism without having any real idea of what it should be doing, and how it should go about doing it. Nevertheless, there are benefits to this: had the 'experts' who drafted the treaty really known what was involved in practice (and Professor Cassese, who himself was one of the drafters of the ECPT, had, I believe, little prior experience of undertaking preventive visits to places of detention before his election to the CPT), then the business of drafting the ECPT might have been a lot longer and more complicated than it was. Indeed, it might never have happened. The ECPT is a sparse text that contains more by way of general outline than practical detail. Those details have been developed through practical experience, and that is no bad thing. When drafting an international agreement, focusing too much on detail can be unhelpful when what is really being sought is the endorsement of an idea. This was very much the experience of drafting the OPCAT.

Professor Morgan went on to accompany the CPT as an expert during its first visit to Austria, and on many other visits thereafter. The day after I heard him speaking on the radio, I knocked on the door of his room along the corridor from mine in the Bristol Law Department (today it seems odd that one might genuinely expect to find an academic colleague in their office, but that was the way it was) and explained that I had heard and been interested in what he had said. Thus began our research collaboration concerning the work of the CPT, which continues to this day. That work included researching and writing a full-length book on the European Convention and the early years of the CPT (Evans and Morgan, 1998).[14]

We started from our knowledge of the Convention text and early practice but had relatively little knowledge of the history that lay behind it. Our research into its origins almost immediately brought us into contact with the Association for the Prevention of Torture (APT), as the Swiss Committee against Torture (SCAT) had recently been renamed, since it was the 'godparent' of the European Convention, without which it would never have come into being. Over time, our academic research developed into supportive engagement. For Rod Morgan, this largely meant further work with the CPT. For me, an international lawyer, this meant greater involvement with the APT, culminating in my becoming a member of its Board of Management, a position I relinquished when I was elected to the SPT in 2009. Initially, my involvement with the APT was largely in relation to its work supporting the CPT but this soon shifted to the process of getting the OPCAT adopted.

Understandably, the OPCAT trail had 'gone cold' at the UN since the tabling of the Costa Rica Draft of an Optional Protocol back in 1981, but much else had happened at the UN level. In 1981, the UN General Assembly established the 'Voluntary Fund for Victims of Torture',[15] and in 1982 the UN Human Rights Committee issued a 'General Comment' concerning torture which, importantly, pointed out that 'the scope of protection required goes far beyond torture as normally understood'.[16] It had also begun considering individual communications, and many of these concerned allegations of torture. The mandate of the UN Special Rapporteur on Torture was established in 1985, initially for only a year but then for three-year periods, and that mandate continues to this day (Méndez and Nicolescu, 2020). The UN Convention which had been adopted by the UN General Assembly in 1984 entered into force in 1987, and the Committee against Torture (known as the CAT) had been established and commenced its work. Yet the UN was in no hurry to return to the OPCAT, and in 1986 and again in 1989 it postponed further consideration of it.

Nevertheless, now that the ECPT had been adopted, entered into force and the CPT had begun its work, the time seemed right to press the issue and in 1991 Costa Rica presented to the UN Commission on Human Rights a new draft of an Optional Protocol to the UNCAT,[17] drafted with the APT and drawing heavily on the European experience. This was hardly surprising, given the role played by the SCAT/APT in developing both the original Costa Rica proposal in 1981 and the decision of the Council of Europe to develop the ECPT. At its 1991 session, the Commission on Human Rights again deferred the matter, and the frustration this produced is well reflected in comments made in a submission by a large group of NGOs prior to the Commission's 1992 session. They argued that it was high time the draft was considered 'quite simply because the idea of a system of preventing torture through visits to places of detention is an idea to which nobody can reasonably object ... Honestly, who – in a forum such as the Commission on Human Rights – could say that such an idea does not deserve to be examined?'[18]

The short answer was that many states did not really want this discussed, and as became obvious, there were plenty of objections to such a system.

But for now, the Commission finally gave way and agreed that the draft should be considered and established an 'open-ended working group', which, with a break in 2000, met annually for two weeks each year from 1992 until 2002, reporting annually on its progress to the Commission. Progress was slow and difficult.[19] This is not the place to consider the drafting history in detail, but it clearly showed that, despite the lip-service paid to the idea, few states were truly enthusiastic at the prospect of establishing an international body able to visit places of detention in order to try to prevent torture and ill-treatment. Moreover, while a modest number were cautiously supportive, a considerable number of states were just plain hostile. Some – such as the United States[20] – tried to mask their hostility behind suggestions which purported to be constructive but rarely were. Others, such as Egypt, made no effort to hide their hostility at all.

The Commission on Human Rights sought to work on the basis of consensus, and the only thing on which there appears to have been consensus was that the discussions were going nowhere, slowly. Although there was agreement on a number of relatively minor points of detail, there was no meeting of minds on the central issue – whether the international visiting body should have unannounced and unfettered access to places of detention. While many states appeared willing to accept this as an abstract proposition, most were only prepared to do so if it was hedged with caveats and restrictions which ran the risk of defeating the entire point of the exercise. The process was, in effect, deadlocked, and the only reason why it rumbled on was that no-one seemed to want to take responsibility for killing it off (Evans and Haenni-Dale, 2020, pp 28–37). But this could not carry on for ever. Out of this impasse emerged what has now become generally recognised as the OPCAT's single most significant contribution to the prevention of torture and ill-treatment – described by some as the 'Jewel in the Crown' of the OPCAT system (Steinerte, 2014). At the time, however, it appeared to many supporters of the OPCAT project to be a thoroughly retrograde step and not an advance at all.

To try to break the negotiating deadlock, the session of the Working Group scheduled for October 2000 was delayed until February 2001 and, following intensive informal soundings and discussions, a radically different proposal, known as the 'Mexican Draft', was presented to the Working Group on behalf of the Group of Latin American and Caribbean states, known as the GRULAC.[21] This completely reworked the draft Optional Protocol so that it no longer focused on visits by an international body. Instead, it proposed that states should establish a *national* system of preventive visits, which would be supplemented by visits from an international body should this prove necessary because the National Preventive Mechanism (NPM) had not commenced its work within two years, or if the state agreed to its doing so.

It was in this way that what have since become known as NPMs were introduced into the OPCAT framework – and this provoked a very hostile response from some NGOs[22] and states. The lunchtime after these proposals were put before the Working Group, there was a stormy meeting at the offices of the APT (then the fondly remembered but rather dysfunctional 'Cabane', not the rather more appropriate and impressive building which the APT today occupies on the same site close to the Palais des Nations) at which I was present, and it turned out to be pivotal moment in the OPCAT story and for torture prevention.

The reason the proposal drew hostility from some of the leading NGOs – from Amnesty International and Human Rights Watch in particular – and from the EU[23] was that it seemed to fly in the face of many of the 'received orthodoxies' of international human rights protection, which is based on the idea that the rights record and performance of countries should be scrutinised by international bodies, not national ones. Far too many 'independent' national human rights bodies were (and are) not really independent at all – and allowing states to set up their own 'independent' bodies to scrutinise their own conduct smacked too much of allowing states to 'mark their own homework'. The fear was that substituting an independent body of international experts for a group of domestics might result in the creation of sham bodies which would be ineffective and fail to challenge the conduct of the governments that created them and to whom they were beholden. Worse, nationally created bodies might act as apologists for abusive states, drawing a veil over their conduct, offering a degree of unwarranted legitimacy and reducing the opportunities for international protection; they might be more of a fig-leaf than a revelation.

As will be seen, these fears were not without foundation. But the proposal was not to replace effective international visiting with ineffective national visiting. It was to establish effective national visiting bodies, while also establishing an international body which would 'support and supervise' their work and, crucially, which could undertake visits itself if the national body was not actually set up or did not undertake any visits. Moreover, the NGOs who were most affronted by this change of direction were not those which had followed the experience of the European Convention and the CPT in much detail.

The NGOs whose work was more closely focused on torture – and torture prevention – had the advantage of having scrutinised the now ten years' worth of work by the CPT and had come to realise the limitations of what a system of regular visits by an international body could actually achieve. In a nutshell, it could never visit regularly *enough*. On average, the CPT could at that time visit any given state for no more than up to about ten days about once every four or five years. Some were visited more often and for longer, but others less often and for only a few days. The prospect of a UN body, operating in many more countries, doing any better than this was clearly remote – for which might be read non-existent. National bodies, at least in theory, could do better than this. That was the argument and that was sufficient to blunt the initial hostility of those states who were supporters of the project and keep them on side. However, the more hostile NGOs never really displayed the same enthusiasm for the OPCAT after that stormy lunchtime meeting.

With the benefit of hindsight, a great deal more subtlety can be read into the thought processes around this proposal to establish national mechanisms of prevention than can really be justified. Indeed, even the argument just given was, in some ways, an almost immediate *ex post facto* justification for what, at the time, was largely seen as a necessary concession to get things moving. For example, I myself was one of those who advanced this justification at the time, but I had had no prior warning of what was going to be proposed at all, let alone the reasons for it. To this day, I cannot honestly say if this really was one of the reasons for making the proposal or not. It certainly became so, and perhaps that is enough.

The proposal also had some unexpected, though positive, consequences. For example, it is hardly controversial to say that national-level mechanisms have a role to play in protecting human rights. What is controversial is granting independent national bodies access to all places of detention – something which was not (and still is not) the case in very many states. During the discussions, however, many states which were really opposed to permitting access to places of detention *at all* chose to focus their objections to the OPCAT on its granting *international* experts the right of unannounced and unfettered access, highlighting concerns related to national sovereignty (always a fertile argument in state-centric circles) and 'problems' that might result from allowing biased and hostile foreigners into their detention facilities. Very few states had objected to the idea of preventive visits to places of detention *as such*. They did not need to, since they could hide behind largely spurious concerns such as these, knowing that other states were bound to have to take them seriously even when they knew them to be groundless. However, once the idea of mandatory 'international visiting' was taken off the table, it became much more difficult for such states to object to visits by national bodies since these concerns did not apply. They were, in effect, blindsided by the change of focus, which deprived them of one of their principal arguments against the OPCAT – even if it was not the real reason for their opposition. Was this foreseen? Was this 'the plan'? Probably not: it was meant to be more of a concession than a trap, but it certainly turned out to be a shrewd move on many levels.

Despite the furore it generated, the proposal to include national as well as international visiting mechanisms within the OPCAT succeeded in creating a new way forward and paved the way for its adoption by the UN General Assembly in December of the following year, 2002.[24] But it was hardly as simple as that short timeframe might suggest. Although the use of national mechanisms was almost certainly intended to address concerns about visits being undertaken by an international mechanism, it quickly became accepted that there was going to have to be a role for both. The real question became the relationship between them, and the task of working out how to strike the right balance was given to the Chair of the Working Group, Mrs Odio Benito of Costa Rica. The balance she struck is the balance that is found in the text of the OPCAT and will be set out in the following chapter. The story of its final adoption can be told quite quickly, remarkable in its own way though it is.

Extensive and largely private consultations took place across the remainder of 2001 and leading up to the tenth and final meeting of the Working Group in February 2002. When the meeting commenced it was known that a new text had been drafted, but that text was not yet made available. There followed a week of intense debate concerning what a text combining both a national and international mechanism might look like, conducted largely in ignorance of what was about to be proposed. Doubtless this was intended to allow the draft to be amended to reflect those discussions – though it is equally possible that it was not changed at all and listening to the discussions allowed the Chair to gauge how best to present it. At the start of the second week, the Chair's Draft was revealed, and following another week of intensive and often heated discussion it was annexed to the report of the Working Group, basically unchanged.[25]

The report of the Working Group was considered by the UN Commission on Human Rights in April 2002 and it is fair to say that no-one was really expecting a great deal to come of it. For reasons which remain not entirely obvious, Cuba then proposed a 'no-action' motion, that is, it proposed that the matter be not considered. This motion was defeated on a contested vote, with the result that the report containing the draft text fell to be voted upon. This was unusual: the purpose of having the matter considered by a Working Group was to seek consensus on a text, and the one thing that was obvious was that no consensus had been achieved. This was reflected in the vote that followed: of the 51 members of the Commission, 27 voted for the text, ten voted against and 14 abstained. Nevertheless, this meant that the text had been adopted by the Commission – and so the matter passed up the UN chain of consideration to the Economic, Social and Cultural Council (ECOSOC) in New York in July of that year, and the 53-member ECOSOC again approved the text: by 35 votes to eight, with ten abstentions. And so it moved forward to the General Assembly in December 2002, where it was adopted by 127 votes to four, with 42 abstentions.

Had this been the 'plan', or even a hope, less than a year earlier? Almost certainly not. Indeed, one key player in the process described to me the plan around that time had been to give the then current text 'a first-class funeral'. But if that was the expectation, a resurrection had occurred. The Optional Protocol was now a reality – though it would only come into force once

20 states had agreed to be bound by it.[26] That threshold was finally passed when both Bolivia and Honduras ratified on 23 May 2006, meaning that the OPCAT entered into force for those first 20 states on 22 June 2006. These pioneer countries deserve to be listed, and they were: Albania, Argentina, Bolivia, Costa Rica, Croatia, Denmark, Georgia, Honduras, Liberia, Maldives, Mauritius, Mexico, Mali, Malta, Paraguay, Poland, Spain, Sweden, United Kingdom of Great Britain and Northern Ireland, and Uruguay. Other ratifications soon followed apace, and by the end of the year, a further 10 states had become parties.[27] But what had they agreed to?

Notes

[1]   There are now a range of works which explore the background to and drafting of the OPCAT from various perspectives. Key texts include Haenni, 1997; Evans and Heanni-Dale, 2004; Murray et al, 2011, chapters 2 and 3; Nowak et al, 2019, pp 700ff.

[2]   The equivalent article in the ECPT is rather different, Article 17(3) providing that '[t]he Committee shall not visit places which representatives or delegates of Protecting Powers or the International Committee of the Red Cross effectively visit on a regular basis by virtue of the Geneva Conventions of 12 August 1949 and the Additional Protocols of 8 June 1977 thereto'.

[3]   OPCAT, Article 16(4) provides that '[i]f the State Party refuses to cooperate with the Subcommittee on Prevention according to articles 12 and 14, or to take steps to improve the situation in the light of the recommendations of the Subcommittee on Prevention, the Committee against Torture may, at the request of the Subcommittee on Prevention, decide, by a majority of its members, after the State Party has had an opportunity to make its views known, to make a public statement on the matter or to publish the report of the Subcommittee on Prevention'.

[4]   Press releases made at the end of a visit are available on the UN website at https://www.ohchr.org/en/treaty-bodies/spt. To give an example, on 6 October 2022, following a visit to Ecuador, the SPT said in a press release that '[w]e are gravely concerned about the dire situation in various detention centres and prisons in Ecuador ... The recent violence is the consequence of decades of state abandonment. Detainees have been living in a state of tension and constant fear, in prisons lacking essential services and basic resources. Some spaces in these prisons are self-governed by detainees who are members of criminal organisations.' This does not exactly pull its punches and is not dissimilar to the views expressed by other UN mandate holders at the conclusion of their visits.

[5]   It is worth noting that the European Committee for the Prevention of Torture, the CPT, which can also issue public statements, has been quite parsimonious too, issuing only ten in over 30 years, and against only four countries, Bulgaria (three times, in 2015, 2017 and 2019), Greece (once, in 2011), Turkey (twice, in 1992 and 1996), the Russian Federation (four times, in 2001, 2003, 2007 and 2019). See https://www.coe.int/en/web/cpt/public-statements

[6]   Optional Protocol to the International Covenant on Civil and Political Rights (adopted 16 December 1966, in force 23 March 1976), 99 UNTS 171.

[7]   E/CN.4/1409, 6 March 1980. For text, see Nowak et al, 2019, p 1195.

[8]   Berrier Report, Council of Europe Doc AS/Jur (33) 18 of 9 September 1981, para 13, adopted by Council of Europe, Parliamentary Assembly Recommendation 971 (1983).

[9]   European Convention for the Prevention of Torture and Inhuman or Degrading Treatment or Punishment (adopted 26 November 1987, entered into force 1 February 1989), ETS no 126.

[10] For a relatively up to date overview of the work of the CPT, see Bicknell et al, 2018. The 31st CPT General Report indicates that it had undertaken 503 visits to the end of 2021. See CPT/Inf(2021)5, appendix 5.

[11] For example, to the end of 2021, Turkey had received a total of 32 visits and Russia 30.

[12] To the end of 2021, 436 of the 471 reports that had been sent to states following visits had been published. See CPT/Inf(2021)5, para 26.

[13] He subsequently published a book – not entirely dissimilar to this book – based on his experiences (Cassese, 1996).

[14] Others include an edited collection of essays (Morgan and Evans, 1999) and a work more focused on the standards of the CPT (Morgan and Evans, 2001), a substantially reworked version of which appeared some years later (Bicknell et al, 2018).

[15] See UNGA Res 36/151 (adopted 16 December 1981). This was a reconfiguration of a trust fund previously established for those whose human rights had been violated due to detention or imprisonment in Chile.

[16] CCPR General Comment no 7: Article 7 (Prohibition of Torture or Cruel, Inhuman or Degrading Treatment or Punishment), 30 May 1982, para 2. It also pointed out that 'the safeguards which may make control effective are provisions against detention incommunicado, granting, without prejudice to the investigation, persons such as doctors, lawyers and family members access to the detainees' (para 2) – all of which have subsequently become familiar as 'fundamental safeguards' in the context of prevention. This general comment was subsequently replaced by CCPR General Comment no 20, Article 7, Prohibition of Torture, or Other Cruel, Inhuman or Degrading Treatment or Punishment (1992), UN Doc A/47/40 pp 193–5 (10 March 1992), para 11 of which sets out an extensive list of procedural safeguards.

[17] E/CN.4/1991/66, 5 January 1991. For text, see Nowak et al, 2019, p 1196.

[18] Written statement submitted by a coalition of NGOs, 4 February 1992, E/CB.4/1992/NGO/27, para 1(1).

[19] For the drafting of the OPCAT, see Evans and Haenni-Dale, 2004; Murray et al, 2011, chapters 2 and 3; Nowak et al, 2019, pp 700ff.

[20] For example, the United States submitted a radically different text of an 'Alternative Optional Protocol' (E/ CN.4/ 2002/ 78, annex II E) for consideration just as the final version of the compromise text was about to be tabled and discussed in the Working Group in January 2002 and which could have knocked the entire process off course, had it been taken seriously. Fortunately, its purpose was sufficiently transparent for it not to have any traction at all. For text, see Nowak et al, 2019, p 1221.

[21] The 'Alternative Preliminary Draft Optional Protocol to the Convention against Torture and Other Cruel, Inhuman or Degrading Treatment or Punishment Submitted by the Delegation of Mexico with the Support of the Latin American Group (GRULAC)', E/ CN.4/2001/67, annex I. For text, see Nowak et al, 2019, p 1201.

[22] The approach was strongly supported by the APT, International Federation of ACAT (FiACAT) and the International Rehabilitation Council for Torture (IRCT), but other leading NGOs, including Amnesty International and Human Rights Watch, had major reservations.

[23] The EU almost immediately submitted a counter-proposal that was heavily weighted towards the work of the international body while acknowledging a subsidiary role for NPMs, subject to tight conditions of independence. See 'Proposal of New and Revised Articles to Be Included in the Original Draft Optional Protocol to the Convention against Torture and Other Cruel, Inhuman or Degrading Treatment or Punishment, Submitted by the Delegation of Sweden on Behalf of the European Union at the Ninth Session of the Working Group in 2001 (EU Draft)', 22 February 2001, E/ CN.4/ 2001/ WG.11/ CRP.2. For text, see Nowak et al, 2019, p 1209.

24 See UNGA A/RES/57/199 (adopted 18 December 2002).
25 I recall being a member of a group which met with the Chair to argue for the removal of a single comma from the text in one of its provisions. The comma remained.
26 OPCAT Article 28(2).
27 These being Armenia, Benin, Czech Republic, Ukraine, Serbia, Moldova, Senegal, Peru, Liechtenstein and Estonia.

4

What the Optional Protocol
to the United Nations Convention
against Torture Requires

Introduction

For all my talk of simplicity, the Optional Protocol to the United Nations Convention against Torture (OPCAT) is a rather complex text. It is unlike all other UN human rights treaties, and it is not surprising therefore that some in the human rights world have found it difficult to work out quite what it means in practice. Indeed, as someone who has worked as closely as it is possible to work with the OPCAT system for very many years, I must admit to not really understanding what some of it means in practice myself. But there are good reasons for this.

As we saw in the previous chapter, the compromise text proposed by the Chair of the Working Group early in 2001 was adopted by the General Assembly at the end of 2022 basically unchanged. In many ways, that text was, however, still a 'work in progress'. While it offered a way forward on most of the major, structural elements – the international and national visiting mechanisms and the relationship between international and national visiting, for example – there were many other issues which would have benefitted from further thought or clarification. The drafters were aware of this, but at the time it seemed more important to settle the major issues of principle than continue to debate the finer points of detail, and doubtless this was entirely correct. However, it does mean that there are some matters which could have been made clearer, and others which are something of a problem. More positively, the open-textured nature of some of the key provisions has allowed room for some real creativity which has greatly enhanced the effectiveness of the OPCAT system.

This chapter is not intended to be a legal 'commentary' on the text – this has been done by others (Nowak et al, 2019). Rather, it focuses on some of the key elements of the OPCAT framework and how they have come to be understood in practice. The text of the OPCAT is divided into seven separate parts. Part I sets out the general principles of the system (Articles 1–4), while Parts II (Articles 5–10) and III (Articles 11–16) concern the establishment and mandate of the UN Subcommittee on Prevention of Torture (SPT). Part IV (Articles 17–23) concerns the work and mandate of the National Preventive Mechanisms (NPMs), while the remainder address various cross-cutting matters.[1] The remaining chapters in this part of this book adopt a similar approach, looking at the basic principles and then turning to the work of the SPT in Chapter 5 and to the work of the NPMs in Chapter 6. The cross-cutting issues will be considered where relevant. These chapters attempt not only to set out what the OPCAT says and what that means, but also how they have come to be understood in practice.

The basic principles of the OPCAT system

Article 1 of the OPCAT sets out in seemingly clear language the basic purpose of the OPCAT. It provides that

> [t]he objective of the present Protocol is to establish a system of regular visits undertaken by independent international and national bodies to places where people are deprived of their liberty, in order to prevent torture and other cruel, inhuman or degrading treatment or punishment.

In truth, almost every phrase of this gives rise to difficulties: what is a 'system of regular visits'? What is an 'independent' body (national or, indeed, international)? What is a 'place where people are deprived of their liberty'? Indeed, what is a 'place' and what is 'deprivation of liberty'? And, of course, we have already seen how difficult it can be to determine what torture, inhuman or degrading treatment or punishment might mean, and what is meant by prevention. The OPCAT gives guidance on some of these key questions, though not as much as might be assumed.

To fulfil these tasks, Article 2 the OPCAT provides for the establishment of the SPT, which will be considered in more detail in this chapter. Article 3 then goes on to provide that '[e]ach State Party shall set up, designate or maintain at the domestic level one or several visiting bodies for the prevention of torture and other cruel, inhuman or degrading treatment or punishment (hereinafter referred to as the national preventive mechanism)'. These, then, form the two pillars of the preventive system; the international and the national visiting mechanisms. But what is the relationship between them and between their visiting programmes?

As was seen in the previous chapter, NPMs were originally introduced as an alternative to international visiting, and it was this that prompted such a negative reaction to the proposal. As the drafting process developed, it became clear that an approach which gave primacy to visits by NPMs, with the international mechanism as either a 'default' mechanism if the NPM was not established or as an optional extra, would not be acceptable and the idea emerged of making the international mechanism something of a 'back-up', to be used where effective visiting was not being conducted.[2] The next phase of the discussions came to centre on the balance between them. With the benefit of hindsight, this approach was not a good idea at all and it would have caused all manner of difficulty. On what basis would the SPT decide that an NPM was not conducting effective visits, so triggering its own visiting mandate? What would be the threshold, and the evidence base? While sounding reasonable enough in theory, it would have been a practical nightmare. The entire business would have become fraught and confrontational – the very antithesis of preventive work.

Fortunately, in this instance the answer to this very contentious question was far better than many had feared and, in truth, better than many had dared to hope. Rather cleverly slipped in, almost as an aside, Article 4(1) goes on to say that '[e]ach State Party shall allow visits, in accordance with the present Protocol, by the mechanisms referred to in articles 2 and 3. ...' The placement of this and the reference to both mechanisms in the opening articles setting out the 'general principles' of the OPCAT system is all important. It means that state parties *must* allow visits by both the international and the national visiting bodies, by both the SPT and the NPMs. It was not to be an 'either/or' approach after all, and neither was the international mechanism only to have residuary powers. This doubtless came as an unpleasant surprise to those who had sought to blunt the edge of the OPCAT system by supporting a switch towards national visiting. They had ended up with both.

The residue of a concession concerning visits by the international body is found in Article 24, which provides that:

1. Upon ratification, States Parties may make a declaration postponing the implementation of their obligations under either part III or part IV of the present Protocol.
2. This postponement shall be valid for a maximum of three years. After due representations made by the State Party and after consultation with the Subcommittee on Prevention, the Committee against Torture may extend that period for an additional two years.

What this means is that when a state ratifies the OPCAT, it has a choice. It can either accept all the obligations at once or, alternatively, it can either delay the powers of the SPT to undertake visits or it can delay its obligation to establish its own NPM, and hence visits to places of detention by the NPM, for up to three years. It can also seek to extend that period for a further two years, but it is not automatically entitled to a further extension beyond the initial three year period. As we will see later, the OPCAT says that a state must establish its NPM within one year of ratifying the OPCAT. The result is as follows. If it wishes to do so, a state can prevent the SPT from visiting it for three years, and potentially for up to five years. However, if it does, it must set up its NPM within one year, and the NPM should be able to start its own visiting immediately. There is, then, potentially a 'gap' of up to a year in which the SPT cannot visit and an NPM might not yet have been established. This will then be followed by up to two or four further years in which only the NPM might be able to undertake visits in the country, but after this both the SPT and NPM would be able to do so.

Although in theory excluding the international mechanism in this way is unfortunate, it does not result in a significant 'gap' in preventive visiting overall and so is not very much of a concession or a loss at all, bearing in mind that some states wished to exclude international visiting altogether. As will be seen later, it is even less of a concession in practice, as the capacity of the SPT to swiftly visit states is limited and while the delay may be frustrating, it may not be that material. Moreover, few states ever choose to postpone SPT visiting in this way. To the best of my knowledge, the only state ever to have done this was the Philippines, which became a party to the OPCAT in April 2012.[3] The SPT undertook a visit to the Philippines in May 2015.

I should love to be able to say that this is a great example of the SPT getting into a country at the very first moment that it was able to do so following the expiry of the three-year period of delay. Unfortunately, I cannot. When the decision to visit the Philippines was taken and the timing of that visit internally agreed upon, the existence of the Declaration had been completely overlooked. Indeed, it appears to have been completely overlooked by the Philippines as well, as I do not recall the precise timing of our visit being raised by them when it was announced at the end of the previous year that we would be visiting them at some point in 2015. I do remember my sense of relief when this came to light that we were just the right side of the three-year period by a matter of days – as by then virtually all our plans were in place and flights booked ...

It is doubtless the case that some states have not become a party to the OPCAT because they do not want the SPT to be able to visit their country. It is equally clear that the 'concession' of delaying SPT visits has not been much of an incentive to draw reluctant states into the system. As a result, it may not seem to have been worth the angst that was invested in it during the drafting process. But it was certainly worthwhile to the extent that it opened the door to the establishment of NPMs. Perhaps surprisingly, states have been somewhat keener to delay their obligations to establish NPMs than to postpone SPT visits – but even so, only seven countries have done this, and only two of these – Romania and Australia – have sought (successfully) to extend that period.[4] In general, the twin pillar system, with visits to be conducted by both international and national bodies, has been accepted – at least in theory. But visits to whom, and to where?

Deprivation of liberty

Readers of a certain age (now an increasingly advanced one) might still recall a popular advertising campaign for an alcoholic drink which boasted that it could be enjoyed 'any time, any place, anywhere'. While as regards the beverage in question that might be something of an exaggeration, this has often been used as a convenient summary of the visiting mandate of the SPT and of NPMs, and, while not entirely accurate either, it certainly conveys the gist of the matter. Nevertheless, while extremely broad, the scope of their visiting mandate is not limitless. The matter is addressed by the last of the 'general provisions' in Part I of the OPCAT, Article 4.

Article 4 provides that:

1. Each State Party shall allow visits, in accordance with the present Protocol, by the mechanisms referred to in articles 2 and 3 to any place under its jurisdiction and control where persons are or may be deprived of their liberty, either by virtue of an order given by a public authority or at its instigation or with its consent or acquiescence (hereinafter referred to as places of detention). These visits shall be undertaken with a view to strengthening, if necessary, the protection of these persons against torture and other cruel, inhuman or degrading treatment or punishment.
2. For the purposes of the present Protocol, deprivation of liberty means any form of detention or imprisonment or the placement of a person in a public or private custodial setting which that person is not permitted to leave at will by order of any judicial, administrative or other authority.

In some ways, these are the most important paragraphs in the OPCAT, setting out where the SPT and the NPMs can go and who they can see. Since they are also possibly the most confused and confusing paragraphs that it contains, I always took the view that, if possible, it was best to avoid discussing them. The SPT is, however, currently engaged in drafting a 'General Comment' on the scope of Article 4(1) concerning the definition of places of deprivation of liberty, and the length of time that this is taking is an indication of how tricky this is proving – I am not surprised – and when Chair, I did my best to deflect the suggestion that this be done, although I was ultimately unsuccessful in that. The problem is simple: it is just too difficult to define. Some things clearly are places of detention, but just about anywhere *can* be: if you were tied to a tree in the middle of a forest by security forces, this might convert the forest – and possibly even the tree – into a place of detention. And since the right to visit extends to anywhere where people *may* be deprived of their liberty, then there is no real limit at all to the types of places that can fall within the scope of the visiting mandate.

In principle, it would be entirely legitimate for the SPT or an NPM to turn up anywhere 'just to check' that no-one was being deprived of their liberty as defined by the OPCAT, if it thought that they might be. Indeed, the SPT has done so. For example, on our visit to New Zealand we went to a hostel for asylum seekers. We knew that those living there ought to be free to come and go, in accordance with the usual types of rules that might apply to any form of hostel-style accommodation, but we had reason to think that this might not have been the case. It was not a 'place of deprivation of liberty', but it might have been acting as one.[5]

The difficulty in pinning down the precise parameters of the visiting mandate is that the OPCAT approaches this question in two different ways, which partly overlap but are fundamentally different. Article 4(1) focuses on the *places* where people are, or might be, detained by, or at the behest of, or with the connivance of, or under the authority of the state. Potentially, that really can be anywhere. Even private and personal premises can be places of detention for these purposes. Unlikely as it may seem, what if a police officer were to be keeping detainees in the basement of their house because the police cells were full? From what I have seen around the world, I could not say that such a thing could never happen. Would that basement be a place of detention under the OPCAT definition in Article 4(1)? The answer is clearly yes.

It is important to realise that the words 'jurisdiction and control' in Article 4(1) do *not* refer to places which the state owns or runs. These are words commonly found in international treaties and concern the *territorial scope* of an obligation.[6] If a place of detention is in an area over which the state in question exercises 'jurisdiction and control'[7] – that is, if it is able to exercise its authority over it – then that is all that is required. On this basis, every building,[8] every forest, every cave and every chasm within a state's territory will normally be covered by this. In addition, there may be situations in which the state exercises jurisdiction and control over places *outside* of its territory – extra-territorial jurisdiction – and in such cases they would be covered too. This could include detention facilities run by a state's military forces in other countries, and military vessels at sea or in foreign waters would also be included, and so on (Murray et al, 2011, pp 79–81). There really is virtually no limit to the range of places that potentially fall within the scope of the Article. What is necessary, however, is that such a place might be used for the purposes of detention 'by virtue of an order given by a public authority or at its instigation or with its consent or acquiescence'. But if that is the case, then if you are not allowed to leave such a place, then that is a place of detention.

Turning to Article 4(2), this takes a very different approach and focuses not on the place of detention but on what deprivation of liberty *is*. That is to say, *who* is a detained person? To recap, it says that a person is a detained person when they are in 'any form of detention or imprisonment or the placement of a person in a public or private custodial setting which that person is not permitted to leave at will by order of any judicial, administrative or other authority'. This has always been a very problematic paragraph because it is so easily misunderstood. Indeed, some have even suggested that it means the OPCAT only applies to those who are held on remand, to sentenced prisoners or to others detained on the basis of some express official 'order'. Obviously, this would make a nonsense of the entire idea of preventive visiting – not least because those at most risk of torture or ill-treatment are likely to be those who are held illegally, incommunicado, and without any form of 'official' authorisation at all. It would also contradict the thrust of Article 4(1).[9] In truth, the position is really quite simple. What it is saying is that anyone who is 'not permitted to leave' a place of detention because they are prevented from doing so by someone in, or based on some form of, officially sanctioned authority over them is, for the purposes of the OPCAT, a detained person. Or, even more simply again, 'if you are not allowed to leave, then you are detained'.

This, I must admit, may be an example of my preference for simplicity in the interests of prevention. And it is perfectly clear that taking these approaches to Article 4 means that there are many examples of situations which might be considered to be places of detention, or people considered to be detained persons, which and who are manifestly and obviously no such thing. Is a public sector worker who is told they cannot leave the office early a detained person, and their workplace a place of detention? I would think not. What about a person on a bus, travelling between stops? I cannot be the only person who, stuck on a bus in a traffic jam, has been 'not free to leave' because the driver will not open the doors. I am detained, and not free to leave …

I Such *reductio ad absurdum* examples should not be used to undermine the breadth of the definitions, which, if more narrowly understood, might deny potential protection to many vulnerable people. But I mention these examples only because I have had them thrown at me when trying to exercise the SPT mandate in practice. For example, in one country we were wanting to travel on board a bus which was being used to forcibly remove migrants from a holding centre to an airport where they were due to be put on a repatriation flight. We were not allowed to do so, and I took this up immediately with the national authorities as I considered it to be a breach of its OPCAT obligations. We had seen the migrants concerned being transferred to the bus, screaming for help, with some – obviously sedated in advance – being carried limp-like over a shoulder onto the bus.

We followed the bus to the airport in our own vehicle but, unsurprisingly, were not allowed to follow the bus on to the tarmac by the airport security staff. I was told that 'a bus is not a place of detention', and so it fell outside our mandate. It was not a place of detention because bus passengers could not be allowed to get off at will for safety reasons and could always get off at the next bus stop. All this is true: but that did not mean that *this* bus was not a place of detention, or that *these* were 'bus passengers' and that they were 'free to leave'. Obviously, they were not.

To use another example, what about a child who is kept in after-school detention and not allowed home for an additional period of time, or who is not allowed outside during a breaktime? Perhaps that is not so clear: children *are* ill-treated at times in school settings. The SPT (nor to my knowledge, NPMs) have ever chosen to probe such issues – though in appropriate cases I see no reason why they should not, in situations where there are reasons to believe that ill-treatment of children might also be occurring – and there are plenty of such situations. For example, if the state permits a school to operate and there are concerns that children are beaten and abused by their teachers, why not visit? Orphanages which are run or licensed to operate by the state are also within the scope of the visiting mandate – though I can recall one country in which we were unable to gain access to an orphanage run by a religious organisation that denied that it was.

These definitions of places of detention and of detained persons sound to the casual observer to be far more restrictive than they really are. This has been a particular problem when visiting hospitals. Surely hospitals are places of healing and care, not of torture and ill-treatment? Not always. Clearly, some secure and psychiatric hospitals may have patients who are detained by court order and so are very much not free to leave. Some may be liable to be given forms of treatments which they have not consented to, due to their lack of capacity. This clearly falls within the visiting mandate. But what of general hospitals? It is quite usual for prisoners to be transferred to general hospitals for surgery or other forms of care which prison medical services may not be able to provide, or for those arrested to be taken to hospital due to their medical condition at the time of arrest. This does not mean that hospitals are places of detention, but it does mean that from time to time they are places where people might be deprived of their liberty. This example helpfully illustrates the difference between the two approaches found within the OPCAT concerning the scope of its visiting mandate.

It is certainly true that the SPT had encountered difficulties in visiting general hospitals, since those in charge simply do not see them as being places of detention or of housing detained persons. This often requires lengthy explanation. Yet we came across cases of patients from prisons being handcuffed to their beds to prevent them from escaping: in one case, with no keys available on site, as the keys to the handcuffs were kept by the officer who had brought the person to the prison – and when we tried to contact them, discovered they were now 'on leave'.

The lists and examples can go on and on. Faced with the question of whether social care homes for the elderly run by private institutions could also fall within the mandate, the SPT finally decided to set out its approach in writing, in the form of an 'Advice' to NPMs. In that Advice, it said:

1. Article 4 contains two paragraphs that must be read together and that place within the scope of the Optional Protocol any public or private custodial setting under the jurisdiction and control of the State party, in which persons may be deprived of their liberty and are not permitted to leave, either by an order given by any judicial, administrative or other authority or at its instigation or with its consent or acquiescence.
2. The preventive approach underpinning the Optional Protocol means that as extensive an interpretation as possible should be made in order to maximize the preventive impact of the work of the national preventive mechanism.
3. The Subcommittee therefore takes the view that any place in which persons are deprived of their liberty, in the sense of not being free to leave, or in which the Subcommittee considers that persons might be being deprived of their liberty, should fall within the scope of the Optional Protocol, if the deprivation of liberty relates to a situation in which the State either exercises, or might be expected to exercise a regulatory function. In all situations, the national preventive mechanism should also be mindful of the principle of proportionality when determining its priorities and the focus of its work.[10]

To my mind, this advice just about sums it all up. It was issued in response to a request for guidance from an NPM, hence the reference to NPMs in the final sentence. But that final sentence applies equally to the SPT too. And what that final sentence is really saying is 'don't overdo it', or 'use your common sense': the mandate is enormous, the possibilities almost endless – but don't forget what this is really all about. It is easy to get distracted by theoretical possibilities and hypothetical argument. In most cases most of the time, it does not take a complex textual exegesis to tell the difference between someone who is or is not being deprived of their liberty, or whether something is or is not being used as a place of detention. It is usually obvious, and when it is not obvious, then the principles of prevention suggest that one should err on the side of inclusion.

Thus in response to the COVID-19 pandemic, the SPT said that

[t]he Subcommittee has ... issued guidance confirming that formal places of quarantine fall within the mandate of the Optional Protocol

to the Convention against Torture and Other Cruel, Inhuman or Degrading Treatment or Punishment (CAT/OP/9). It inexorably follows that all other places from which persons are prevented from leaving for similar purposes fall within the scope of the mandate of the Optional Protocol and thus within the sphere of oversight of both the Subcommittee and of the national preventive mechanisms established within the framework of the Optional Protocol.[11]

And in case it was thought that this was going too far, the SPT added that

[t]he overriding criterion must be that of effectiveness in securing the prevention of ill-treatment of those subject to detaining measures. The parameters of prevention have been widened by the extraordinary measures that States have had to take. It is the responsibility of the Subcommittee and of national preventive mechanisms to respond in imaginative and creative ways to the novel challenges they face in the exercise of their mandates related to the Optional Protocol.[12]

Simple.

The SPT

I have already said a good deal about what the SPT has said, but not very much about what it is. These matters are addressed in Part II of the OPCAT, which concerns the establishment, composition, and internal working of the SPT, and these will be looked at in the remainder of this chapter. What the SPT is meant to do and how it is meant to do it is set out in Part III of the OPCAT, and this will be looked at across the chapters that follow.

Texts are impersonal things, and textual provisions concerning committees can make those committees and their members seem rather impersonal and abstract too. Obviously, that is not the case. Members are people, and with that comes all the usual baggage. The work of any committee is irrevocably influenced by not only the knowledge and experience of its members, but their personalities too. That is even more so of a body such as the SPT, whose members come from different countries with different personal and professional backgrounds and who are expected to spend extended periods in each other's company, often travelling long distances in discomfort, tired and hungry, visiting some of the worst places that can be imagined and listening to individuals whose day-to-day lives are almost unimaginable. And then also spending time in formal committee rooms, engaging in the general 'politics' of committee life, on matters great and (more usually) small. Unfortunately, collegiality and sociability are not highlighted as essential election criteria. Fortunately, most members during my time on the SPT demonstrated both qualities – for which I shall be forever grateful.

Members are elected by the states parties from a list of candidates that they themselves have nominated. The OPCAT Article 5 sets out a range of factors which Article 7(1)(a) says states should give 'primary consideration' to when electing members. The first is that members should be 'chosen from among persons of high moral character, having proven professional experience in the field of the administration of justice, in particular criminal law, prison or police administration, or in the various fields relevant to the treatment of persons deprived of their liberty'. The background or experience of most members nominated or elected can fairly be said to fall within this suitably broad-brush descriptor. Most tend to have had a legal or medical background, experience of working in NGOs or in national institutions on human rights matters, academics working in matters of criminal justice, and so on. The ranges of medical experience span forensic doctors, psychiatrics, psychologists – frankly, an unusually large spread of deep expertise directly relevant to the job in hand.

As time went on, more and more members had direct experience of working for NPMs. This could be a little difficult at times, and this did result in some potential conflicts of interest which had to be carefully managed, but the benefits of having that experience outweighed any occasional delicacies, difficulties or awkwardness. We also had a number of members with political and diplomatic experience – and though usually frowned on in human rights circles, having some members with such experience was also useful given the particular need of the SPT to work confidentially and – yes – diplomatically with states in the exercise of its mandate. While the 'balance' between different cohorts of experience was not always optimal, the range of experience available usually was. Naturally, and as with any group of 25 people, some were somewhat greater assets than others, but during my time on the SPT most of the members, most of the time, were indeed assets – and we were fortunate in this.

We were also fortunate in other ways. The OPCAT Article 5(3) also says that 'consideration shall also be given to balanced gender representation on the basis of the principles of equality and non-discrimination'. While at first the number of female members was low, this rapidly changed and for most of my time as Chair the SPT was about as perfectly gender balanced as it was possible to be, being composed of either 13 women and 12 men, or vice versa. Apart from its first years, it has never been seriously 'out of kilter' – something that cannot be said of some of the other UN human rights bodies, although the most recent election in October 2022 has resulted in the slightest of tilts towards a more female-dominated committee, with 11 men and 14 women.[13]

The final factor to be taken into account according to OPCAT Article 15(4) is 'equitable geographic distribution and to the representation of different forms of civilization and legal systems of the States Parties'. The anachronistic reference 'different forms of civilisation' in a 21st-century text is a real embarrassment. Beyond that, there has always been a struggle to achieve this, for several reasons. Obviously, you can only elect members from states parties, and if there are not many states parties from certain parts of the world then there will not be members from them on the SPT.[14] That is unavoidable: the changing pattern of membership reflects the changing patterns of states parties.

Another point is that this is the UN. And the UN thinks in terms of regional blocs, not real geography. This means that its understanding of what is equitable in terms of geographic distribution does not necessarily make much sense to anyone else. The UN still works based on five blocs – Africa, Asia, Eastern Europe, Latin American and Caribbean (the GRULAC) and Western European and Others (WEOG). This is beyond rational comprehension. The European Union, for example, has member states in three UN groups (as Cyprus is in Asia, apparently), and of course Australia and New Zealand are in Western Europe ... There is no grouping drawing together the important Middle East and North Africa (MENA) grouping, and so on.

Nevertheless, and despite these UN geographic fictions, the outcome of elections has been largely satisfactory in terms of a rough reflection of the composition of states parties, bearing in mind that many do not choose to put up candidates at all. In general terms, the Americas have tended to be overrepresented in recent years relative to the number of states parties, whereas Africa and Asia have been underrepresented, though increasingly this is not true of Africa. While the two European (and other) groups at one time dominated numerically, this was possibly an underrepresentation proportionally. But taken in the round, the pattern of membership has not been radically out of line with reasonable proportionality over time and following the most recent elections seems reasonably representative given the overall makeup of states parties.[15]

In terms of expertise, gender and representativeness, the SPT has, in my view, done well, and probably better than most elected UN human rights treaty bodies. This is as much luck as judgement, however. The extent to which states really do think of these factors as 'primary consideration' when voting is not for me to say. I am sure that a commendable number do, or do to an extent, but it is blatantly obvious that some do not and vote on the basis of broader political issues[16] and trade votes with other states not only for election to the SPT but for a whole host of other elections across the UN system. It is a minor miracle that the outcomes have been so generally positive as they have been. And although the SPT – like all other human rights treaty bodies – found itself criticised from time to time by states due to its perceived lack of representativeness, gender balance, expertise and so on, those self-same states never bothered to add that they were the ones responsible for any such imbalances; there was nothing the SPT could do about it. But states at the UN can be very good at blaming other people for problems of their own making.

From theory to practice

The first elections took place towards the end of 2006 and the ten founding SPT members met for the first time in February 2007. Since most of the original states parties were from Europe and Central and South America this meant that the members would be from these regions too, and the first elections resulted in four members from the Americas – Argentina, Costa Rica, Mexico and Uruguay – and six from Europe; though in UN parlance three were from the WEOG, from Denmark, Spain and the UK, and three from the Eastern European Group, Croatia, Czech Republic and Poland. Perhaps most significantly, four of the six European members elected either had been, or still were, members of the European Committee for the Prevention of Torture (CPT), and its former President – Silvia Casale, from the UK – was elected the first Chair of the SPT. Inevitably, this meant that the experience of the CPT informed thinking about how the SPT should go about its work. With the benefit of hindsight, that might have been unfortunate. Perceptions matter in the UN, and no matter how good that model was, the 'European' inspiration of its working practices provided a mental barrier for some, who either could not or would not come to terms with things being done in the 'European' way. For good or ill, the legacies of this initial tension between regional styles of working have been enduring, even as the SPT's membership base has broadened and diversified.

Ultimately, this broadening and diversification has been the result of the increasing number of states parties, but in two ways. Not only does it mean that more states can nominate candidates and be involved in the elections, but under the terms of the OPCAT Article 5(1), once 50 states had ratified, then the number of members was to increase from ten to 25. Members are elected for periods of four years and can be re-elected once, a total period of eight years.[17] However, to achieve a more regular turnover, the first period of office of half of the original ten members was reduced to two years, meaning that elections now take place every two years when those terms of office expire.[18] That threshold was reached in 2010, and so at the end of that year there were 20 vacancies to be filled! The first full term of half the original ten members had finished, to which the additional 15 new places were added.

It was the first time that any UN human rights treaty body had more than doubled overnight. It meant that there were more people sitting around the table who knew next to nothing of how the SPT really worked than those that did. It was not a terribly comfortable experience, and it is to be hoped it will never be repeated. To make matters more difficult again, the 'Bureau' of the SPT – its Chair and the then two, and since the enlargement, four Vice Chairs – must be elected every two years as well. In effect, this means that when the newly elected Committee meets in the February of the year following an election, it also must elect its officers. The new members often will have very little working knowledge (and sometimes none) on which to make their decision, and this can be a source of considerable difficulty and can set things off for the next two-year cycle of SPT activities on a rather poor footing, with relationships (and egos) fractured from the start. As I say, members are human.

For completeness, I should add that although members are only permitted to be 're-elected once', implying a maximum of eight years as a member, this is not strictly accurate. If a member resigns, then the state of that resigning member can nominate a person to fill that position for the remainder of the term. If they then stand for election, then that is their first election in their own right and so can be re-elected again. It was on this basis that I was nominated by the UK as a member in 2009, when the UK member resigned, and was first elected in my own right in 2012 and then again in 2016, my second term ending in 2020, a total of 11 years. In addition, it has become an accepted practice that there is no bar on former members being nominated to a new term of office and to be eligible for election following a break in continuous membership. There are now several members who have been on the SPT for two terms of membership, have had a 'break' for two years until the next election and have then been elected and then re-elected again. Their eight years thus becomes sixteen, with a two-year hiatus, and potentially more ... As I used to joke, there were four categories of SPT members: the replacement, the elected, the re-elected and the resurrected. I have been three out of those four, with only the latter eluding me (and it is a status to which I do not aspire, in this context at least).

The idea of increasing the size of the membership from ten to 25 was to ensure that there were enough members to carry out the increasingly large number of visits that would be required as the number of states parties increased. Frankly, it is almost laughable to reflect on this reasoning now, given that the number of visits that the UN funded in the year that followed the expansion remained the same as it had been from the beginning – which was three. With 25 members understandably anxious to be sent on a visit, this meant that the SPT ended up sending teams of eight or nine members on visits in 2011, accompanied by a veritable army of interpreters, Secretariat, drivers, security: this was a logistical nightmare and completely inefficient – in some police stations, there were considerably more members than detainees to speak with. This did not happen again.

This speaks to a deeper, and somewhat more troubling truth. Article 5(6) of the OPCAT highlights the need for members to be 'independent and impartial'[19] and much is rightly made of this, not only on the SPT but on all UN human rights bodies.[20] In my experience, this has been overwhelmingly the case as far as members of the SPT have been concerned. But while it is possible for the SPT as a body to be impartial, it is not possible for it to be fully 'independent'. It can be relatively 'independent' in terms of *how* it does what it does – but it certainly cannot be independent in terms of *what* it can do. Those constraints come from two sources: what I would term the 'legitimate constraints' which flow from the scope of its mandate, and the 'insidious constraints' which flow from the financial and operational control exercised over it by states and by the machinery of the UN. Both will be illustrated in the chapters which follow.

There is one other manifestation of member independence that ought, perhaps, to be mentioned, and this is linked both to their interests and expertise and to the dearth of visiting opportunities in the early years of the SPT. It can hardly be denied that in the first few years following the expansion of the SPT to 25 members in 2011 there was not really enough visiting to do. Similarly, the numbers of NPMs in existence was still relatively small, and the opportunities to work with them effectively was equally limited. Perhaps this explains why at that time there was something of a flood of suggestions that the SPT produce statements on various matters concerning their mandate.[21] As has been seen, it had by then already produced what still remain its two seminal documents, on the Concept of Prevention and the NPM Guidelines. It had also set its face – rightly, in my view – against generating further sets of abstract standards, which already existed aplenty and on which it was free to draw. Instead, and very much at the prompting of individual members and largely reflecting their particular concerns, the SPT decided to draft a series of what might best be described as 'reflections' on torture and the prevention of torture in a variety of settings, relating to various vulnerable groups or to particular issues.

I should like to say that this was the product of careful organisation and selection, but in truth it had more to do with the enthusiasms of the proposers than careful strategic planning. Yet in some cases the results were impressive and have been of considerable importance. For example, the SPT issued a document on the links between torture and corruption in 2014,[22] a full five years before the UN Special Rapporteur on Torture issued a report on the topic.[23] This was innovative, controversial at the time and, like all these documents, it was directly inspired by what the SPT had encountered in its visits. It also produced important papers in 2015 on torture and LGBTI,[24] and in 2016 on torture and women deprived of their liberty[25] and on medical treatment without informed consent.[26] None of these aimed at being prescriptive or standard setting, but in common with SPT papers at that time, sought to raise awareness and reflect on what prevention 'meant' in these various and varied contexts.

This wave of activity petered out around 2016. In part, this was because the numbers of visits had increased significantly and there was just less time;

in part, it was because the initial enthusiasm for drafting such papers had, regrettably, begun to take on something of a competitive air; it was also the case that not all projects agreed upon by members in haste had proved as successful as others, with some never quite seeing the light of day. A final factor – inevitably – concerned changing UN policies on publication of documents. Initially, SPT papers, such as the Guidelines and the Concept of Prevention, were issued as separate official documents and also in the SPT Annual Report – the former making them more accessible, the latter more visible. This worked well. However, it was decided by the UN that this amounted to publishing the same document twice, and this was therefore no longer permitted. This led to discussions about how and where to publish, and if it were in the Annual Report this could result in long delays. There were also increasing difficulties in getting translations of drafts of such papers to enable members to work on them. Increasingly, papers were not translated until their near final form, making it difficult for those not able to read them in the original language to effectively contribute to the process.

Rather than bringing members together in a common enterprise, suddenly the changing rules on such matters meant that the drafting was becoming problematic, even divisive. At that point, it was best to stop. More positively, perhaps, the increased focus on visits was also creating a new demand for internal working tools, checklists and guidance to assist SPT members and to encourage methodological consistency over time within its work. As a result, less was produced that was 'public facing' – though some important advice was issued to NPMs from time to time in response to their direct requests and which was of general relevance, culminating in the various public documents issued during the COVID-19 pandemic. But above all else, what drove the change in focus was the increasing emphasis on visits, and it is to the SPT's visiting mandate than we shall now turn.

Notes

1   Part V is composed of Article 24, concerning Declarations, Part VI, comprising Articles 25–6, concerns financial provisions, and Part VII, comprising Articles 27–37, covers a range of final provisions, largely, but not exclusively, concerning the technical workings of the OPCAT.

2   The key article, and the bone of contention, was Article 22 of the 'Mexican Draft' (which provided that '[t]he States Parties to the present Protocol undertake to accord the Subcommittee all the powers granted to national mechanisms for the prevention of torture under the provisions of articles 5 and 6 if, within two years of ratification of the present Protocol, a national mechanism has not started to visit places of detention'. For text, see Nowak et al, 2019, p 1207. For discussion, see Evans and Haenni-Dale, 2004, pp 38–41.

3   The text of this currently unique declaration reads: 'In accordance with Part V, Article 24 of the Optional Protocol to the Convention against Torture and Other Cruel, Inhuman, or Degrading Treatment or Punishment, the Republic of the Philippines hereby declares the postponement of the implementation of its obligations under Part III of the Optional Protocol, specifically Article 11(1)(a) on the visitations by the Subcommittee on Prevention

to places referred to in Article 4 and for them to make recommendations to States Parties concerning the protection of persons deprived of their liberty against torture and other cruel, inhuman or degrading treatment or punishment.' Available on the UN Treaty database, https://.treaties.un.org

4   The seven countries to have done so were Australia, Bosnia–Herzegovina, Germany, Hungary, Kazakhstan, Montenegro and Romania. Germany, Hungary and Montenegro established their NPM within the extended period, while Kazakhstan did so very shortly afterwards. Romania further extended its period by two years and established its NPM very shortly after that period elapsed. Bosnia and Herzegovina should have established its NPM by the end of November 2012 and is yet to do so. It was visited by the SPT for the first time in 2022, meaning that no OPCAT took place for 14 years following its entry into force. Australia should have established its NPM by the end of January 2023 and is yet to do so. As has been noted already, the SPT visit to Australia in October 2022 was suspended because of a lack of cooperation. All information and supporting documentation is available on the SPT website at https://www.ohchr.org/en/treaty-bodies/spt/national-preventive-mechanisms

5   Obviously, one must avoid a *reductio ad absurdum*: to pick up on the example in the previous paragraph, no-one would seriously suggest it would be appropriate to visit forests to ensure no-one had been tied to a tree by security forces. Ultimately, it all comes down to the strength of the suspicion in unusual situations.

6   The precise meaning of 'jurisdiction and/or control' for legal purposes is one of the most fraught topics in international law, on which courts and tribunals have, and continue, to differ fundamentally. It is beyond the scope of this book to delve into this and – for the reasons given in this chapter – largely unnecessary.

7   The OPCAT speaks with different voices on this. The text appears in six different official UN languages, each one of which is legally authoritative. Yet while four texts refer to jurisdiction *and* control, two refer to jurisdiction *or* control. This is almost certainly an error. The usual international legal language is of jurisdiction *or* control, and this is the preferred approach, which is reflected in the SPT practice. For example, in 2016 the SPT attempted to gain access to detention facilities in Donetsk which at that time was under the de facto control of local powers and which were described by Ukraine at the time as 'uncontrolled territories'. The legal basis for its doing so was the jurisdiction which Ukraine was entitled to exercise, despite its not currently exercising control. See also Nowak et al, 2019, pp 749–51.

8   A possible exception concerns foreign diplomatic premises, an issue that arose when the OPCAT was being drafted and was largely avoided rather than resolved. To the best of my knowledge, no attempt to visit diplomatic premises has been made by the SPT, though in principle it seems clear that the diplomatic premises of a state party to the OPCAT located in another country, even another country that is not a state party to the OPCAT, would fall within the scope of its visiting mandate, and that of that state's NPM (Murray et al, 2011, p 79).

9   Because of this, it has been argued that this potential contradiction is to be addressed by the application of the principle of 'systematic interpretation' of treaties, which would then give prominence to Article 4(1) as being more reflective of its object and purposes. See Nowak et al, 2019, p 749.

10   'Compilation of Advice Provided by the Subcommittee in Response to Requests from National Preventive Mechanisms I. Scope of Article 4 of the Optional Protocol', CAT/OP/C/57/4, p 19.

11   'Advice of the Subcommittee to States Parties and National Preventive Mechanisms Relating to the Coronavirus Disease (COVID-19) Pandemic', CAT/OP/10, 7 April 2020, para 5.

[12] 'Advice of the Subcommittee to States Parties and National Preventive Mechanisms Relating to the Coronavirus Disease (COVID-19) Pandemic', CAT/OP/10, 7 April 2020, para 15.

[13] See https://www.ohchr.org/en/events/events/2022/9th-meeting-states-parties-2022-elections. As the vast bulk of remand and sentenced prisoners are male, it is important that this does not become a more serious imbalance as a result of future elections.

[14] For example, when the SPT was first established and had ten members, six were from Europe and four from Central and South America, there being few states parties at that time from other parts of the world.

[15] Thus after the most recent elections in October 2020, there are now seven members from Western Europe, six from Eastern Europe, six from Africa, four from Central and South America and two from Asia. This spread of members is now not greatly dissimilar to the spread of states parties.

[16] I recall being told by the representative of one state in the run up to my re-election in 2016 that I was doing a great job as Chair and was greatly respected, but of course there was no way he could vote for me given the political disputes between his country and the UK on various matters, all entirely unconnected to the election. I took that as the kindness that doubtless it was meant to be and was not at all surprised. It was, however, indicative of how the system works.

[17] OPCAT, Article 9. The European Convention originally had the same limitation, but in the light of the experience of the dislocation caused by an ever-changing membership this was changed to allow CPT members to be re-elected twice, and so serve for a maximum of 12 years. This is a far better approach, and it is unfortunate that the drafters of the OPCAT failed to learn from this lesson. See Protocol no 2 to the European Convention for the Prevention of Torture and Inhuman or Degrading Treatment or Punishment (adopted, 4 November 1993, in force 1 March 2002), ETS no 152.

[18] OPCAT, Article 9. In effect, this means that every two years an election is held for either 12 or 13 members, and at each election a given number will not be eligible for re-election, ensuring that there are at least some new members joining every two years.

[19] Article 5(6) provides that '[t]he members of the Subcommittee on Prevention shall serve in their individual capacity, shall be independent and impartial and shall be available to serve the Subcommittee on Prevention efficiently'. On taking their place as a member for the first time, members must make a 'solemn declaration' to this effect. See SPT Rules of Procedure, CAT/OP/3/Rev.3, Rule 14. I always thought it strange and slightly unfortunate that this emphasises efficiency, rather than effectiveness.

[20] The independence of treaty body members has been a contentious issue during the various inter-governmental processes for 'strengthening' the UN human rights treaty bodies. See Evans, 2001, pp 103–4. In 2012, the Chairs of the treaty bodies endorsed a common approach, which has been reflected in the working practices of most of the ten human rights treaty bodies. 'Guidelines on the Independence and Impartiality of Members of the Human Rights Treaty Bodies ("the Addis Ababa Guidelines")', A/67/222, annex I.

[21] Although more were commissioned and produced, a total of seven were ultimately both completed and made public, the last in 2016. Today, they can be found on the SPT website at https://www.ohchr.org/en/treaty-bodies/spt/approaches-prevention

[22] 'The SPT's Views on the Relationship between Torture Prevention and Corruption', CAT/C/52/2, section V.

[23] For which, see the Special Rapporteur on Torture, 'Report on the Relationship between Torture and Corruption', A/HRC/40/59.

[24] 'The SPT's Views on Prevention of Torture and Other Cruel, Inhuman or Degrading Treatment or Punishment of Lesbian, Gay, Bisexual, Transgender and Intersex Persons', CAT/C/57/4, section V.

[25] 'Prevention of Torture and Ill-Treatment of Women Deprived of Their Liberty', CAT/OP/27/1.

[26] 'The SPT's Approach regarding the Rights of Persons Institutionalized and Treated Medically without Informed Consent', CAT/OP/27/2. The drafting of this was particularly difficult and put the SPT at loggerheads with the UN Committee on the Rights of Persons with Disabilities with whom it had consulted for quite some time. The draining nature of the experience doubtless contributed to the diminishing enthusiasm for undertaking such exercises.

5

The Visiting Mandate of the UN Subcommittee on Prevention of Torture

Introduction

The mandate and the powers of the UN Subcommittee on Prevention of Torture (SPT) are found in Part III of the Optional Protocol to the United Nations Convention against Torture (OPCAT). The centrepiece of this is Article 11, which sets out the three key tasks that the SPT is to undertake and relate in turn to (a) visits, (b) to National Preventive Mechanisms (NPMs) and (c) to other international and regional bodies working towards the protection of persons against torture and ill-treatment. These are, in effect, the tools that the international community has placed at its disposal to prevent torture and ill-treatment, and the SPT is to be judged by the way in which it uses them. As will be seen, the SPT can do a very great deal. Yet it is not a free agent, and in practice it can only do what it is permitted to do by those who exercise operational control over it. In a very real sense, it is free to do what others permit. But when the SPT can act, its powers are formidable. This chapter and the next trace that tension, setting out what the OPCAT permits the SPT to do and what it has been able to do in practice. The focus of this chapter is the SPT's visiting mandate. It sets out and reflects on how the mandate operates in practice. A more personal view of the realities of undertaking visits with the SPT is reserved for later.

This entire book has been leading up to this moment: the earlier chapters considering what is torture, the need for prevention, the idea of visiting as a means of prevention and the history of the OPCAT all coalesce in Article 11(a), which laconically provides that the SPT shall '(a) Visit the places referred to in article 4 and make recommendations to States Parties concerning the protection of persons deprived of their liberty against torture and other cruel, inhuman or degrading treatment or punishment.'

For something so central to its raison d'être, it is somewhat surprising that the OPCAT has so little else to say about visits. This is not a criticism though, and the flexibility that the OPCAT permits has been extremely valuable as it has allowed the SPT to experiment with different approaches as it seeks to find out how best to go about its business. One crucial question that the OPCAT *does* address concerns the places which are to be visited – these being the 'places referred to in article 4' – and the previous chapter has already considered this at length, highlighting just how broad a range of places this is; indeed, potentially limitless. While very welcome, this exacerbates the problem of how to go about the task of visiting them.

A system of 'regular' visits?

Article 1 of the OPCAT says that the object of the Protocol is to establish a system of 'regular' visits – but nowhere does it say what is meant by this. Surprising as it may seem, this ambiguity is central to the effective functioning of the SPT in practice. In a nutshell, it can refer to either time or shape: a 'system of regular visits' could be a system of visits which takes place according to a regular cycle, such as every two, four, five or however many years, much like the reporting cycles to other treaty bodies.[1] 'Regular' in this sense is referring to periodicity. Alternatively, the idea of a 'regular' visit could refer to what the visit looks like: that is, there is a form of visit of a 'regular' sort, which the SPT undertakes whenever it happens to decide to visit a particular state. This latter understanding of 'regular' may seem completely disingenuous at first sight, but it makes complete sense when it is appreciated that there is another form of visit which is not mentioned in the OPCAT at all – and that is an 'ad hoc' visit.

The European Convention for the Prevention of Torture (CPT) expressly recognised two types of visits – 'periodic' and 'ad hoc'.[2] This came to be understood as meaning that some visits would take place within the context of a 'regular' programme of 'periodic' visits, which could be supplemented by other 'ad hoc' visits conducted outside of the 'regular' programme when this was called for. This resulted in a system in which the CPT would 'announce' a programme of regular visits for the coming year but would supplement that with other, shorter, visits which were not pre-announced and were not a part of the regular programme of periodic visits. In effect, regular visits were 'pre-programmed', whereas 'ad hoc' visits, as the name implies, were not.[3] Moreover, 'periodic visits' did not imply that such visits were 'regular' in terms of frequency.

This is essential background for understanding the OPCAT, since rightly or wrongly this pattern of CPT practice became part of the subliminal background thinking. For some, it was vital that the SPT should not be limited to a formalistic programme of visiting akin to the reporting processes of the other UN human rights treaty bodies: that would mean that it would have to complete a full cycle of visits to all states parties before it could return to any of them. It would also mean that it might be many years before a particular state was visited at all, depending on how far down the list it was. The only way of preventing this, it was thought, was by allowing the SPT, like the CPT, to have the freedom to undertake 'ad hoc' visits outside of the 'regular' programme, so that it could respond to situations of pressing concern. Without wishing to spend more time reviewing the drafting history, it suffices to say that states were having none of this, and there is no mention of 'ad hoc' visits in the OPCAT, only a 'regular' system (Evans and Haenni-Dale, 2004, pp 33–4, 45–6). There is only one, slight, nod in the direction of greater flexibility, when in Article 13(4) it adds that '[i]f the Subcommittee considers it appropriate, it can propose a short follow-up visit after a regular visit'. To whom it is to propose this, and to what purpose, is entirely opaque, and this is a matter to which we shall.

The other provision in the OPCAT which bears on the idea of what a 'regular' system of visits might look like is Article 13(1). This says that the subcommittee 'shall establish, at first by lot, a programme of regular visits to the States Parties in order to fulfil its mandate as established in article 11'. This implies rigidity rather than flexibility. Indeed, on a strict and narrow reading it seems to suggest that the SPT is to construct a programme of visits to all states parties by drawing lots, to which, presumably, subsequent states parties would be added in due course. To their great and eternal credit, the first-elected members of the SPT – doubtless drawing on their CPT experience, and assumptions – did something completely different and which paved the way to making the SPT's system of visiting as flexible as it could ever possibly have been.

In its first year the SPT was told that it would only be able to undertake three visits. To be fair, this was not unreasonable for a newly established body and for a UN Secretariat learning how to run an entirely unfamiliar system. But which countries should these be? Article 13(1) says that the programme of regular visits was to be chosen by lot. It said nothing about the timespan that the 'regular programme' was meant to cover. The SPT took the view that, like the CPT, it would produce annual 'regular' programmes – and since it had to choose its 'first' annual[4] programme by lot, it put the names of states parties 'into a hat' and drew out Mauritius, the Maldives and Sweden. It is difficult to believe that these would have been the countries it would have chosen if left to its own devices. But the critical point is that having decided on its first 'annual' programme in this way, it decided to leave the lottery system behind and instead adopted what it termed 'a reasoned process'.[5] Henceforth it could decide which countries it wished to visit – this became its 'regular' programme. It is unlikely that this is what many states expected, but it did not meet with any challenge and is now firmly embedded in its practice that each year the SPT chooses the countries it plans to visit.

Visits to where?

But how does it choose? This is probably the question the SPT is most frequently asked, certainly by states, and it does not admit of an easy answer. As Chair, there were many times when I thought that a lottery might not be such a bad idea after all. The comparison with the European system is pertinent to help grasp the difficulty. Since Russia left in 2022, the ECPT has 46 states parties, including several very small countries, and some with few formal detention facilities at all. The CPT therefore has up to 46 members, a substantial Secretariat,[6] a reasonable budget, and works in only two languages. It is now able to undertake about 15 or so visits each year. All the states are relatively proximate, with a time difference of no more than three hours between them.

Some large or problematic countries, such as Turkey, the Russian Federation and the United Kingdom, have been visited by the CPT more or less every year (either with a regular or an ad hoc visit), most are visited every four or five years and some of the smaller countries, such as Luxembourg, Liechtenstein, Andorra and San Marino, every six or seven years or so or even less. Quite frankly, with a decent spreadsheet it was possible at that time to more or less work out what the CPT visiting programme for the coming year might plausibly look like. Indeed, in my early years as Chair, I wanted to know where the CPT was planning to go in the following year, so as to better inform the SPT's own programme planning. As the CPT's programme was at that stage still confidential, the Executive Secretary of the CPT would not tell me. This did not surprise me, so I asked him whether the list of countries I was about to read out was or was not a fair bet. When I finished, he asked who had leaked their confidential programme to me: I think I had got one country wrong. It was not rocket science.

It cannot be said that the SPT's visiting programme displays a similar degree of foreseeability, and there are many reasons for this. The most obvious concerns the number of states parties to be visited related to the visiting capacity of the SPT. There are currently 92 states parties, and the SPT now visits about eight, perhaps nine or ten, countries per year if it can. That seems to be about the maximum that it is possible to sustain on the basis of current resourcing, though there have been years in which it has done more and at one point there was an aspiration to build towards a programme of 12 visits per year, though this was never quite reached.[7] The SPT has recently reiterated its aspiration to have the capacity to visit countries about once every eight years on average, implying a need to be able to visit about 11 to 12 countries each year. This is just about feasible, but whether it is really possible in practice remains to be seen.[8]

On the basis of a programme of eight visits per year, if all countries were to be visited on a cyclical basis this would mean that each state might expect to be visited about once every ten or 11 years. However, even this has not been achieved in practice, and at the end of 2022 the SPT had only undertaken a total of around 80 visits in its 15 years of work. Moreover, it had visited 17 states at least once (including 14 of the 18 countries it had visited in its early years to the end of 2012).[9] At the end of 2022 it had officially visited 64 of its then 91 states parties, meaning that there were 27 it was yet to visit at all, including a considerable number of long-standing states parties.[10] This is both a weakness and a strength. Obviously, it is a weakness in that all states parties should be visited. But it is a strength because it has forced the SPT to be 'strategic' rather than 'mechanical' in how it organises its visiting programme. Even if the SPT were to have a dramatic increase in its visiting capacity, this would not change and it has recently stressed that 'a multi-year plan cannot include a list of country visits to be undertaken, but only a number of visits, in abstract', with such an agreed number providing a benchmark for its strategic planning.[11]

Although the SPT now says it identifies the countries to be visited through a 'reasoned' process, it has said little about those reasons. Elements of that reasoning are as follows.

Not all countries need a visit as much as others. For example, if a country has established an NPM and that NPM is working well and is in regular contact with the SPT, then there is less need for the SPT to conduct a visit than if the NPM has not been established or if it is having difficulties in going about its work for some reason. Similarly, the OPCAT itself says in Article 31 that

> [t]he provisions of the present Protocol shall not affect the obligations of States Parties under any regional convention instituting a system of visits to places of detention. The Subcommittee on Prevention and the bodies established under such regional conventions are encouraged to consult and cooperate with a view to avoiding duplication and promoting effectively the objectives of the present Protocol.

Decoded, this means that the SPT and CPT should avoid unnecessary duplication – and given the SPT's global reach but limited capacity, this rather suggests that the SPT should not spend too much of its time visiting European countries which could also be visited by the CPT.[12] This was certainly what happened in the early years, when the only European country which the SPT visited was Sweden in its first year when drawn by lot. It was not until 2011 that the next European country was visited – this being

Ukraine – and 19 of the 27 states parties which the SPT has not yet visited are in Europe.[13]

The difficulty with this generally sensible approach was, however, that it did not seem to reflect another 'mantra' of the OPCAT and of the UN human rights world more generally, which is that the SPT should, according to Article 2, be guided 'by the principles of confidentiality, impartiality, non-selectivity, universality and objectivity'. Given that 40 of the now 92 states parties are members of the Council of Europe, and in the early days the percentage was closer to two thirds, spending most of the time visiting countries in Africa, the Americas and Asia appeared to be decidedly partial, selective, non-universal and subjective. And in truth it was, and with good reason – though that rarely matters in UN circles, where appearances count for far more than they ought. However, this is far from the full story and when I joined in 2009 the perception within the SPT was that it was spending much too much time on European countries, whereas the perception of many states and other observers was that it was not spending enough. The reasons will become apparent when we turn to the work of the SPT in relation to NPMs in the chapter that follows.

Practical constraints

But there are other, more prosaic, influences on the SPT's visiting programme, all of which are legitimate in their own way but perhaps less easy to explain. A first is language. It is all very well for a committee to meet in Geneva with simultaneous translation in its meeting rooms. It is quite another for a delegation of that body to be working together in often remote locations for long periods and not be able to talk to each other. It just does not work. A major constraint, then, is the linguistic competence of members, bearing in mind that this has to be one of the six official languages of the UN – though committees are only permitted by the UN to operate in one of three 'working languages' of their choice (exceptionally a fourth may be permitted), these being Arabic, Chinese, English, French, Russian and Spanish. In the real world, this meant that the working language of a visit has always had to be either English, French or Spanish, being the three working languages chosen within the SPT. When it is decided to visit a country, it is also not always obvious which language will be used, and there were times when we were slightly wrongfooted by the preferred working language of the country to be visited (which we would, of course, always try to accommodate).

How many visits in each language can be undertaken in a year ultimately depends on the linguistic skills of the members, and that varies greatly over time. During my early years as Chair most visits were in English or Spanish, with only an occasional visit in French, as these were the dominant languages in which members could work. Over time, this changed, and French become more prevalent and Spanish less so. Initially, if we were doing six visits a year, three could be in English, two in Spanish and one in French: then this became one in Spanish and two in French, while retaining three in English. The more visits that were undertaken, the more English, and latterly French-speaking visits there would be. This obviously affects which countries you can go to. It may seem like the 'tail wagging the dog', but if all members were to go on visits (and that was, as far as the members were concerned, pretty much non-negotiable) then than was the way it was. For example, it was no accident – nor was it bias – that Spanish-speaking countries in the Americas have been visited more frequently than might otherwise have been expected. Spanish was not widely spoken elsewhere at a time when there were a considerable number of Spanish-speaking (including only Spanish-speaking) members on the SPT.

Linguistic ability is one thing, the mix of expertise is another. In principle, there really ought to be a medically trained member on every visit. But what if your medical members do not between them speak one of the three working languages, or cannot make themselves available for a visit in the 'relevant language'? And then there is gender. Ideally, you want a balanced team – but again, language constrains this. As a result, certain 'groups' tend to emerge, who end up visiting together and tend to visit countries in the same geographic areas together. For example, some of the relatively small group of Spanish-only speaking members were largely limited to visiting countries in Central and South America, and the French-only speaking members parts of North and West Africa, given the countries that were a party to the OPCAT system. While English-only speaking members tended to be able to work in more countries, this also meant that it was more difficult for them to visit in these regions, though sometimes needs must (I participated in the French-language visit to Senegal, for example, and was able to lead the delegation to English-speaking Belize – my only visit in the Americas).

This is not ideal, by any means. One of the major benefits of being an international body is the cross-fertilisation of experience from different systems around the world and exposure to the realities of detention and ill-treatment within them. If members end up with a partial exposure – and worse, if that is limited to those regions, systems and structures with which they are already fairly familiar – this can result in a lack of challenge to the status quo, or to a lack of proportion regarding the relative significance of an issue being addressed from a preventive point of view. It also makes trying to generate a universal appreciation of what might be an appropriate preventive recommendation very difficult. As we will see in later chapters, things which are appropriate in one context may end up looking and sounding ridiculous in another. What, for example, is the point of insisting upon a person being taken in person before a judicial authority within 24 hours in a country where this is a physical impossibility for reasons of geography and transport? It is, then, important when putting visiting teams together to try whenever possible to include members from different regions. This then has an impact on which countries can *usefully* be visited.

A key factor is indeed the 'usefulness' of a visit, and this has several dimensions. Frankly, if a country has no real interest in preventing torture and ill-treatment or of engaging seriously with the SPT then the only point in going there lies in the symbolism of having done so – though the significance of this should not be underestimated. It is, in my view, absolutely appropriate to visit some countries simply to draw attention to the need for action. But at the end of the day, SPT reports are confidential, and the impact of visits depends on the willingness of the state to take our recommendations seriously. I considered it was far better to spend time in countries where we thought we could potentially make a difference, rather than in countries where we could not, particularly when we were able to make so few visits anyway.

Again, there are more prosaic elements to usefulness too. If a state is in the middle of the process of establishing its NPM, then that might be a very good moment to visit, to influence and assist in that process. Similarly, if that process appears to be stuck, or running into the sand, a visit from the SPT can help focus the mind and prompt action – this certainly appears to have been the case in Australia, where the weeks before the very long-delayed SPT visit in the autumn of 2022 and the then fast approaching (extended) deadline for establishing the NPM at the end of January 2023 prompted a flurry of activity, albeit to no great effect as it turned out. On the other hand, if a state has just passed legislation establishing an NPM but it is not constituted, up and running, then it might be better to wait until it is before visiting.

If there are about to be elections in a country this might not be the best time to visit: there have certainly been cases in which a report given to a newly elected government has been more or less dismissed on the basis that 'that was them, and we are different' – and although a change of government is highly unlikely to have much of a difference on preventive practice, it is a difficult argument to counter without current evidence. Even more basic are practical questions such as the weather: is there really any point in going to countries in rainy seasons when it is going to be physically impossible to access remote detention facilities? Having been stuck in floods, on broken roads and washed away dirt tracks on numerous occasions, this is not an irrelevant consideration and can result in a visit being largely wasted. Add into the mix public holidays, the availability of the Secretariat members to support and accompany a visit, not to mention the physical availability of members given the need for them to be able to clear their diaries for up to two weeks to undertake such a visit (and additional time to recover afterwards), and it borders on the miraculous that visiting occurs at all. The process of constructing a workable and useful SPT visiting programme was hardly a predictable process, and all this gives a flavour of why. It is certainly a 'reasoned' process, but some of those reasons might surprise.

It is obvious from all of this that the business of determining a visiting programme is a complex operation. When I joined the SPT this seems to have been conducted by the three-person Bureau, and in my first SPT session in November 2009 we were simply handed a piece of paper with the names of three countries to be visited in 2010 – they were Bolivia, Lebanon and Liberia. The reasons – and doubtless there were reasons – were those of the decision-makers, which I was not one of at that time. These were two English-language visits (both of which I ended up taking part in),[14] and one was Spanish. None were in Europe.

During my time as Chair, this system changed. To get through the ever-increasing workload, we decided to spend part of our week-long sessions in four 'Regional Teams' (a poor choice of title, a bad decision for which I was entirely responsible). More will be said of these later, but the practice became that the regional teams – based on their more in-depth knowledge of the countries in the regions they covered than was had by the Plenary as a whole – would suggest which countries they thought were priorities for visits. These suggestions would then be reviewed by the Plenary as a whole and scrutinised by the Bureau and the Secretariat to see what was feasible, and the extent to which particular combinations of these priority countries was compatible with the various considerations outlined earlier. Overall, this approach was very successful (though it did produce some unexpected outcomes from time to time). The process – led by one of the four SPT Vice Chairs whose focus was on delivering the visiting programme – resulted in a fairly well-balanced programme, covering all regions of the world and so was certainly universal and, I believe, impartial. I cannot say it was not 'selective', but it was selective for all the right reasons, whereas being either random or rotational would have been 'non-selective' for all the wrong reasons. I dread to think what a waste of work might have resulted had it been otherwise.

Announcing visits

Choosing which countries to visit is one thing, undertaking a visit is quite another. This will be looked at in Chapter 7, but there is one issue which should be considered here and that concerns announcing which countries are to be visited. In a sense, the entire question is somewhat awkward since visits are meant to be 'unannounced' – the fundamental idea is that the SPT can turn up where and when it likes.[15] Once again, fine though this is in theory, trying to do this in a literal sense would be nigh on impossible, and rightly so. For example, you can hardly have an effective police service or prisons service if it would allow anyone who just said they were a UN official to rock up and look at their paperwork, go into cells and talk confidentially to those in custody without this running the risk of seriously undermining the integrity of the criminal justice system. Similarly, in the real world a UN delegation cannot just 'appear' in a country out of nowhere and expect to see senior members of the government on demand. They might not even be in the country at the time. There must be some form of advanced communication to make a system of 'unannounced' visits workable.

Building once again on the experience of the CPT (for which see Bicknell et al, 2018, pp 44–9), the SPT adopted the practice of announcing its annual programme of visits in advance, usually just after the conclusion of its one-week session in November each year, this being the session during which the programme was decided upon. Letters would be sent to the Permanent Missions in Geneva of those countries to be visited just before a press notice was issued listing those countries, so they would not be caught off-guard. While this let them know that they would be visited in the course of the coming year, they were not told when that would happen. Indeed, at the point when those letters were sent and the press release issued, the SPT would not really know itself, as it would not have had time to work this out. It was, then, more a notification of a statement of intent.

Once plans were in place, the practice grew of inviting the Permanent Mission of a country to be visited to meet the Head of the visiting delegation a session or two before the visit was due to take place. The delegation could be briefed on what was expected by way of facilitation of the visit, iron out any misunderstandings relating to the SPT's mandate, and help build a working relationship around the visit. Sometimes during this we discovered some information that caused us to decide to 'fine tune' when we would visit, but these were never 'negotiations' about whether we would be visiting or the dates of the visit – though some states did try to turn them into that.

As with the CPT, the SPT announced publicly the precise dates of its visit a little in advance of its start. This could be quite flexible, but for the SPT it was usually about three months ahead of the visit. This allowed civil society to know in more detail when to pass information to us, allowed us to fix up official meetings and to make the many other practical arrangements that were necessary. Flights must be booked, hotels and transport arranged, interpreters hired, and so on. Most importantly, many members may require a visa to travel to a country they are to visit. This, of course, kills off the idea of completely unannounced visits from the start. And some states during my time certainly tried to use the formalities of issuing visas to try to delay or hamper a visit. Several times I can recall setting off on a long flight without knowing if the visa would be granted on arrival, as had been 'promised'. It almost always was – but it added to the stress, and this was almost always deliberately done to be difficult and potentially cause a visit to be postponed. In one highly unusual case, it was – with the decision being taken literally while some members were en route to the airport. The reality is that it is all but impossible to go through the process of organising even an 'unannounced' visit without putting the state on notice as to when the delegation is arriving. If a state wants to know, it has plenty of ways of finding out. And some did.

What was most important, however, was giving states the time necessary to be able to inform the services responsible for running places of detention that the SPT might be visiting and that we had to be given immediate access if we did. This often took a lot of explaining and training: merely issuing and circulating a general notice to this effect would rarely be sufficient to get the message across. Because of this, we also asked for detailed 'letters of credentials' from the relevant government departments which we could show to prove we were who we said we were when we sought access. Often, we did not really need these, as the information that we might be coming had already been spread around the various systems effectively. But preparing all this takes time, and since it is essential if a visit is to be successful, it is necessary to allow the state adequate time to do it. As a result, you cannot just 'appear from nowhere', like Superman or Wonder Woman, no matter what the text of an Optional Protocol might say.

In the real world – or in the real world of the UN – it was just about impossible for us to get a visit off the ground in less than about three or four months. And states needed no more than this to prepare for our visit. It finally dawned on us that there did not seem to be any good reason why we were issuing 'annual' programmes of visits for the coming calendar year at all. All it did was lock us into a 'straightjacket' – if these were the eight or ten countries we had said we were going to visit that year, then we had to visit them.[16] As financial difficulties closed in on the UN around 2017–18, and given the difficulties we faced getting visiting teams together at times and the increasing number of visits we were trying to do, the effect of announcing an annual programme simply made things more difficult for the SPT than they needed to be. As a result, while each November we still agreed upon our 'annual' programme, we moved towards only announcing the next 'tranche' of visits – the next three or four visits that we needed to announce to get the planning underway and 'the ball rolling' with the various states concerned, as well as to keep civil society and others informed. This remains the current practice.

This brought us closer to the original intention of the OPCAT, which was that visits would be undertaken with as little advance notice as possible. It also meant that we could, if we wanted to, change our minds about which countries to visit if priorities changed. If a visit had not been publicly announced it need not be conducted, and if we came to the view that a different visit was preferable then we could insert another country into our running order at relatively short notice. No-one would ever know, and this certainly happened. In effect, by the simple expedient of changing when we announced to the world what our visiting plans were, we had – almost by accident – created the possibility of undertaking the closest thing to 'ad hoc' visits that the SPT was ever likely to be able to undertake, if they were to include visits to places of detention. In effect, the SPT managed to turn the text of the OPCAT around and remedy what was once considered one of its key weaknesses – the inability to undertake visits at comparatively short notice. All it took was for the SPT to think differently about some bureaucratic matters, despite all the controversy this had generated when the OPCAT was being discussed.

This built upon previous experience of innovation around the nature of visits. One example of this concerned 'follow-up' visits. As has been mentioned already, OPCAT Article 13(4) says that '[i]f the Subcommittee on Prevention considers it appropriate, it may propose a short follow-up visit after a regular visit'. On several occasions, we felt that it was very important to be able to return to a country and visit places of detention again to see for ourselves what progress had been made. Rather than 'ask' whether we might do so, we simply informed the country that we were 'proposing' to visit them again and then just did so as if it were any other visit. Only once did a state suggest to us that we needed their permission to do so. By then, however, we had already visited numerous countries more than once, and so we simply decided to conduct a second regular visit instead. I do not think the SPT has formally conducted a 'follow-up visit' since, and there does not seem to be a need to do so. It can just visit, and as a result Article 13(4) is something of a dead letter.[17] Once again, a provision that was originally intended by states to keep the SPT at arm's length has not worked out that way in practice. There have been many other forms of innovation which are more significant and dramatic than this. These will be discussed later, when looking at the SPT's work with NPMs and how it responds to problems which arise during its visits.

The aftermath of a visit

A visit is not an end in itself. The purpose of a visit is to allow the SPT to see what is happening and to 'communicate its recommendations and observations confidentially to the State Party and, if relevant, to the National Preventive Mechanism'.[18] Although it is not stated quite as clearly as might be expected, Article 16(4) then places the state under an obligation to 'take steps to improve the situation in the light of the Subcommittee's recommendations'. At the end of each visit the SPT delegation meets with representatives of the state and presents comments, usually orally. This is then followed by the transmission of a written report sometime later. This generally takes between six to eight months, though sometimes it has taken considerably longer. The state is then usually given six months to produce a written response. Both the report and response are confidential, unless the state gives its permission for one or both to be published. Although a state is entirely free not to agree to this, the SPT has made no secret of its wish that reports are published, as is obvious from this being a standard recommendation found in many published reports. A gratifyingly large number have been published – 63 out of the 96 visit reports at the end of 2021[19] – confounding those who thought that states would simply bury and ignore reports they could keep confidential.

Yet the reports themselves are hardly comprehensive: they cannot be. When I first joined the SPT, reports could be of any length. Shortly afterwards, a decree went out from the powers that be that no single document produced by a treaty body could be longer than 10,700 words. And if a document submitted was longer, it would not be translated and not be issued. That is not a lot of words with which to address all that might be wrong and to set out and explain the rationale for the recommendations made. However, I was not entirely sorry about the word limit. It made reports shorter, crisper and focused and led to the exclusion of a lot of pointless UN jargon-ese and flummery. Nevertheless, it was still a real constraint, and at times difficult decisions had to be made about what to include and what to exclude. And as the only 'native English speaker' on the SPT or in its Secretariat, hours of my life were spent redrafting sentences to cut out the odd word or two from so that a report would be under the limit. Charles Dickens' Mr Micawber would have understood it perfectly: 10,699 words, an excellent report, translated and transmitted; 10,701, a terrible report, sent back for correction and pushed to the back of the production queue.

As this suggests, reporting is a very formalistic process and, while clearly necessary, is best supplemented by more constructive forms of contact. Predictably enough, state responses, particularly if they are to be published, tend to be rebuttals of what the SPT has said and while they may also chronicle some changes and improvements, even when they do they tend to be rather grudging and along the lines of 'we were going to do this anyway'. There appears to be relatively little kudos associated with accepting and implementing a preventive recommendation of the SPT and few are embraced with enthusiasm, even when they are adopted. But this is to be expected in formal written exchanges which, if made public, become available for scrutiny and use by others. Written responses to UN reports are not ideal places for states to admit to major failures and shortcomings.

As a result, my preference was always for oral discussions, which could be much franker and more open and allowed you to 'gauge' how best to make your points in a way which might strike home and potentially make a difference. Handing over an elegantly phrased written recommendation does not have this effect, and while it is a necessary baseline – establishing what it is you think ought to be done – it can rarely set out the full nuance and reasoning behind why it is being made, nor really convey your real thoughts. That needs the addition of a look, a pause, an emphasis, a hesitation, a tone of voice, with a rising and a falling. There is a degree of theatre involved, for all its seriousness. This can help build relationships and move things forward in a way which a written report often cannot. Indeed, they run the risk of doing the opposite. They invite the recipient to pore over them to look for errors which can be used to prise them apart, or discredit them in some way, thus avoiding the essential truth of what is being said.

Moreover, the very business of producing reports and responses to reports results in a sense of 'closure': the SPT has spoken, the state has replied and the matter is now closed, until the next time. And if there is not going to be a 'next time' – that is, another formal visit – any time soon, then there is little pressure on the state to do very much at all about the recommendations which have been made. It comes as no surprise, then, that when this is the case, little happens.

One of the most dispiriting experiences that I think I ever had was when I participated in a second visit to a country I had already visited some years before. The first visit had been a formative experience for me since, while I had seen many bad things before, I had never seen anything quite like the first prison we went to visit. It was the one and only time when, on entering a particular and notorious cell block, the stench was such that I almost immediately found myself wrenching and vomited on the floor. I was not the only one to do so. Naturally, there were 'recommendations' about the place. Returning some years later, I do not know what I really expected to find, but as soon as we arrived outside that same prison once again, I knew with an overwhelming sense of certainty that nothing, but nothing, was going to have changed. And it had not. I cannot go into the full details since, perhaps unsurprisingly, the report is confidential. It is painful to have to say that, since what that report recounts is an affront to humanity, at every level. It ought to be required reading for anyone who thinks that preventive visiting is not important. But it remains forbidden reading – and I can see why.

But *is* it important if, as was so clearly the case here, our visit had prevented almost nothing? At the very least, it might be argued, it meant that at least *some* now knew. But the problem with such an argument is that *some* always did. In fact, many must always have known – or have known enough to know: those who are held there, their families and the local communities; those who work there, who routinely go there in the course of their work, including lawyers, doctors, delivery staff, workers, NGOs, religious figures and so very many more (no prison, in truth is completely closed to outside scrutiny in some way); those involved in its day-to-day management and those who have administrative responsibility in relation to it (why is so little spent on food, cleaning, sanitation, basic maintenance and so on and so forth?). Add to that the very many in the international community who have had ample opportunity to become aware of what is likely to be going on and thus know in general terms, if not in specifics, what might reasonably be expected as a result of their very many interactions with the country concerned in matters such as technical assistance, reform initiatives, aid and assistance programmes and so on. *Of course* plenty of people knew, or knew enough to know the rest. So what does it add, to add the SPT to that list?

There are answers to that question. As the primary purpose of the SPT is to try to prevent such things, the SPT ought not to be so easily deflected from focusing on what it finds as, perhaps, others might be. It should be able to have access to those in authority and ensure that these matters are drawn to their attention, and to insist that they at least talk with the SPT about it. That is what the OPCAT requires. But what if they do not? I do not recall meeting a single person on that second visit who had even heard of, let alone read, our previous report. Certainly, a copy certainly could not be found in the country – we provided them with a new one. And of course, the report was not available on the UN website; after all, it was confidential. Did they ever even get as far as thinking about making that initial report public? Somehow, I doubt it. Indeed, I doubt whether the content of the report was ever thought about at all, by anyone. Or possibly even read.

The OPCAT does have an answer, of sorts. Article 16(4) says that

> [i]f the State Party refuses to cooperate with the Subcommittee on Prevention according to articles 12 and 14, or to take steps to improve the situation in the light of the recommendations of the Subcommittee on Prevention, the Committee against Torture may, at the request of the Subcommittee on Prevention, decide, by a majority of its members, after the State Party has had an opportunity to make its views known, to make a public statement on the matter or to publish the report of the Subcommittee on Prevention.

It was not until 2022 that this 'ultimate sanction' was first used, in relation to Nicaragua.[20] Why? The reason is that, thanks to a terrible piece of drafting, it is not the SPT's sanction at all. It belongs to the Committee against Torture (CAT) – and on what possible basis could the CAT make such a decision? They have not visited; they have not been party to the 'dialogue', or to the lack of it. They should not have even seen the report in question. After all, it is confidential, even from the CAT. Although it had been thought about, these reasons had previously stood in the way of its use. The situation in relation to Nicaragua in 2022 was somewhat different.

Nicaragua had refused to appear before the CAT itself earlier in the year, which then issued its own concluding observations on the country. Nicaragua then refused to cooperate with the SPT concerning its previously announced visit to the country, and indeed went out of its way to denounce the entire UN human rights system. As a result, there was, probably for the first time, an immediate shared experience of non-cooperation by both bodies which doubtless helped fuel the process. The result is that the SPT's confidential visit report arising out of its 2014 visit has now been made public against the wishes of the state – the first time such a thing has happened.

Is this a harbinger of a new dawn, concerning the use of Article 16(4)? Possibly – though possibly not. In a sense, the almost simultaneous refusal of Nicaragua to cooperate with both the CAT and SPT made this a relatively 'easy' case as there was a common, if not exactly shared, experience of flagrant non-compliance. It may well be that this is an outlier rather than an 'icebreaker'. In a rather paradoxical sense, this might be just as well. The OPCAT is, ultimately, about working with states, and issuing formal public condemnations does not really help improve a broken relationship. It might be cathartic, but it is unlikely to be productive. In their joint press release announcing this move, the Chair of the SPT hoped that the forced publication of the report of its earlier visit would have a preventive effect, but if it does so that is unlikely to be any time soon. It can be better to play the long game – recognising that is the price of working towards long-term prevention. But it is a price that others must pay, and that is not a comfortable thought at all. It is difficult to see how the use of Article 16(4) aids effective prevention, though there are times when its use may be all that is possible – and if that is the case, and if it is also possible to use it, then why not? Yet it remains what it is: a mark of failure, which fortunately remains exceptional and might best remain so.

Notes

1   Most other UN human rights treaty bodies consider reports which are submitted to it by states in accordance with a fixed period set out in the relevant convention, which can vary from between two and five years, the most common period being every four years. This is more often honoured in the breach, with many states reporting late, some extremely late and infrequently and some not at all.

2   ECPT Article 7(1) provides that '[t]he Committee shall organise visits to places referred to in Article 2. Apart from periodic visits, the Committee may organise such other visits as appear to it to be required in the circumstances.'

3   Initially, most CPT visits were 'regular', in the sense of being a part of the pre-announced programme, but this has shifted over time. For example, in 2021 the CPT conducted 15 visits, nine of which were 'regular' and six 'ad hoc'. See the CPT 31st General Report, CPT/INF(2021)5, para 1. See also Bicknell et al, 2018, pp 44–7 for discussion, including why this shift may have occurred.

4   'Annual' is also something of a misnomer. In its early years, the announced programme was undertaken over a roughly the next 12-month period, from around about May until

the March of the following year. Efforts were later made to try to complete the announced programme within the calendar year, but this was often difficult to achieve for various practical reasons.

5   First Annual Report of the Subcommittee on Prevention of Torture and Other Cruel, Inhuman or Degrading Treatment or Punishment, CAT/C/40/2, para 14.

6   According to its latest General Report, its full Secretariat complement is 24 persons strong. See CPT 31st General Report, CPT/Inf(2021)5, annex 4.

7   The record is as follows: 2007, two visits; 2008, three visits; 2009, four visits (including a short two-day 'follow-up'); 2010, three visits; 2011; two visits; 2012, five visits; 2013, six visits; 2014, seven visits; 2015, eight visits; 2016, 11 visits; 2017, ten visits; 2018, six visits; 2019, seven visits; 2020, no visits; 2021, one visit; 2022, eight visits.

8   See 'Statement of the Subcommittee on Prevention of Torture and Other Cruel, Inhuman or Degrading Treatment or Punishment on the 2020 Review of the Process of Strengthening the Human Rights Treaty Body System', 15th Annual Report of the Subcommittee on Prevention of Torture and Other Cruel, Inhuman or Degrading Treatment or Punishment, CAT/C/73/2, annex, paras 9–10. It suggests that this should be 'temporary' pending a move towards a doubling of this, equating to a visiting cycle of every four years – something which is highly improbable.

9   The four to which it has not yet returned are Mauritius, Sweden, Mali and Moldova.

10   This includes some states which had ratified before the OPCAT entered into force in June 2006, such as Albania, Croatia (which is now due to be visited in 2023), Denmark and Georgia. Other countries which had not been visited by the end of 2022 despite having been a state party for over ten years included (with the date of their becoming a party) Estonia (2006), France (2008), Liechtenstein (2006), Luxembourg (2010), Montenegro (2009), Serbia (2006), Slovenia (2007).

11   See 'Statement of the Subcommittee on Prevention of Torture and Other Cruel, Inhuman or Degrading Treatment or Punishment on the 2020 Review of the Process of Strengthening the Human Rights Treaty Body System', 15th Annual Report of the Subcommittee on Prevention of Torture and Other Cruel, Inhuman or Degrading Treatment or Punishment, CAT/C/73/2, annex, para 8.

12   This is now partly addressed through the reciprocal positions of the CPT and SPT reflected in the Chairs' Statement in 2018 in which it was agreed 'to consult each other in future ahead of visits as well as on the potential benefits to be gained by the SPT carrying out visits in Europe'. See 'United Nations and Council of Europe Torture Prevention Bodies to Strengthen Cooperation', joint statement of 26 July 2018, available from: https://www.coe.int/en/web/cpt/-/united-nations-and-council-of-europe-torture-prevention-bodies-to-strengthen-cooperation

13   Of the other eight, six are in Africa (one of which, Madagascar, is to be visited in 2023) and two in Asia (one of which, the State of Palestine, was due to be visited in 2019 but had to be postponed the day before it was due to commence, and so it is perhaps inappropriate to include it in this list: it would have been visited by now but for external factors).

14   I was not originally intended to participate in what turned out to be my first SPT visit to Lebanon in May 2010 but was asked to do so at very short notice since the visit had to be postponed from its original date in April to the closure of much of Europe's airspace due to the eruption of the Eyjafjallajökull volcano in Iceland.

15   This was a hotly debated and highly contentious matter during the drafting of the OPCAT, and it is true that nowhere in the OPCAT is the 'unannounced' nature of SPT visits expressly reflected. Article 4 says that the state 'shall allow visits', Article 11(1)(a) says that the SPT shall 'visit the places referred to in article 4', while Article 12(a) provides that states undertake '[t]o receive the Subcommittee on Prevention in their territory and grant it access to the places of detention as defined in article 4 of the present Protocol'.

To that must then be added Article 13(2), which provides that '[a]fter consultations, the Subcommittee on Prevention shall notify the States Parties of its programme in order that they may, without delay, make the necessary practical arrangements for the visits to be conducted'. Article 14(e) adds that the SPT has '[t]he liberty to choose the places it wants to visit and the persons it wants to interview'. Perhaps most importantly, Article 14(2) then restricts the ability of the state to object to a visit to a particular place of detention to very limited circumstances. Taken together, there is enough here to support the understanding that visits are to be unannounced, but only just. See Evans and Haenni-Dale, 2004, p 46; Nowak et al, 2019, pp 828–31.

[16] This is still true enough and explains why in 2022 the visits undertaken by the SPT were largely those which had been announced in various tranches back in 2018 and 2019 and which remained to be conducted.

[17] Follow-up visits nevertheless remain listed as a potential form of visit on the SPT website, which is of course true. Nowak et al, 2019, p 847 suggest that permission is not required for follow-up visits but since 2017 have been deprioritised for budgetary reasons. This is does not accord with my understanding or experience.

[18] OPCAT Article 16(1). This is not as simple as it sounds since some NPMs are, regrettably, not as reliable, or as independent of other influences, as one might wish. Consequently, this can only be decided on a case-by-case basis, rather than done as a matter of routine. While it does happen, it is probably correct to say that it happens infrequently.

[19] See 'Fifteenth Annual Report of the Subcommittee on Prevention of Torture and Other Cruel, Inhuman or Degrading Treatment or Punishment', CAT/C/73/2, paras 18–19. The reason why the number of reports transmitted is higher than the number of visits undertaken is that some visits result in two separate reports being sent, one to the state and another to the NPM, each of which can agree or withhold publication of the report which it receives. This is discussed further in Chapter 6.

[20] See https://www.ohchr.org/en/statements/2022/11/nicaragua-two-un-rights-committ ees-deplore-refusal-cooperate-and-lack. See also https://www.ohchr.org/en/press-relea ses/2022/11/un-torture-prevention-body-announces-upcoming-visits-2023

6

The UN Subcommittee on Prevention of Torture and National Preventive Mechanisms

Introduction

This chapter introduces the work of the National Preventive Mechanisms (NPMs), which is set out in Part IV of the Optional Protocol to the United Nations Convention against Torture (OPCAT). Article 19 sets out their three key roles:

(a) To regularly examine the treatment of the persons deprived of their liberty in places of detention as defined in article 4, with a view to strengthening, if necessary, their protection against torture and other cruel, inhuman or degrading treatment or punishment;

(b) To make recommendations to the relevant authorities with the aim of improving the treatment and the conditions of the persons deprived of their liberty and to prevent torture and other cruel, inhuman or degrading treatment or punishment, taking into consideration the relevant norms of the United Nations;

(c) To submit proposals and observations concerning existing or draft legislation.

In order to fulfil these roles, NPMs are to have essentially the same powers as the UN Subcommittee on Prevention of Torture (SPT): to be able to undertake visits to places where persons are deprived of their liberty at a time of their choosing and to have unfettered access to all detainees and to all relevant materials, to be able to interview in private and confidentially and to make recommendations to those in authority concerning both the places visited and concerning matters relating to detention and preventive safeguards more generally.[1] This requires the NPMs to have appropriate expertise at their disposal, as well as sufficient funding and operational autonomy. Above all else, it requires that they are independent – something which in practice has turned out to be a far more complicated idea than I think was ever imagined.

I have already stressed the importance of NPMs, which form a central part of the OPCAT. Indeed, it is the 'twin pillar' approach, based on the interplay between the international and national mechanisms, which makes the OPCAT so unique. This chapter looks at NPMs through the 'lens' of the SPT, since that is the 'lens' through which I have seen them. Unlike some of my former SPT colleagues, I have not been a member of, or directly worked for, an NPM, so I cannot say what that is like. What I can say is what the SPT thinks 'its other half' within the OPCAT system *should* look like – and unsurprisingly it tends to think that they should look rather like the SPT, but ideally without the constraints under which it, the SPT, labours. Neither states nor NPMs always agree with this, however.

Moreover, one of the key tasks of the SPT is to play both 'midwife' and 'parent' to NPMs: it is meant to help bring them into being and guide them in their work – and as in any such relationship, there will be frictions. It also is called on to form a view of their work and to seek its improvement where it believes improvement is needed, thus exercising a form of critical scrutiny. Although NPMs are meant to be independent national bodies, they are not independent of the SPT's view of them. Indeed, it is the opinions of the SPT that have caused many of them to be the way they are, or which provide the model of what they should become. As a result, I am a somewhat biased observer when it comes to NPMs, and if I can only really speak of what the SPT thinks NPMs should be like, then it is best to look at how the SPT has exercised its mandate in relation to them. Others will write of the experience of being an NPM, and they will doubtless have things to say about the views of the SPT concerning them.

It is very important to stress at the outset that some NPMs which in some important respects do not really conform to the SPT's preferred model do a very good job, the French and the UK NPMs both being cases in point. For example, the UK NPM must be about the most complex entity in the entire OPCAT system, embracing over 21 separate statutory bodies operating in England and Wales, Scotland and Northern Ireland, often in very different ways.[2] But the point about NPMs and the SPT all being a part of one system is that they should listen carefully to what each has to say about the other, if they are to be as effective as they might be in preventing torture and ill-treatment. And the SPT has certainly learnt a lot from both the French and the UK NPMs, both of which have been very helpful in supporting and establishing NPMs in numerous other countries and contributing greatly to the OPCAT system through spreading their learning and experience. Although the SPT did not necessarily recommend the models they reflect, it certainly commended their work. In a sense, that sums up the OPCAT approach: what matters is what works, even if it is not necessarily what might be expected. Such an approach is not normal across the human rights world, where substance so often takes a back seat to form.

The protean forms of an NPM

It is far better to have things which look rather unusual but which do the job they are intended to perform than it is to have things which look the part but which fail to do so – and the NPM world is replete with examples of both. However, while the SPT undoubtedly has views on what an NPM ought to look like, it has never had one clear preference, nor should it, nor could it (Murray, 2008). Indeed, the OPCAT expressly mandates otherwise.

Article 3 the OPCAT provides that '[e]ach State Party shall set up, designate or maintain at the domestic level one or several visiting bodies for the prevention of torture and other cruel, inhuman or degrading treatment or punishment (hereinafter referred to as the national preventive mechanism)'. It then repeats (in slightly different language) and elaborates further on this when in Article 17 it goes on to say that

> [e]ach State Party shall maintain, designate or establish, at the latest one year after the entry into force of the present Protocol or of its ratification or accession, one or several independent national preventive mechanisms for the prevention of torture at the domestic level. Mechanisms established by decentralized units may be designated as national preventive mechanisms for the purposes of the present Protocol if they are in conformity with its provisions.

There is a lot in here. First, states are to 'maintain, designate or establish [in Article 3, 'set up'] their NPM', which are all rather different things and takes us back the way in which NPMs were brought into the OPCAT system at a late stage in the drafting process. Perhaps unsurprisingly, many states which were supportive of the OPCAT and of establishing a system of international visiting already had systems of visiting in place at the national level (indeed, and as we have seen, many in Europe were already subject to visiting by the CPT too). Equally unsurprisingly, many of those who were opposed to establishing an international visiting mechanism did not. Understandably, those that had such mechanisms did not want to have to create additional bodies which would either replace or duplicate their work – why should they?

As a result, it was agreed that those states which already had domestic bodies visiting places of detention would be able to keep ('maintain') them, while those that did not would have to establish (set up) such a body. 'Designate' is something slightly different again and sits between the two. Quite what it was originally meant to mean in this context is not entirely clear, but it has come to refer to the situation in which a body which already exists is given the role of acting as the NPM. It is not 'maintaining' its visiting role, as it previously did not have one; it is certainly not being 'established or set up', as it already exists, but it is being asked – 'designated' as the body which henceforth will fulfil that function. Too much should not be made of these different forms of establishment, however, since in practice there is usually a degree of all three involved. For example, many states have long-established systems of inspection or oversight of places of detention but might not be exercising, or see themselves as operating, a 'preventive' mechanism in relation to torture and ill-treatment (Evans, 2020, 258).

In the UK, a good example might be OFSTED, the school's inspectorate which, together with HMIP, the prisons' inspectorate, visits secure children's homes; and the Care Quality Commission, which visits care facilities. Neither needs to be established – they exist. They are maintaining their work; but by being 'designated' as a part of the UK NPM they assume, for the first time, a clear role in relation to the prevention of torture and ill-treatment that they previously did not have. To that extent, they are being 'set-up' through their designation to maintain their work, but to view it and to develop it in a different way. The mechanism might not be new, but the task is.

Whether NPMs are 'maintained, designated or established' in this role is all rather secondary. What matters is that it is a role they are now expected to fulfil, and to fulfil under the broader mantle of the OPCAT. The OPCAT is also very clear that there can be 'one or several' such independent mechanisms operating within a state, and that 'mechanisms established by decentralised units' can also be designated.[3] As a result, it is somewhat misleading to speak of 'a' national preventive mechanism, as if it were a single body or entity, and it would probably be more accurate to speak of national preventive *systems*. All this means that it is difficult, if not impossible, for the SPT to tell a country what its NPM should be like. That is for the state to decide.

In practice, several dominant approaches have emerged.[4] Many OPCAT states parties, particularly in Europe, had well-established Ombudsman's offices and these were frequently asked to take on the NPM role, which often means amending the mandates to allow for this. In an increasingly large number of states the NPM function is given to an existing (or newly established) National Human Rights Institution (NHRI). As both Ombudsman's offices and NHRIs are traditionally seen as 'human rights defenders' (and in some countries they are called 'the Office of the Public Defender') this may seem a very natural thing to do. However, this has often proven surprisingly problematic.

Prevention is often confused with investigation (Evans, 2020, p 276). Naturally, preventive visits have 'investigatory' elements: the visiting body will be asking questions, looking at documentation, following up on information and so on. But this does not mean that the purpose of a visit is investigatory in nature. Prevention is not about investigating, nor is it about holding people to account, although it may very well result in that. This can be a particular problem in those countries which have designated Ombudsman's offices, and in some countries NHRIs, as their NPM, since such institutions often see themselves primarily as 'complaints' mechanisms, which investigate allegations of individual or institutional failure or abuse.

At its most extreme, this can mean that some NPMs work *as if* they were complaints investigators and may even think it necessary for them to have received a complaint before they can undertake their work. I have visited some detention facilities with members of an Ombudsman's office who were acting as the NPM in a country and heard for myself them telling detainees that what they should do if they thought they were being ill-treated was to submit a formal complaint to their office and then they would come and investigate it. Rather than themselves taking the initiative and responding to what they were seeing by themselves making recommendations, they had converted their preventive visits into little more than an opportunity to 'drum up' formal complaints. This is not what an NPM should be doing.

Admittedly, it was unusual to find NPMs working in this way, but it was not unusual to find that Ombudsman's offices and NHRIs continued to focus on the cases of individuals that they met during their visits, seeking to resolve them as if they were investigating a complaint. This meant that detainees tended to think of the NPM as being a complaints investigation body and treated it as such, asking it to explore their cases and try to get some form of individual remedy for them. This often put such NPMs in a difficult situation, since while this is not their role as an NPM, it might well be their role as a member of an Ombudsman's office or NHRI. It is difficult to expect staff to operate in such very different ways at the same time. We certainly found examples of members of Ombudsman's offices who worked for the NPM only a day or two each week and for the rest of their time were involved in complaints investigations in the same prisons that they were also visiting as an NPM. This is confused, confusing and, in practice, nigh impossible. For all these reasons, the SPT tended to recommend that if a body with a complaint investigation mandate was designated as the NPM, the NPM function should be allocated to a separate unit with its own staff and operational autonomy, so that it could develop its own working practices, ethos and identity.[5] Preventive visiting is not the same as complaints-based work.

In other countries, a different general approach is adopted. Many countries already have a plethora of existing inspectorates, and these have been given the NPM role collectively – the UK being an example. Once again, this might seem entirely appropriate. Preventive bodies are often described as undertaking 'inspections', and once again, in a general sense they are. But the inspectorial function, properly understood, is subtly but significantly different from preventive visiting (Evans, 2020, p 277). Inspectors generally inspect to standards, the purpose being to determine whether those standards, or expectations, are being complied with. At the end of an inspection the institution will normally be given feedback on the extent to which those standards are being met. It will then be for the institution, or the authorities responsible for them, to seek to address the failings identified.

The other side of the 'inspectoral coin' is that those standards will be known in advance, and so the institution should know what is expected of it. The result is that inspection visits can become more about compliance with standards than with prevention. Preventive visiting goes beyond this, allowing those undertaking visits to think creatively about what ought to be done in the light of the circumstances which they encounter and to make recommendations accordingly. For example, we encountered numerous examples of small police cells being used for the purposes of medium-term immigration detention. While those cells might have been acceptable for short overnight stays, there was no way they could be suitable places to hold people for weeks on end. Their suitability needed to be judged in the light of what they were being used for, not on the basis of what they were – yet that was not the case. It seemed that they fulfilled the standard for being a suitable holding cell, and that was sufficient. Clearly, it was not.

There are other potential difficulties too. The first relates to the sheer scope of the potential work of NPMs and the way in which independent national oversight mechanisms are configured. The breadth of the definition of places of detention and of persons deprived of their liberty means that the range of places that an NPM must be able to access is huge. Many existing mechanisms tend to be sector specific: they look at prisons, policing, heath care, education and so on. They may also have geographical constraints, operating in some parts of a country but not in others – this is particularly true of federal states and other countries with devolved structures and often reflects constitutional, legal, historical, political, cultural and many other factors besides. As a result of all this potential complexity, there is a real danger of 'gaps' occurring. Another potential problem is that not all components of NPMs which are composed of multiple bodies may be working in the same way. Indeed, some parts of an NPM might not really see their work as being primarily about prevention at all, even if what they do may have a preventive effect in some way or another: the mantra 'business as usual' comes to mind, with taking on their new role making little practical difference to what they do and how they do it.

While existing mechanisms fulfil important roles, including in the prevention of torture and ill-treatment in places of deprivation of liberty (Daems and Robert, 2017), the SPT found that the work of relatively few really reflected the essence of preventive visiting as it understood it. For the SPT, preventive visiting is, simply put, the process of exploring, through visits, discussion and examination, the practical experiences of those in detention in order to inform the making of recommendations by the visiting body on how best to reduce the likelihood of torture or ill-treatment. It has been surprisingly difficult to get this message over to NPMs who are just not used to working that way, many of whom seem to think that it is all a lot more complicated than it really is.

Working with NPMs

It may well have been the first ever NPM visit conducted in Africa. We were in a meeting at the offices of the designated NPM. There were bookshelves with copies of the various guides on visiting places of detention produced by NGOs and others. We were told of the international seminars the NPM had participated in during the first year of its existence, and the help that it had received from international partners in developing its own operation procedures and visiting manual. It was all very impressive. The only slight issue was that the NPM had never actually undertaken any visits. Why? We were assured that there were some profound obstacles that stood in the way of it doing so, largely of a budgetary nature. This perplexed us somewhat: after all, we were sitting in its reasonably smart offices in a central location in the capital city that was reasonably well equipped, meeting with salaried members of the NPM staff who had received training in what to do. The problem, it seemed, was a shortage of cars.

This is not a trivial issue when it comes to visiting detention facilities in far-flung locations. But we did wonder why it had stood in the way of their visiting any place of detention at all for the best part of a year. The main central police station was – literally – around the corner from its offices. So rather than spend more time discussing the modalities and protocols of undertaking visits, we had a better idea: the delegation said that it would just pop around that corner and visit the place – and suggested they came along too. In truth, they had little choice, and their reluctance was palpable. We went by foot. We arrived, explained who we were and why we were there, and, within a very short period, we were all at work, moving around the premises, looking at documentation, talking to detainees and to staff. It was a revelation. Initially, the NPM members who came with us were standing back, reluctant to do anything. Before long, they were fully participating, and by the time we left, were taking the lead. We returned to the offices as we had left – on foot. We agreed to meet that afternoon at a prison on the outskirts of the city, with the NPM members making their own way there. It was a successful afternoon too. A good day, all in all. Not that it was what we had planned to do when we set off that morning.

This experience stayed with me. I think the NPM was reluctant to get 'out and about' – and there were numerous reasons for this, and not all of them related to the availability of cars. Perhaps none of them did. There were clearly some political sensitivities at play, and the lack of transport may have offered a plausible excuse – I would not want to pass any judgement on that. We only know what we know. The important points were, for me, twofold. First, the 'idea' of what was involved in preventive visiting had been projected to the NPM in such a way as to make it seem very technical and difficult, the handbooks and guidance being long and complex. Obviously, visits need to be undertaken with understanding, delicacy and care. But these are not the same things. We needed to make the task seem doable, not daunting. The second point was that much had been made about the importance of the SPT visiting places of detention in order to properly understand the situation of detainees. But this was also true of the SPT's meetings with NPMs as well. If we were to be offering them advice on how to undertake their work, we needed to know more about them individually, the challenges they faced in doing their work and what might – practically – be done about it. Were we, the SPT, going about this in the right way?

There was – and remains – a fundamental problem concerning the work of the SPT in relation to NPMs. Some NPMs may not have budgets for elements of their work, but the SPT does not have a discrete budget for its work in advising and assisting states with the establishment of NPMs and advising and assisting NPMs in their work *at all*, despite these being core tasks mandated by the OPCAT itself. The SPT is funded to meet in Geneva, currently for up to four weeks per year, and to undertake its country visits – but nothing else. Whatever it does to fulfil its mandate in relation to NPMs has somehow to be built into these two forms of funded activities. And not everything that could or should be done can be.

The NPM Guidelines

Perhaps inevitably, the first thing which the SPT did was to develop Guidelines, at first a set of 'provisional' guidelines[6] which were replaced by its 'Guidelines on National Preventive Mechanisms', adopted at its session in November 2010.[7] These have stood the test of time and currently remain unchanged, though they have been further supplemented by other documents offering guidance to NPMs, notably an 'Assessment Matrix' which is itself annexed to an important Handbook produced by the Office of the High Commissioner for Human Rights (OHCHR) in its Professional Training Series (OHCHR, 2018). The 2010 Guidelines themselves lie at the heart of that Handbook, and they are routinely referred to in SPT reports and have formed the basis of a technical assistance manual produced by the OHCHR. It is fair to say that they have become almost canonical.

The Guidelines are divided into three sections, 'Basic Principles', 'Basic Issues regarding the Establishment of an NPM' and 'Basic Issues regarding the Operation of an NPM', and there is little in them that should surprise. Inevitably, they reflect the preoccupations of the SPT at the time when they were adopted. For example, the first of the ten 'Basic Principles' is that '[t]he NPM should complement rather than replace existing systems of oversight and its establishment should not preclude the creation or operation of other such complementary systems'.[8] This now seems to be rather an odd opening principle as it seems to downplay, rather than stress, the importance of the NPM. But at the time the Guidelines were written this was a very real problem, as some states were arguing that if they established a new NPM then they could stop the work of existing oversight mechanisms and exclude NHRIs and inspectorates from working in places of detention in order to avoid duplication or overlap. This would have been quite wrong, since their roles are very different, and it was extremely important to make this point as clearly as possible.

This is not a commentary on the NPM Guidelines – but one important element of them concerns independence, which, as a key component of the OPCAT framework, should be touched on because it is rather more complex than it sounds.[9] Everything must be set up by something, and if it is to have a budget, it must receive it from somewhere, and it is not unreasonable (indeed, it is entirely right and proper) that the NPM be accountable for its work and expenditure. But accountable to whom? If it is to a governmental department, then clearly its independence is potentially compromised. However, if the NPM function is given to an NHRI, an Ombudsman's office or an Inspectorate, it will still be subject to the budgetary and operational parameters which are set by its parent body and so not 'independent' of it – even if that parent body is itself independent.

As a result, the NPM Guidelines add an important element to the central idea of independence, which is 'operational' independence, or operational 'autonomy'.[10] It is unrealistic to expect an NPM to be entirely free of operational constraints – but it ought to have independence in how it works within them and, of course, be fully independent in what it says. This too has been an issue, even within independent institutions. I recall encountering a situation where an NPM which was a part of the Ombudsman's office was unable to issue its reports to the state because they had not been approved by the Ombudsman. That is not operational independence. Perhaps the most difficult issue which I felt concerning independence was the following: what did it mean in a country where, like it or not, virtually every institution was in some way a part of the apparatus of governance, or – even more difficult again – only those with the ear of those in power were ever going to be heard? Like it or not, in some countries 'independence' means 'irrelevance', and that hardly assists prevention. Understandably, however, the Guidelines do not address this.

As regards the 'Basic Issues Regarding the Establishment of NPMs', two elements deserve particular mention. The first is that the Guidelines stress that '[t]he NPM should be identified by an open, transparent and inclusive process which involves a wide range of stakeholders, including civil society. This should also apply to the process for the selection and appointment of members of the NPM, which should be in accordance with published criteria.'[11] Experience suggests that in many countries this is essential if the NPM is to have credibility and win the confidence of those with whom it will be working. If the NPM is not trusted, then it is unlikely that it will be able to do a good job.

The second is that 'the NPM should ensure that its staff have between them the diversity of background, capabilities and professional knowledge necessary to enable it to properly fulfil its NPM mandate. This should include, inter alia, relevant legal and health-care expertise.'[12] This seems self-evident, but often it is not the case, particularly when the NPM mandate is given to an existing institution such as an Ombudsman's office whose staff may be excellent lawyers but may not include those with other relevant skills. At the very least, the NPM ought to be able to have access to those with additional skills when necessary, but often this does not happen. Although the Guidelines do not say so expressly, language and interpretation skills are often also necessary, and by no means all NPMs have access to these either.

The final part of the Guidelines, 'Basic Issues regarding the Operation of an NPM', is subdivided into two parts, the first concerning 'Points for States' and the second 'Points for NPMs'. Although this was certainly not foreseen when the Guidelines were drawn up, this division ultimately became mirrored in a major innovation in the working practice of the SPT, the establishment of 'NPM visits'.

NPM visits

Much of what is of greatest value in the OPCAT and in the work of the SPT has been a byproduct of an attempt to address an unrelated difficulty, and the creation of NPM visits is an excellent example of this. There is no mention of them in the text of the OPCAT as such. Their origins lie in a project supported by the Council of Europe in the early years of the SPT and which involved, inter alia, its funding members of the SPT to attend seminars and workshops in Council of Europe countries. During those seminars, presentations would be given on the OPCAT and the work of NPMs, and those bodies which had been given the NPM mandate in the country concerned would then visit a place of detention, accompanied by international experts (not necessarily SPT members) who would then offer them feedback on the way the visit had been conducted. They were, in effect, 'on the job' training sessions in which SPT members were invited to participate.

They were certainly not SPT visits, and the SPT was not involved in producing any reports arising out of them. Indeed, it was something of a bone of contention (and rightly so) that the SPT did not even get to see the reports which were written by the project team. Moreover, as all these exercises were, inevitably, held in European countries, this simply served to reinforce the feelings of some within the SPT that too much time was being spent on European matters. While this was probably true, it was also true that there was no funding to undertake such an exercise anywhere else – and the inability to do it elsewhere was hardly a good enough reason for not doing it all. It also meant that the SPT was able to use its own visits to go to other countries at a time when it was still only receiving enough funding to undertake around three visits per year.

When, as previously explained, the SPT expanded in size from ten to 25 members in 2011, and with more than 50 states parties, it became untenable for it to continue to undertake so few visits. The experience of trying to take eight or nine members on a visit had been salutary and was never again repeated. To increase the number of visits being undertaken, some members argued – entirely reasonably at first sight – that it might be possible to visit more than one country at a time. Would it not be more economical to visit two neighbouring countries when the SPT was in the area, linking a visit to a larger country with a visit to a smaller country? The answer received from the OHCHR to the suggestion of undertaking what were described as 'combo' visits was a resounding no, since the complexities involved in organising the infrastructure to visits places of detention and exercising the SPT's mandate in each of the countries to be visited would remain the same.

Against this background, the question was asked: but what if we don't visit places of detention then? Recalling the experience of the European NPM Project, what if the SPT just visited the NPMs to learn more about their work and, if the NPM was able to organise it, accompany them when they visited places of detention and offer them feedback, as members had done in the context of the Council of Europe project? But – came back the answer – if it is an SPT visit, the OPCAT says that a report must be submitted following a visit to the state, not the NPM; and it would be wrong to give feedback on the performance of an NPM to the state. To which the SPT came up with the ingenious (!) suggestion of producing two reports – one to the state concerning any aspects of the functioning of the NPM which it was in a position to address (such as issues concerning the legal framework, the NPMs' mandate, funding, and the response by the state to its recommendations) and the other to the NPM itself concerning its visiting practice, and how it might be improved. There were several (in fact, quite a lot) of other 'buts' – but in the end, it was agreed to give this a try. And so the idea of the NPM visit was born – as the slimmed down residue of an attempt to economise on the costs of undertaking visits to neighbouring countries.

In fact, it never really worked like that anyway. When we tried to come up with two neighbouring countries which would be quick and easy to travel between, and one of which had an NPM, it rapidly became clear that there really were not very many such pairings to be had at the time that either had not already been visited or which were not in Europe. And the last thing that was wanted was to spend even more time in Europe and less elsewhere. And it also became clear that for a UN team there is no such thing as an easy cross-border crossing. As a result, the idea that the two sorts of visits – the 'regular' and the 'NPM' visit – be somehow linked was abandoned as causing more problems than it solved, and we moved from a programme of three visits a year in 2011 to one of five conducted in 2012, three of which to this day remain highlighted on the UN website of the SPT as having a 'focus on NPMs'.[13] Something else crucial changed in the process of planning these visits too. It became clear that it really was not all that difficult to seek credentials to let the SPT visit places under its own mandate during such visits, and this would be a lot easier than asking the NPM to arrange to take an international team into a place of detention with it. So although the original plan had been to only visit places of detention with the NPM, we were in fact able with relative ease to do so ourselves under our own mandate if we wanted to. And generally, we did.

But what of countries which were yet to establish an NPM? We could not visit something that did not exist – and some of our greatest concerns were precisely such countries. We had a convention mandate to advise and assist, but unless we were able to visit we seemed to have no real means of doing so, other than through written exchanges or meetings with Permanent Missions in Geneva, which, generally speaking, knew next to nothing about what we were speaking of. It was therefore decided to 'push the envelope' a little further and visit a country which had not established an NPM – in what was called an 'NPM Advisory Visit'. Only one such visit ever took place – to Nigeria in 2014: and this was able to be done partly because it was rather unclear whether there was or was not an NPM in existence at all. In a sense, we went to find out. Although this is still listed as a discrete type of visit on the SPT website, it is doubtful whether such a thing will ever take place again.

The visit was extremely short, only a couple of days long, and did not involve any visits to places of detention. It was largely limited to meetings with government officials and to a body which appeared to hold the NPM function. As Nigeria is still listed by the SPT as a country that does not have an NPM, it gives away nothing that is not already known to say that we concluded that it did not.[14] The hope had been that this might ultimately have been something of a bridgehead into a new range of activities in which a handful of members (only two participated in the visit) went out to visit states on the back of the SPT visiting mandate to hold discussions concerning the establishment of NPMs, allowing us to fulfil that part of the mandate in a more innovative and effective way. States are – as we will see – usually obliged to establish their NPM within one year of becoming a party to the OPCAT system, but apart from sending them materials there was no structured way of offering them that assistance without a visit. However, this was overtaken by events, and the possible precedential value of this 'Advisory' visit as a means of addressing this rather fundamental shortcoming in the SPT's armoury was diminished when it was realised that was possible to do much the same thing by other means – basically, by using a colleague's laptop in breakout sessions during the Plenary meetings in Geneva, on which more will be said shortly.

Nevertheless, the largely failed 'NPM Advisory Visit' concept has now metamorphosed into yet another new variant: a short visit focused on 'High Level Talks' concerning a discrete issue that merits such a visit. The first such visit, lasting a few days, took place to Brazil in 2022. This was originally planned for 2020 but had to be postponed due to the pandemic. The aim was to discuss changes to the funding and structure of the NPM in Brazil, an issue that the SPT had long been concerned about and on which, in yet another innovation, it had already issued a detailed statement in the form of an Advice to the NPM about proposed changes and its effect upon them.[15] Obviously, this was intended as a contribution to the vigorous domestic debate about these highly controversial proposals. Such visits are not mentioned in the OPCAT itself, and this is yet another example of the SPT acting innovatively within the OPCAT framework to best fulfil its mandate.[16]

Regional teams

Returning to my colleague's laptop, writing today it is almost too embarrassing to recount what now follows. It has already been mentioned that towards the end of 2011, the SPT began to spend part of its time meeting in 'regional teams', and the primary reason for this was to allow it to have the time to examine what progress was being made in the establishment of NPMs, and how established NPMs were going about their work. This could not be done in the main Plenary sessions of the SPT as there simply was not enough time in our then weeklong sessions, held three times each year.[17] The regional teams met on the Monday afternoons and Tuesday mornings. Each member was asked to take primary responsibility for keeping in contact with the NPM in around three or four countries, and to report back on this to the team at each session. This provided a practical means of considering, even if only briefly, the situation regarding the NPM in every state party at every SPT session and, overall, it worked quite well.

Each regional team would then report back to the Plenary on any specific issues which it felt everyone ought to know about or matters that required following up. One way of following up on matters was to decide to invite the NPM to come to a session of the SPT and spend time either with the Plenary or with the regional team itself. The difficulty with this approach is, however, obvious. Many of the problems faced by NPMs came down to a shortage of money, and we were asking them to spend considerable sums to come to Geneva to explain this to us. Paying their costs to come was of course completely out of the question. As rarely could more than an hour be spent with each of those we invited, this was hardly a cost-efficient exercise for anyone. The same was true when it came to raising detailed questions with states about their progress in establishing their NPMs. Although we continued to do this from time to time when it seemed appropriate, we found another way: Skype.

Huddled around a member's laptop, members of a regional team would be able to talk to two or three NPMs or states during their team meetings, which was much more efficient all round. Translation was not possible of course – that was only available in the Plenary meeting room and in respect of things said in the meeting room. One of the most embarrassing moments I have ever had at the UN was chairing a meeting with the NPM of a French-speaking country – for once, in the Plenary room – but which could not be translated as the words were not being *spoken* in the room. Our French-speaking Secretariat thus helped out by repeating what they were saying, and because it was now being said 'in' the room, it could be translated.

Even the use of Skype was not a fool-proof solution: regional teams could only do this at first if they were meeting in a first-floor room in the Palais Wilson – on the shores of Lake Geneva, at the centre of the UN human rights world, there was no Wi-Fi available for us to use on the upper floors at the time. Post-pandemic, it is incredible to recall what a struggle it was – a mere five or six years ago – to be able to use electronic communication to bring us closer to the NPMs and states; but we did. It was considered risky and risqué. The SPT – and NPMs – owe a real debt of gratitude to both members and the SPT Secretariat who went out of their way to try to make this work at a time when the very idea of such a thing was considered by some as being at best eccentric and, at worst, downright dodgy. This quickly led to us holding longer online workshops with states and NPMs outside of our session times too: after all, domestic legislative timetables do not turn on the dates of SPT plenaries. So when the work of the treaty bodies went 'online' in March 2019, we were already well versed in what to do.

Of course, while this was all valuable, there is no replacement for face-to-face engagement, and we were fortunate that in some countries either the OHCHR, the United Nations Development Programme, the Council of Europe, the Organization for Security and Co-operation in Europe, other organisations or agencies, sometimes civil society and sometimes states themselves, would organise seminars and roundtables to which we might be invited to discuss progress, at the inviter's expense.[18] Some thought such entrepreneurship problematic, believing that all such activities should be planned and coordinated through the UN and the SPT Secretariat. Personally, I welcomed each and every opportunity to meet with NPMs and states in order to fulfil the SPT's mandate – whether it was online from Geneva, online from my home, whether it was in the country concerned, and irrespective of who paid for it. The sad truth was (and remains) that if we waited for the UN to come up with the financial resources to fully facilitate this work, we would be waiting for ever.

Those first fragile steps on skype paid dividends and completely transformed how the SPT was able to help states establish NPMs and help NPMs in their work. All it took was a laptop and a bit of imagination.

'Egregiously overdue …'

Article 17 of the OPCAT says that states are to establish their NPMs within a year of becoming bound by the convention, while, as already discussed, Article 24 allows them to delay that obligation for up to five years, allowing a maximum period of six years for those who seek to do so. As must be clear by now, while the idea of an NPM is quite a simple one to grasp, setting one up is not so simple and takes time. Some states do not want to join the OPCAT system until they are ready to do so and have spent many years thinking about how best this might be done. Ireland is a case in point: I have lost count of the number of times I have been to Dublin to discuss progress on this – and although the outline of their plan has been settled for many years, the detail still is not, and so they have not yet done so. The situation in Belgium is similar.

However, while it can be difficult, it is not *that* difficult, and there comes a point when pleading the difficulty of the exercise becomes more of an evasion than a reason. If this is true of states which are thinking of ratifying, then it is even more so of states which have already chosen to become bound by the OPCAT but have not established an NPM as they are obligated. For example, Australia spent several years thinking about how to structure its NPM, and yet there is still no NPM established in many parts of the country over five years after they ratified the OPCAT, and in January 2023 it missed its already extended deadline for doing so. There are plenty of other examples too. No-one made such states become a party of the OPCAT system: it was their choice, and they ought to have known what they were committing themselves to – although the SPT has also run into a considerable number of states who seemed surprised that this was really expected of them, and it is well known that many states make human rights commitments which they have no intention of fulfilling.

Moreover, states are not currently asked to do very much. All that the SPT Guidelines ask is that a '[s]tate should notify the SPT promptly of the body which has been designated as the NPM'.[19] Once it has been notified, this is listed on the SPT's public website. There is no 'accreditation process', and the SPT does not at that point consider whether the body designated as the NPM fulfils the OPCAT criteria. All it asks is the absolute minimum: that something be designated. As it says in its introduction to the NPM Guidelines:

> It is the responsibility of the State to ensure that it has in place an NPM which complies with the requirements of the Optional Protocol. For its part, the SPT works with those bodies which it has been informed have been designated by the State as its NPM. ... [T]he SPT does not, nor does it intend to formally assess the extent to which NPMs conform to OPCAT requirements.[20]

Moreover, and although the NPM Guidelines do not say so, the SPT has always taken a fairly relaxed approach to the one-year deadline, understanding that it is better that states spend time to get it right, rather than rush something through which is inadequate but which is then going to be difficult to change. However, there does come a point when patience wears thin, and as a result, in 2016 the SPT initiated a process which involved the publication of a list highlighting those countries which were slow to designate their NPMs.

The elliptically entitled 'List of States Parties Whose Compliance with Obligations Set Out in Article 17 of the Optional Protocol to the Convention against Torture and Other Cruel, Inhuman and Degrading Treatment or Punishment (OPCAT) Is Substantially Overdue' names those states which are more than three years late in establishing their NPM, from whatever date it ought to have been in place. For most, this will be four years. For others, who made declarations under Article 24, it will be longer. For example, Australia would only be eligible for inclusion on the list if it has not established its NPM by January 2026, fully eight years after it ratified the OPCAT. In addition, before a state is put on that list, it is written to and given the opportunity to explain why it ought not to be – which in practice allows the SPT to confirm whether there still is no NPM in place, though it also delays the listing a little more again.

Although all that the list does is highlight information which is already in the public domain, it has had a significant and positive impact, since several states were keen not to be listed, and some of those listed were keen to make progress in setting up their NPM in order to be removed from it. The criteria for removal from the list are not particularly onerous and, again, do not involve any element of evaluation by the SPT of the NPM which is put in place. All that is required is that the state notify the SPT of:

1. The fact of such establishment;
2. A copy of the legal instrument establishing the national preventive mechanism, whether by legislation or another act;
3. The name of the head of the national preventive mechanism;
4. The postal address of the national preventive mechanism;
5. The email address and phone number of the national preventive mechanism.

In other words, all that is required is some minimal supporting evidence and some information on how the NPM can be contacted. It is not a lot.[21]

Nevertheless, at the end of 2022 14 states remain on this list. They are Belize, Benin, Bosnia and Herzegovina, Burundi, Central African Republic, Democratic Republic of the Congo, Gabon, Ghana, Liberia, Nauru, Nigeria, Philippines, South Sudan and State of Palestine. Although it does not appear in the formal list on the SPT website, as Chair I used my annual statement to the UN General Assembly to go slightly further again by listing those which I considered to be 'egregiously overdue', this being more than ten years late in establishing their NPM. At the time of writing in 2023, six would fall into that camp – Benin (15 years), Bosnia and Herzegovina (14 years), Democratic Republic of the Congo (11 years), Gabon (11 years), Liberia (11 years) and Nigeria (12 years).[22] Clearly, the 'NPM Advisory Visit' to Nigeria did not lead to much; Benin was first visited by the SPT in 2008, the year when its NPM should have been established, and again in 2016. Liberia was visited in 2010 and again in 2018 … In many ways, it is a rather depressing list, being a catalogue of failure.

Accentuating the positive

Nevertheless, one must never give up on the NPM process. Several countries – including Chile, Lebanon and Mongolia – appeared on the 'substantially overdue list' and were subsequently removed when their NPM was finally established. Burkina Faso was 'egregiously overdue' – but it too has since been removed as well. Above all else, however, it is vital to stress that the SPT website also lists the 72 states which *have* designated their NPMs, some of which were not required to have done so at all when they did so. This is a very high rate of compliance indeed and is a major achievement that needs to be trumpeted and celebrated. While by no means all these NPMs are quite what might have been hoped for, they can all be worked with. And many do an extremely good job indeed.

There are now probably thousands of members of NPMs established within the OPCAT framework, conducting tens of thousands of visits to places of detention each year, probably meeting with hundreds of thousands of detainees and making goodness knows how many recommendations to help prevent torture and ill-treatment. This is a tremendous achievement and well beyond the contemplation of those who initiated the OPCAT project. The SPT should take some of the credit for this: by constantly seeking new ways of keeping the pressure on, year in, year out, to get NPMs established and to ensure that they operate as best they can. Even if this has been a bit of a struggle at every step of the way, it has really made a difference and has achieved what it was meant to achieve: it has helped prevent torture.

Notes

1   See generally OPCAT, Articles 18–20 and see Murray et al, 2011, pp 117–19.
2   For an overview of the UK NPM and its work, see its latest Annual Report, 'Monitoring Places of Detention during COVID-19 12th Annual Report of the United Kingdom's National Preventive Mechanism 2020/2021', 2022, CP 609. This and much other information is available from: https://www.nationalpreventivemechanism.org.uk/
3   See OPCAT, Article 17, which provides that '[e]ach State Party shall maintain, designate or establish, at the latest one year after the entry into force of the present Protocol or of its ratification or accession, one or several independent national preventive mechanisms for the prevention of torture at the domestic level. Mechanisms established by decentralized units may be designated as national preventive mechanisms for the purposes of the present Protocol if they are in conformity with its provisions.'
4   The Association for the Prevention of Torture maintains an excellent NPM database with interactive links to relevant legislation, as well as descriptive overviews of various forms of NPMs. See https://apt.ch/en/opcat-database/
5   SPT Guidelines on National Preventive Mechanisms, para 32: 'Where the body designated as the NPM performs other functions in addition to those under the Optional Protocol, its NPM functions should be located within a separate unit or department, with its own staff and budget.'
6   The 'Preliminary Guidelines for the Ongoing Development of National Preventive Mechanisms' were set out in the First Annual Report of the Subcommittee on Prevention of Torture and Other Cruel, Inhuman or Degrading Treatment or Punishment, CAT/ C/40/2, para 28 (a)–(n).
7   Fourth Annual Report of the Subcommittee on Prevention of Torture and Other Cruel, Inhuman or Degrading Treatment or Punishment, CAT/C/46/2, paras 63–102. See also the front page of the SPT website, under key documents at https://www.ohchr.org/en/ treaty-bodies/spt. For the record, these were in fact drafted by myself, Rachel Murray and Elina Steinerte, two colleagues at the Human Rights Implementation Centre at the University of Bristol, and adopted largely unchanged by the SPT.
8   NPM Guidelines, para 5.
9   Para 18 of the NPM Guidelines provides that '[t]he State should ensure the independence of the NPM by not appointing to it members who hold positions which could raise questions of conflicts of interest', and this is matched by para 19, which provides that '[m]embers of NPMs should likewise ensure that they do not hold or acquire positions which raise questions of conflicts of interest'.
10   Para 8 of the NPM Guidelines provide that '[t]he operational independence of the NPM should be guaranteed'. This is one of the 'Basic Principles' set out at the head of the document.
11   NPM Guidelines, para 16.
12   NPM Guidelines, para 20.
13   The first such visits were in 2012, to Honduras, Senegal and Moldova. In 2013, NPM visits took place to Germany and Armenia; in 2014 to Ecuador and Malta; in 2015 to the Netherlands and Turkey; in 2016 to Cyprus, this being the last to be flagged as such.

[14] This list is discussed subsequently, and for which see https://www.ohchr.org/en/treaty-bodies/spt/non-compliance-article-17

[15] See 'Views of the Subcommittee on Prevention of Torture on the Compatibility with the Optional Protocol to the Convention against Torture of Presidential Decree no. 9.831/2019 Relating to the National Preventive Mechanism of Brazil', 19 December 2019, CAT/OP/8. Available from: https://www.ohchr.org/en/treaty-bodies/spt/national-preventive-mechanisms/advices

[16] The visit has similarities with the 'High Level Talks' which the CPT introduced some years ago and which it now conducts fairly frequently. See Bicknell et al, 2018, pp 56–7.

[17] In 2018, it was agreed that one of these sessions should be increased to two weeks, but the first time that proved possible was in 2021. The SPT therefore now meets in Geneva for four weeks each year, for a week in February and November and two weeks in June.

[18] The inviting organisation would have to cover all costs as the OHCHR had no budget to pay the costs of members to do such things – though it could send staff members from time to time. Sometimes members paid their own way. Sometimes members while visiting a country for entirely different reasons – including when on holiday – might take the opportunity to meet and talk. Some, including some members, frowned on this, but if it was the only way to have a conversation that needed to be had, then so be it, in my view.

[19] NPM Guidelines, para 23.

[20] NPM Guidelines, para 2.

[21] Details of the process, setting out these criteria, are available from: https://www.ohchr.org/en/treaty-bodies/spt/non-compliance-article-17. Importantly and helpfully, this was updated in June 2022 to clarify and make public the criteria for removal from the list, something which previously had been somewhat opaque and not entirely uncontentious.

[22] The current Chair has not continued this practice, but the time constraints which affect the length of the presentations appear to have increased considerably. The practice of including in that statement the longer list of those not in compliance continues, however. For the latest Statement to the UN General Assembly, on 14 October 2022, see https://www.ohchr.org/en/statements/2022/10/chairperson-subcommittee-prevention-tortures-statement-77th-ga-session

PART II

The Problem

7

Visits: An Insider's Story

Introduction

Hoteliers must have hated us. We were among the worst sorts of guests, and at our very worst at breakfast. Just about every member of the delegation would be feeding themselves up for the day on enormous quantities of just about whatever there was to feed on: and then – worst of all – would leave with as much secreted in their bags and pockets as possible. Some limited themselves to fruit, especially bananas (there is a reason for this). Others would be busy making up sandwiches out of rolls, meats and cheeses for themselves, and others. I doubt the hotel kitchens could have done a better job. Indeed, in some instances I know they could not. We once asked if the kitchens might provide us with some take-away sandwiches. They did. But when the packets were opened (amazingly, during the course of a helicopter flight being taken to reach a particularly remote part of a country) they were full of cockroaches. Some hardy souls removed them and pressed on with what remained. Others did not. The desperation to eat was real enough. There would be no other opportunity for the rest of an extremely long and hard day.

At least there *were* cockroach sandwiches. Another visit, another hotel – the only one that was available for us to stay at. No chance of helping ourselves from the breakfast buffet as there wasn't one. Indeed, I cannot now recall whether there was any breakfast available at all. I suspect not. After all, there was only hot water for an hour or so a day, and electricity intermittently. There was a 'restaurant' attached to it, but it was rarely open. One evening, returning from a visit around 7 pm (no breakfast, no lunch), the restaurant was closed. The only other was twenty minutes' drive away. A flat tyre later, we arrived around 9 pm, and the kitchen was closed. Ultimately, we had to prevail on the manager to ask the cook to come back, and we ate whatever there was.

Another 'no breakfast' morning – but we had a meeting with the local authorities at the airport so we could eat there instead. No café, or shop. But we were meeting the local officials in the VIP lounge, so – jelly babies only. The long flight of five hours: biscuits with a drink. The airport in which we were changing fights – we were late, had to run for the connection. An internal flight and no food: a biscuit of course. Arrive at our hotel – no food available. Rush out to find a McDonald's still open at 11 pm. Made last orders – double burgers, double chips, double anything. Welcome to the 'other' world of UN Subcommittee on Prevention of Torture (SPT) visiting.

Visiting in practice

There is not a manual yet written on visiting places of detention which does not stress the importance of advance planning, of logistical arrangements, of having clear plans and protocols on what to do within places of detention, setting out the structure of an ideal visit and how to conduct it and so on. I should know as I have helped write a fair number of them, written with National Preventive Mechanisms (NPMs) particularly in mind. Over time, I have become increasingly coy about doing so since they simply do not reflect my personal experience, and it feels somewhat hypocritical to be peddling the 'don't do what I do, do what I tell you' approach all of the time. Yet it is not that the theory is necessarily wrong: the problem is that the theory does not always work in practice – and in the practice of the SPT, hardly ever.

I do not know whether to be embarrassed by this or not. There are good reasons – or at least, reasons – why this is so. First and foremost, a visit by the SPT is not the same as a visit from an NPM, which is based in the country concerned. As has been seen, a visit to a country by the SPT is a rarity – perhaps once every seven or eight years, sometimes less, sometimes more. In 2010, my first year on the SPT, I visited two countries – Liberia and Lebanon. I returned to Liberia again in 2018, and the SPT returned to Lebanon in 2022. Other countries visited have been returned to sooner but, other than for states in the Americas (and for reasons already given), that is rare. Given that SPT members, in principle, can serve two four-year terms – usually, then, a maximum of eight years – relatively few members will ever return to a country they have visited for a second time – so a visit is likely to be a 'one off' experience. The same is likely to be true for many members of the Secretariat.

As a result, every visit has a sense of 'finality' about it. This is the *one* opportunity for the delegation to see what there is to be seen and to make its recommendations. What it does not do *now* it may never be able do at all – and certainly, most of the members of the delegation will not. As members are experts in a broad variety of forms of detention and issues – prisons, policing, health care, psychiatry, women in detention, juvenile detention, immigration detention – and so much else besides, it is extremely difficult to exclude themes and issues and places from a visit. Members want to focus on their areas of expertise, and this is not irrational. Add to this the calls from civil society to focus on matters of concern which they seek to raise and the pressure on the delegation to do far more than may, in truth, be desirable, is both overwhelming and, in truth, irresistible. For example, to leave a country knowing that you cannot really comment on women's prisons because you have not visited one is a terrible thought to take away with you, as it is of anything and everything else that has not been looked at. And a typical visit lasts six to ten days. What can you do in that time? The typical pattern of one of the shorter visits which have come to dominate in more recent years is as follows.

A visit will officially commence on a Monday and end on a Friday. This enables the delegation to meet with senior state officials at both its start and its finish – they would rarely agree to meet on a weekend in most countries, and we could not force them to do so. One can, of course, visit places of detention over the weekend, and so extend the visit accordingly. This may sound sensible and often does occur. Yet it is not exactly as efficient as it sounds. In many countries, weekends are times when detention facilities are also understaffed, or staffed with temporary staff, making access more difficult and visits less productive. Many internal facilities, medical, social, educational and so on, will not be operational. It is not ideal, but 'ideal' is not usually the benchmark. One does what one can. It is more usual for the weekends to be spent transiting from one region to another in larger countries, and this is indeed a more efficient use of time, though it does make for arduous schedules – but little about an SPT visit is not arduous.

The Secretariat will usually arrive towards the end of the week before the start of the visit to confirm arrangements, often collect credentials and to prepare as best they can for the arrival of members over the course of the weekend. As members will usually be coming from several quarters of the globe, it is rare for the full team to be in place much before a Sunday afternoon – when meetings might immediately commence with local briefings, including by civil society groups. When I first joined the SPT, it was considered quite improper to do anything 'substantive' before the first official meetings with the national authorities held on the Monday morning – but that scruple has long since been abandoned. Indeed, one of the lessons learnt during the COVID-19 pandemic is that there is far more that can be done in advance of a visit than was originally thought, and this now includes meetings with NGOs and others. Why wait until you are in the country at all? It is increasingly the case that the SPT delegation now meets online with selected NGOs and civil society groups in advance of the visit, and this is a very much better use of time and resources.

Oddly, in some ways it is something of a return to the practice when I first joined the SPT: about three weeks or so before our visit to Liberia,

I attended a seminar there organised, and paid for, by international NGOs and which was a platform to inform both local NGOs and officials about the visit and to hear from NGOs. It was, then, somewhat bizarre to find myself a few weeks later in the same hotel, with many of the same people, hearing almost exactly the same things. Rather than being a time-saving exercise, it was more of an expensive 'dummy run', though nonetheless useful for that. There is no doubt that online meetings in advance of the visit are a very welcome development – freeing up time and resources for visiting places of detention themselves.

When I first became an SPT member, all visits tended to be longer than many now are – about ten days in total. The first two days, however, would usually be taken up with meetings with officials from various ministries and then with civil society groups, and it was quite usual for visiting to only begin on the third day. About six days would then be spent visiting places of detention, a day then spent on internal meetings and discussions concerning a lengthy statement, often written and extending to some ten or 15 pages which would somehow have to be produced and agreed upon, and then this would be presented at a fairly formal meeting on the final day, after which the delegation would swiftly depart – sometimes straight to the airport for the long journey home.

And everyone participated in everything, attending every formal meeting and visiting every place of detention. This was not efficient; indeed, it was very inefficient. The opening formal meetings had originally been used as a means of acquiring important practical information – but why could this not be acquired in advance? As the length of our visits reduced to more like six to eight days, and some to five, things needed to change. Ultimately, in the visits which I led, these fairly formal first meetings with authorities were slimmed down from half day – or even day-long – events into short meetings of little more than an hour in which we reminded those attending of our mandate and what we expected: to be able to access places of detention upon arrival, move around unhindered and speak in confidence with whom we wished. We would then agree to meet at the end of the visit for a short concluding meeting. We would then move to a range of meetings with different groups with whom we wished to meet to help finalise our plans and our thinking. We might often split up for these, and compare notes later, back at the hotel. This then was mirrored in the conduct of the visits.

By the second day we were usually ready to begin visiting. Delegations were usually of either four, or sometimes five or six members. This meant that we could split into two teams, each accompanied by a member of the Secretariat and a translator, but often with only one security officer. Add a driver, and that is still quite a crowd. Each team would tend to focus on different types of facilities. While we might all go to a large prison together, we would tend to split up to focus on policing, immigration, health-related units or whatever else was the focus. Teams might even go to different parts of the country for several days: in a visit to Ukraine, for example, we all started in Kyiv, but one team then headed to the south and west, whereas another went north and then east, towards the Donbas, already by then an 'uncontrolled territory' as Ukraine described it. I headed up that team, visiting places the names of which are now all too familiar: Kharkiv, Kramatorsk, Zaporizhzhia, Donetsk, Mariupol. Colleagues on the other team went to Odesa, Kherson and elsewhere. When we had visited Ukraine five years earlier, with a team of nine, we probably visited fewer places than we were able to do with half that number on that later visit. Again, we would meet to brief each other at the end of each day if we were staying in the same place and, if not, would do so when we met up again – usually on the penultimate day. This substantially added to the length of time that could be devoted to visiting. Indeed, sometimes, the last visit to a place of detention might be on the morning of, and only a few hours before, our final meeting with the national authorities.

This could only happen because of another major change in practice – an entirely unintentional and unforeseen consequence of the UN's decision to limit our written reports to a maximum of 10,700 words. The 'written statements' which had previously been produced in the dying hours of the visit in its early years had often been not far off this – and as the practice was to tidy these up shortly afterwards and let the state have them as a 'down payment', so to speak, on the final report, it almost amounted to the drafting of a report 'in situ'. This, in my view, was not a good idea. Members were tired, passions were running high, everyone was stressed, and it was not the moment to commit to writing measured reflections and observations arising from the visit. And, moreover, they had not been agreed by the SPT as a whole: the usual approach was for each delegation to agree its draft report, which was then shared with all members, to be discussed and agreed upon at the next Plenary session in Geneva. While the Plenary could not dispute what the delegation found (after all, it had not been there), it might (and usually did) raise questions about the recommendations made.

For all these reasons, I encouraged delegations to abandon this practice and use the final meeting as a moment in which to give oral impressions – raising any urgent matters which required urgent attention – and setting the scene for the next stage of the process, which was the submission of the report and the state's consideration and reaction to that. This might seem to be a 'soft' approach, and a missed opportunity to say some hard-hitting things, but in practice I found it to be the opposite. When you are committing things to writing, and particularly when that is then subject to discussion and a need for consensus, punches are more likely to be pulled and the result perhaps too nuanced or simply too bland to make an impression. I preferred to go into those meetings with an agreed list of points that we wanted to make – and then just speak to those points in the ways that seemed most effective. This enabled you to gauge the response and judge when it was, perhaps, wise to be somewhat circumspect and when you felt it was possible to be very blunt indeed. In general, I found little difficulty with being blunt in such meetings, and I felt that we were accorded more respect for being so. After all, most in the room knew the truth of what we were saying.

There was always a degree of gamesmanship about this, it must be said – on both sides. In one country, we were very well aware that there was a tendency for officialdom to hold forth at length on matters of little importance. To curtail this, we explained that our schedules meant that we could not devote more than one hour for our final, brief, closing meeting. I have to admit that this was entirely untrue. The very senior officials, of ministerial rank, sitting opposite then welcomed us to the meeting and said they would like to say just a few words before I began. Nearly an hour later as they were concluding they expressed their regret that we now had to leave and indicated that as a result they would be looking forward to hearing what we had to say when they received our written report some months hence. As I thanked them for their kindness, I ostentatiously took off my watch, propped it up in front of me and began speaking – doubtless with some repetition, a little deviation but absolutely no hesitation – for the next hour and a quarter, pinning them to the room. As we finally shook hands on our departure, there was a smile on the minister's face, and a slight bow of the head that amounted to his saying touché. We understood each other perfectly. It was what the occasion demanded and could not have been prepared or scripted. And afterwards, at least for a while, some progress was made in enhancing the independence, standing, capacity and the work of the NPM. I like to think there was a connection here; indeed, I believe there was.

Bananas

Bananas were the fruit of choice for the SPT breakfast-buffet thieves for one simple reason: you can peel them without touching what you eat. And they fitted very easily into the pockets of the blue vests the UN insisted that we wore, and which were extremely practical. And that, I am afraid, is where most of the handbooks on visiting places of detention that I have contributed to fall down – what they say should be done is often just not practical for the SPT (and doubtless others) to do.

Let's take lunch. Or rather, let's not. You have travelled two, three or even four hours in a van to arrive at a place of detention. You left at 7 in the morning if you are lucky (you need to allow time for the interpreters, who are recruited and live locally, to come and join you before you set off from wherever you are staying) and so it may already be 10.00 am, or later. You have to get into the place, which may take minutes or a good deal longer. The protocols suggest that you should first meet with the head of the institution – which is both proper and sensible if you are to be able to conduct an effective visit. You need the cooperation of the staff, and that is not going to be forthcoming without the clear and visible blessing of those in charge. In a large institution, this may take a little while. They may be in meetings, or not to hand. You say it does not matter, but to them, it does. So you wait. Some refreshment might be offered at this point, and only a fool would decline it, both for the sake of politeness and practicality. It will probably be the last you have until you leave. Likewise – the toilet! Ask to use the one as close as possible to the Director's office. I can assure you, it is 'downhill' all the way from there. Indeed, if you want an early idea of what to expect within the cell blocks, check out the toilets used by the prison guards. If they are terrible (and they often are), you will know already that what you will be finding in the cell blocks is going to be even more terrible again: they are never going to be better!

It is now 11.00 am: how long do you want to make this meeting last? Ideally, as short as possible. In my early visits, a huge amount of time was spent asking questions of commanders who often would then have to call others in to answer them, and an hour could easily slip by. I tended to try to cut these short, by simply explaining what we hoped to do. Before entering, we would have agreed a 'game plan' – who was to do what – and all we needed to do was explain this and ask for assistance in pointing us in the right direction, and opening and closing doors for us too, of course. For all the talk of 'unrestricted access', no-one is ever going to give the SPT a bunch of keys, nor would you want them to. But when detainees see us being let in and out by their guards, what do they think of us?

At this point, the handbooks tell you what to do. The problem is, despite our best efforts, we rarely could do it. You want to have a general tour of the premises to get a 'feel' of the layout and the overall context. This is valuable, but as you move around, wearing your UN blue vests, you are immediately visible as different. In quite a few of the places I have visited, any external visit would be unusual. Added to which, it is highly likely that detainees have been told ('warned') that we might be visiting – and when we do turn up at a prison, as night follows day, some emergency measures will be taken by the staff whether we like it or not. Perhaps outdoor exercise will be stopped and detainees returned to their cells – or, equally likely, that it will not be taking place at all during the time when we could be visiting. We are a disruption to routine, no matter how we might wish it to be otherwise. Not always in a bad way, of course: often there are quite appealing menus on display when we visit. However, detainees sometimes told us that they had never seen what was on these 'special' menus, and we frequently failed to see food distributed *at all* while we were present. If we were not able to eat during the day, sometimes neither were the detainees. We were certainly not meant to see what was provided – better that we see nothing. And when looking at the so-called 'kitchens' in which food was sometimes 'prepared', we were rather glad of that. Sometimes we did look at the food storage facilities and were able to observe the parasites roaming freely through the sacks of rice and the like. We were not the only ones with cockroach sandwiches. But what was always the case was that, as we moved around, detainees wanted to talk to us. It was impossible to just move on and ignore them, or even to tell them you would be back later to do so – because we knew that might well not be true. So you talk to them. But how?

The handbooks on visiting tell you never to speak with detainees through the bars of a cell or through a grill on a door. It should be open, and you should enter. Absolutely. But if there is no-one to open a door, do you really choose not to speak with a person who wants to talk to you and deny them that opportunity? Who are we refusing to do so *for*? Certainly not for the detainee. When speaking with detainees, it is absolutely the case that you should aim do so out of earshot of the guards, and ideally out of view, so that they do not know who you are speaking with. But really? Out of earshot of prison staff may indeed be possible, but out of sight rarely so. Cell blocks are crowded places, particularly those which are chronically overcrowded, as so many cells that we visited were.

Moreover, talking 'with' a detainee in an overcrowded multiple occupancy cell is something of a misnomer. Remember, in many – most – cases you will be speaking through an interpreter. We might be used to doing this, knowing that it is necessary to speak in short sentences, and allow the interpreter time to do their job before you continue. Most detainees do not know this – or they are just so keen to say what they have to say that they do not do so. And if there are 15 or 20 detainees in a cell (and often there are more), at a minimum six or eight of them will want to speak with you, and usually all at the same time; agreeing or disagreeing with what others are saying, wishing to highlight their point of view, showing you in the precious minutes which may be all that they have of your time and attention *their* mattress, *their* papers, *their* injuries, *their* skin diseases; explaining to you *their* cases, *their* injustices, the toilets and washing facilities *they* use; *their* food, *their* ... All of this is exactly what you want to hear – but you hear it, if you can actually hear anything at all, from four, five, six or more voices at once, all filtered through the sole voice of an interpreter who is trying to listen, to hear, to disentangle, translate and to speak. It is not an interview, it is pandemonium. And what else was it ever going to be?

The handbooks have an answer of course: this is not how it should be done. They all say much the same thing. Having undertaken your initial orientation, you should: (a) consult the registers; (b) identify a selection of detainees representing a range of categories (ideally, perhaps, six to eight of each) of recent admissions, the longest serving, the soon to be released, those who have been subject to recent disciplinary sanctions, and so on; (c) ask if they are prepared to be interviewed in private; (d) do so in a place which is out of sight or hearing of prison officers. Or something like that. This is certainly a balanced, objective approach which can be extremely helpful, and I have found it so. It can also be completely impossible. Let's briefly deconstruct the process.

Let's consult the registers. What registers? We are in a country which has been wracked by civil war, all records are paper-based, and it is extremely hot and humid. Record books have simply decayed for want of being properly stored. Or, equally likely in many countries, they are kept in a central registry which may not be open. Or which is locked, and someone needs to find out who has the key. And surprisingly frequently those with the keys are on duties elsewhere and cannot be found – or it turns out that they only work in the mornings, and by now, of course, it is approaching midday and they have already left … By the time we find the keys, it's another half an hour at least. 13.00 or 13.30?

Let's identify those we wish to speak with. How? The registers are written in the local language you may not be able to understand and are often completed in handwriting that is almost illegible. And let's not assume they have been constructed in a way which makes it easy to identify those we wish to interview. They were written to record, not to be consulted for purposes such as ours. The only person with a hope of helping you understand what they mean and how to find what we are looking for are, in fact, the prison staff. The interpreter will help you, but they need to learn how the books work, and oh yes – the interpreter: how many have we got? If they are helping with the registers, then they cannot be helping other members talking with detainees: and do we want all the members consulting the registers at the same time? Probably not. Its 14.00 pm.

Let's ask those we have identified if they are prepared to be interviewed. How? Do we know where they are to be found within the prison? Is that recorded in the registers we are looking at? Possibly, but possibly (indeed, probably) not. The only people who will know where they are will be the prison officers. So do we ask them? We now know where they are: who goes to ask if they wish to be interviewed? Do we? We need to be shown where they are, taken up to the cell block, find out who is who within the crowded cell, and then ask them if they will speak with us. Why them, they will ask? They may well be suspicious. I recall in one country we undertook an entire process such as this and, completely at random, somehow came up with the most notorious political prisoner in the prison, if not the country. He would not say a word, he was far too suspicious of our motives. And then what of the others in the cells who see what is happening, and who shout out that they want to speak with us? We explain our methodology to them – and they are usually unimpressed and feel ignored (for the good reason that they are being ignored). Why should it not be them ...? So we try to explain ... It's 14.30, if we are lucky.

Let's interview the person in private, out of sound and sight of the prison staff. How? Where do you have in mind? There is no such space in the cell block; really, there is not. And it is hardly a conducive place – and the noise! You want a quiet, private place. There may be offices in the admin block – but to get to the offices, you will have to be escorted by the guards – but as they must know who you are talking to by now anyway, that seems hardly to matter anymore. Better options might be to conduct such interviews in the exercise yards, or visiting rooms if they are not in use (and it is strange that so often when we were in a place of detention, for some reason, no general visiting by family or friends was ever taking place ...), or, best of all, might be the rooms where lawyers might meet with their clients (for most detainees, a fairly unusual setting, then). But the same practical problems instantly arise – do we take them there, and take them back ourselves? That is probably the right thing to do, but it is entirely formalistic in terms of protecting the identity of the person concerned – and, indeed, is possibly quite a bad thing to do, as you are displaying to the entire prison world what has been happening. Though it is hardly as if by now almost everyone did not know already what was going on. Even if the interview is finally held 'out of sight', it will certainly not be 'out of mind'.

And was it worth it – did this person really open up to you? Why should they? How long do you have for them? Twenty minutes perhaps? Rarely more. They have never seen you before and will never see you again. Why on earth should they trust you and tell you want you want to know? They might want to tell you what *they* want to say – and why should they not? But frankly this might be a very different thing. You need to try to build a rapport – you cannot just fire off a list of questions, sounding like an officious data collector. You need to have a conversation, and this takes time. And remember that we were hoping to see six detainees each. Six? That's not many – even if all four members of an SPT visiting delegation are able to be do so (and rarely is this possible). But this amounts to about another two hours, at a minimum. And it's 16.30.

And we have to go. Shifts are changing, curfews are approaching. And, we may have another two-, three- or four hour-long drive back from whence we came. When we arrive back, we might be in time for dinner. Or perhaps not. So where is that banana?

Dealing with the expected and the unexpected

While what I have just described is not unusual, it is not typical for all these problems to be encountered on every visit to each place of detention. Obviously, if members of the delegation can speak with detainees and staff without the need for interpretation matters can be very much easier. Other practical problems remain and, trivial though they might seem, it is usually the banal that can provide the greatest barriers. Once inside a place of detention, how do you communicate with your colleagues? In a large prison, you may be scattered around in different cell blocks, administrative units, medical units and so on. Before entry, you will have agreed a rough division of labour: who is to focus on what, how the team will be divided up and so on. Ideally, after brief introductions some members of the team will immediately leave to look at records and documentation while the remainder commence a general tour of the prison to get a sense of the layout and work out what it is possible to do, where interviews might be held and the like. The full team then need to meet up again to compare initial impressions and confirm the feasibility of the plan for the day and then set about it. Once dispersed within the institution, how do you stay in contact with each other and respond to issues that come to light?

Sometimes we had short-wave radios, but usually these were not permitted. Mobile phones were, of course, out of the question and had to be left behind. Ultimately, if you needed to speak to a colleague – for example, needing the advice of a medical member concerning an injury – then one of us simply had to go and find them; we could hardly ask the guards to do so! And that is just not as easy as it sounds, since how do we know, exactly, where they will be? We therefore usually agreed to rendezvous from time to time, but even this was not straightforward. We would agree how long we would try to spend on each task, to ensure we had covered all that we could by the time we had to leave. But everything was, inevitably, unpredictable – and the need to be flexible was, ultimately, paramount. If you did enter rooms in which instruments of torture were present or if you find a group of detainees being hidden away because of their injuries – and we did – then plans change.

The one thing that was unchanging, however, was the challenge of entering into places of detention at all.

Ridiculous though this sounds, occasionally the challenge was finding where the actual entrance to a building really was – or even finding it in the first place. Without doubt, one of my most embarrassing moments was on our visit to Italy: it had been agreed that one of the groups could get to its destination by taxi to save the considerable expense of hiring a car for the day. This was not a good idea. The taxi duly dropped us off in the right general area but certainly not in the right place. And in city centres, what is or is not a small detention unit is not always exactly obvious. What do you do? Wander up and down the street looking? Pop into a newsagent and ask? (Yes to all, I am afraid – although only after taking off your UN vest; that at least reduced the degree of embarrassment somewhat.) In the end, we were assisted by a passing nun …

That was as unforgivable as it was unforgettable, but sometimes locally hired drivers know less than they claim and have difficulties finding facilities too. Sometimes the information that one has is out of date: although we always asked for information concerning places of detention (prisons, police stations and so on) in advance of a visit, it was remarkable quite how many countries seem to find it difficult to produce such lists and give accurate addresses. I used to think that this was deliberate, but over the years I came to realise – alarmingly – that in a considerable number of cases this was not the reason at all. There was just no easy way of knowing. Some facilities change their use: we can receive information from NGOs, for example, which is simply out of date, and on arrival you discover that a facility has been repurposed for something else. In one country, we found ourselves travelling a considerable distance to visit what we believed on the best of evidence to be a small, remote, high-security prison which on arrival we discovered had very recently been converted into an isolation unit for prisoners with TB. Naturally, we conducted the visit (having donned protective equipment, kindly provided), and it turned out to be valuable to have done so – but it was not what we had anticipated. I am very conscious that this might suggest that our work was slapdash; badly planned and badly executed. I would deny that emphatically. The amount of effort put into trying to get all this right was enormous. The point is simply that, despite the very best of efforts, things do not always go to plan. And given what we were doing, it would be remarkable if they always did.

Of course, sometimes they did not 'go to plan' on purpose. All states should take our visits seriously, but some have taken them seriously in the wrong way. Obviously, the authorities knew we were in their country. Obviously, they knew a part of our schedule – after all, we fixed up meetings with them. While we never shared with them our detailed visiting plans setting out the places of detention we planned to visit, it would have been utterly naïve of us to think that it was a complete mystery. Elements of our plans were bound to be predictable. If you are in a country such as Belize, for example, in which there is just one central prison which holds all sentenced and remand prisoners, male, female and juvenile, it is pretty obvious that we are going to turn up on one of the couple of days in the week during which we are in the country. They might not know the hour of our coming, but they will surely know it to within a day or so. And if preparations are made for our coming, then in the real world there is absolutely nothing we can do about that.

In some places, preparations might include painting walls, improving facilities and so on, and it would be churlish to complain about their having done things that we might well have asked to be done afterwards anyway, or which we would have approved of them doing. Though rarely were we unaware of preparations such as these – detainees would usually tell us anyway.

Some forms of 'pre-prep' were, frankly, farcical: such as the shiny new u-bend toilet placed in a small, cramped, cave-like underground punishment/isolation cell that had virtually no natural light, was filthy, vermin infested and rank: moreover, it was just placed there – not the slightest trace of any plumbing attached to it at all. Had anyone ever tried to use it, that would have been perfectly obvious. And it hadn't been used – naturally. I expect the plan was to remove it within minutes of our departure. Though sad, such things were, in a peculiar way, quite funny really, and one has to smile from time to time, even on an SPT visit.

Other forms of preparation were more concerning. Detainees being told how to behave, being given materials and made to clean their cells, instructed not to speak with us or *to* speak with us and told what to say – and what not to say. Again, all of this was not difficult to spot, though more difficult to deal with. Most difficult of all were those times when detainees told us that they had been told *not* to speak with us but just did so anyway, adding that the consequences for them once we left were worth it. Knowing what some of those consequences might well have been, I would rather not have to make that calculation and can only hope they felt they had made the right decision: we were not always so convinced. Article 15 of the OPCAT makes it very clear that there should be no sanctions or reprisals against those we met or who provided us with information. We would always remind states of this, and we had very clear protocols on how to minimise the risks of reprisals against those with whom we spoke, sometimes requesting specific protective measures be put in place, or simply stopping the visit because the risks to the detainees of our continuing were, in our view, just too great.

In the light of all this, we often changed our plans. On several occasions, we decided to go back to places of detention a second time, just to confirm what we thought: that things were not normally as we had seen them just a day or so before (and yes, the shiny new u-bend toilet had indeed disappeared). Sometimes it would be to check that a person we were concerned might be at risk because of having spoken with us was being safeguarded as we had requested. Sometimes, however, it was clear that we were being monitored from the outset. In one country, for example, it was obvious that our cars were subject to GPS tracking to follow our movements.

Our confidential visiting programme occasionally appeared to have become known to the authorities (having printed copies in bags is unadvisable – bags can be scanned on entry to buildings or be required to be left behind a desk before seeing a senior official). I recall one occasion where the local police chief happened to turn up as if by magic whenever we arrived at a police station. On another occasion, when we arrived at an immigration detention facility we were told by its head 'you are late', and he went on to explain, in a fairly irritated tone of voice, that some of the other officials whom they had intended to be there when we arrived already had had to leave.

And they were right: we had planned to arrive at 11.00, but the journey had been much longer and more difficult than expected, and it was nearly 13.00 before we did so.

Such was the monitoring of our movements during that visit that we ended up deciding precisely which facilities to visit orally each evening, informing the drivers of our destinations only when we were all in the van and then changing them again en route. I recall meeting some hot and flustered senior police chiefs who had spent much of the morning driving around trying to ensure that they were at what they thought were our intended destinations ahead of us. Indeed, we ran into one chap several times in the course of a day, who just 'happened' to be in each of the places we visited, as if by chance. That takes some organisation (or enough luck to win the National Lottery) when we ourselves did not know exactly when and where we would be at the start of the day.

None of this is really in accordance with the spirit – or even the letter – of the OPCAT, but it is to be expected and can be dealt with. Sometimes, however, the level of intrusion reached such a level that it just had to be confronted. And as so often has been the case, the SPT found an innovative way of doing so.

During its visit to Azerbaijan in September 2014, the delegation repeatedly found itself unable to access places of detention in certain parts of the country, despite showing the credentials provided by the relevant government departments and the assistance of the government-appointed liaison officer whose role is to help in such situations. It was as if the OPCAT did not apply, or the writ of the government did not run. After consulting with the SPT Bureau, it was decided that the delegation – who clearly could not undertake their work – should pause the visit while seeking to resolve the situation, and, ultimately, the delegation left the country with its work unfinished: in effect, the visit was put on hold. Further discussions were held to explore the situation, and, once guarantees were received that this would not happen again, the SPT returned to the country in April 2015 and completed the visit. This time it was able to gain access to all places of detention as required. This measured, step-like process had secured a result which a complete stand-off would have failed to secure.

A similar situation arose in May 2016 during the SPT's visit to Ukraine, when we found ourselves, with one exception, serially unable to secure access to premises run by the State Security Services (the SBU), who seemed very well briefed on a minor alternation to the small print in our credentials which we had not spotted but which could be interpreted as inhibiting our right of access. This could hardly have been accidental. Again, we suspended the visit and withdrew from the country. Following very helpful discussions and some in-country engagement with the agency concerned, the SPT returned in September 2016 and was able to complete its visit.

I should add that this information is not confidential as it is found in the report arising from the visit, which was made public with the consent of Ukraine in February 2017.

A similar situation arose yet again in 2017 during the SPT's visit to Rwanda. The delegation again found itself unable to operate without what it considered to be an excessive degree of continual interference and so once again, after requests that such interference cease, paused its visit and withdrew from the country, in the hope and expectation that – as in the cases of Azerbaijan and Ukraine – after a breathing space and time for reflection and perhaps better preparation by the state authorities, the visit could resume. However, this did not prove possible, largely because the Rwandan authorities did not consider that they had done anything amiss. As a result, the SPT felt it had no option but to 'terminate' its visit in June 2018 without producing a report – the first time that the SPT has been unable to exercise its mandate in accordance with the OPCAT in a country it has visited. The SPT did not do this lightly, and the question of why Rwanda did not permit it to resume and conclude its visit remains unanswered.

The same cannot be said of the second such example. On 16 October 2022, the SPT commenced its long-postponed visit to Australia, this having been originally planned for April 2020, but which could not go ahead due to COVID-19 travel restrictions. The visit, which had been long known of and much discussed within the country, was due to last until 27 October, but on 23 October it was suspended because of a lack of cooperation: it was not able to access places of detention in Queensland and New South Wales. The antipathy of these Australian States to the OPCAT in general and to visits by the SPT in particular has been long known and well documented, and the refusals to allow the SPT delegation access to places of detention seems to have had all the hallmarks of being deliberate and premeditated. It therefore came as little surprise that, in February 2023, Australia joined Rwanda in sharing the dubious distinction of having visits to their countries terminated for lack of cooperation, albeit in the case of Australia the responsibility for this was clearly directed at the states concerned, rather than at the country as a whole.[1]

The power of the Protocol

The suspension or termination of a visit remains highly unusual, and the acknowledgement of an inability to conduct a visit at all – as in the case of Nicaragua – currently remains unique.[2] For the most part, states have taken their obligations under the OPCAT seriously, and in the right way. While some have certainly been surprised to discover the scope of the SPT's mandate and what they have committed themselves to permitting, most states most of the time have been generally helpful and cooperative. They have provided the information requested, the credentials that have been asked for; they have identified governmental 'focal points/liaison officers' who can be contacted at any time of the day or night (and yes, the SPT has visited numerous police stations late at night, which is when police stations are usually at their busiest) and who have been very helpful in explaining the need for sometimes incredulous officers to allow the delegation to do what it wants to be able to do. The good thing about members of hierarchical uniformed organisations is that they generally respect the orders they receive, no matter what they might think of them. And for all that has been said, for the most part, this reflects the reality of much of the experience of visiting with the SPT – and because of that, everything else becomes bearable: things which can be dealt with; obstacles, not barriers.

There is power in the Protocol, but it is not magic. What is of prime importance is that the SPT can visit, can enter places of detention and can do its job – not always quite as easily as it might wish or as ought to be the case, but it can do it. Perhaps not in the textbook manner that even the SPT itself prescribes, but it can be done if there is a positive spirit and a willingness to be flexible, innovative and pragmatic. At the end of the day, it is not about the SPT and its members, it's about the detainees and preventing them from being tortured or ill-treated. Remember that, and you can put up with just about anything.

But spare a thought too for those responsible for places of detention, who must work, day in, day out, in the places that we see for just a day or so. Those who work there are rarely monsters, and most only want to do their jobs as best they can, sometimes under almost impossible circumstances. It is not easy. Nor is coping with the arrival of the SPT necessarily easy. I vividly remember arriving one lunchtime at a facility in the very first country I visited. There was a soldier at the main gate with a rifle in his hand who just kept refusing to let us in, to call his superior, or to do anything at all other than tell us to go away. We therefore explained that we were going to have to call the Ministry about it – at which point, this young recruit or conscript burst into tears, sobbing "I've only been in the Army for three days ..." His first solo task: his orders, over lunchtime – "stand at the gate and don't let anyone in". And we ship up, waving our UN imprimatur. You couldn't not feel sorry for him, poor guy.

Notes

[1] https://www.ohchr.org/en/press-releases/2023/02/un-torture-prevention-body-terminates-visit-australia-confirms-missions

[2] This being the case of Nicaragua, discussed earlier, and for which see https://www.ohchr.org/en/statements/2022/11/nicaragua-two-un-rights-committees-deplore-refusal-cooperate-and-lack

8

Accepting the Unacceptable

Introduction

I really do not want this book to be a litany of horrors. They are all too easy to produce and can have the opposite effect to that which was intended. When authors present such accounts as 'horror stories' they are inevitably received as such by readers – as stories. Yet the horror is not the story, but the reality that the story recounts. That is not and cannot be ours, and we cannot 'make it our own'. We might receive and acknowledge the story and accept the knowledge that it conveys. Many – most – of us will then finish our reading and do something else. And how many of us are really prompted into action because we have read about terrible things? Some people are, but, in truth, not all that many. We may recoil from what we have read but, for the most part, we move on. What else are we meant to do? What else *can* we do? We have no particular responsibility for what is recounted or, perhaps more importantly, any authority or very much power to do anything about it even if we wished to. I do not want to put readers in this position, which can be tantamount to some form of veiled accusation, or an invitation to assume some responsibility or accept some guilt. That is not fair.

But some people *do* have that responsibility and have the authority and the power to make things different.

This chapter and the chapter that follows are largely about such instances – situations in which something is very clearly wrong and yet nothing is being done about it by those who have the power to do so. This inevitably requires recalling some very harrowing stories – but the reader must remember that these are not stories to those whose stories they are: these are their experiences, parts of their lives, their past, their present and directly or indirectly, of their futures. They are not 'just' stories. To the extent that I observed these things, the experience of having observed them is now mine, just as the experience of reading about them becomes the experience of the reader. But the experience which is recounted is not that of the author or the reader, for which both author and reader can only be thankful.

Calm and normal

I must start with a visit to a police station; and to a very particular police station, as this was the visit that lies at the root of why I am trying to explain myself in the way that I am. This visit made an indelible impression on me and raised a question in my mind to which I still cannot begin to fathom an answer. There really is not much to tell. We arrived quite late in the evening, around 10 pm I think, at a police station in the capital city of the country we were then visiting. We had already seen enough elsewhere to know that the conditions in which people were being held would be grim, and they were. Indeed, to describe them as inhuman and degrading does not even begin to do them justice. We had no difficulty in entering the police station, in viewing the premises or, the commanding officer told us, in speaking with the detainees if we wished to do so, though he was very clear that he thought it inadvisable for us to enter the holding cell – or, indeed, even to speak to the detainees directly through the bars of the cage-fronted cell in which they were held. The reason, we were told, was that we would be spat at and have things thrown at us, the consequences of which might be serious. Really, we thought? Really.

The holding cell was, from memory, about 5 by 4 metres square, one side completely open but for the floor to ceiling metal bars, with a door of bars in the middle, obviously padlocked. In consequence, when looked at straight on, everything within the cell was completely open to view. Despite its being quite late in the evening, we could hear a low level of sound coming from the cell, punctuated by the occasional shout to which other voices joined, accompanied by a rattling of the bars for a few moments, which soon subsided into silence, until after a few moments, like the swell of the sea, it rose and then fell again. The voices and the sounds belonged to about 20 to 25 men who were standing within it. Standing, and not at that time in the evening lying down, or even sitting. For they could not all have lain down at the same time in any case as there was not enough room, but that was not the point. Nor was it the point that there were no mattresses or blankets on which to lie down on the hard concrete floor. The point was that the floor was splattered in human excrement – almost covered – and the men were standing around and in it. It was that excrement that could have been thrown at us, we were told. And they were right. There was no toilet, or anything like a toilet. There was a barred window at a high level, through which some tried to pass their human waste, scooped up as best they could. The custody register indicated that some of the detainees had been inside the cell for three, four or five days – some possibly even longer. There was nowhere for them to be let out into other than into the remainder of the police station, and so they were kept in that cell for days at a time, waiting for something to happen.

It was neither the first nor the last time we saw something like this – but there was something which marked this out in my mind as different. The police station and its holding cell was routinely visited by an official inspectorate, twice a day, around 9 am in the morning and 9 pm in the evening, every day. There was a record book in the station to prove that these visits had taken place and to record their assessment. And that record book was there in front of us, last completed about an hour before we arrived. And every single entry, for that day and for weeks and weeks and weeks previously, said precisely the same thing: 'Calm and Normal.'

While what we saw might conceivably have been described as 'calm', the question I still cannot answer is how by any stretch of the human imagination could this have been described as 'normal' by the very people who visit such places to ensure that things are? Except that, it seems, as far as they were concerned, it *was* normal and warranted neither remark nor explanation.

Lies, not excuses

The best that might be said of what we saw in that place was that when we raised this with the authorities at the end of the visit (having also pointed out the obvious to those on duty and in charge of it at the time), at least no-one seemed to deny the truth of what we saw. Frankly, how could they? It was what we had seen. Unfortunately, this was not always so, and some seem to find it very easy indeed to deny that things taking place around them which are glaringly obvious are actually taking place at all. I take the view that such outrageous lies concerning what we encountered did not amount to excuses, let alone attempted justifications, although they might sometimes be couched that way.

At the risk of being overly categorical, a plain lie is simply a plain lie and, as far as I am concerned, that amounts to the acceptance of the unacceptable by that liar. This is further compounded in some way by the idea that I – we – were such blithering idiots that we might conceivably believe that the obvious lies we were being peddled could be true. Indeed, such lies betoken the embrace of the unacceptable, rather than the mere acceptance of it. And there were plenty of examples of this. Perhaps those who did this were also lying to themselves as well as to us – though this might be a too generous and unwarranted overcomplication. Most of the cases I am thinking about tended to concern individuals who were likely to have been directly involved in torturing people, and so they had plenty to lie about – to us, and, perhaps one might hope, to themselves as well.

I recall a visit to one rather secretive facility – extending downwards into the ground, bunker-like for several floors. Deep underground, we saw a range of interrogation rooms with mirror windows, allowing the questioning that would be taking place to be monitored and, of course, recorded. The equipment necessary for this was all there, making it abundantly clear what the rooms were being used for. Getting into them had been a bit of a struggle. There was a large metal door, locked with a couple of padlocks that needed to be opened before we reached them. Of course, we were told that there was nothing of interest there; that the person with the keys was not around at the time; then, that they had gone on holiday and taken them with them. In the end, with bad grace, the locks were cut off at our insistence. Gaining access to the room, we also found inside a small, hard metal chair, with a head-restraint and strappings. We knew what it was – obviously it was an electric chair – but we asked anyway: we could hardly ignore it as it was right in the middle of the room – indeed, it was the only thing in the room. It was, we were told, used for taking photographs for ID cards. Ah – never thought of that! Though we never did get around to hearing the explanation for the hook attached to the ceiling, and the metal rings bolted into the floor underneath it ...

Another example. We entered an office in a police station and closed the door behind us. Propped up behind the door was a grisly collection of chains, metal bars and small, crumpled plastic bags, some smeared with traces of blood. We had received plenty of allegations concerning the use of all three during interrogations at that station, and here were such items and implements, just left lying around. Why were they there? Evidence, we were told. They had been recovered from a crime scene and were needed as evidence against those who had been detained in court. Of course, we asked the relevant questions about the case to which they were said to relate, the holding and documentation of such evidence and so on – though knowing full well – as did everyone in the room – of what they were really evidence of.

Both these incidents, and all such incidents of which these are merely examples, were also evidence of something else as well: they were evidence of a clear willingness to accept that torture was occurring on the premises. The blatant lying – and the involuntary smirking that invariably accompanied it – was also proof enough that the use of torture was considered to be perfectly acceptable by those we were speaking with. Indeed, one might even say, perfectly normal.

'It's all fine'

It was not only state officers and officials who accepted the unacceptable without question. We visited a police administration block in a city centre and found inside a group of about 20 or 30 men handcuffed to each other, crouching behind an office counter so that they might not be seen by us. We were, unusually, conducting this visit on a Sunday morning. All of the men had been detained on the Friday evening and were being kept there – all handcuffed together and left alone – over the weekend until they could be taken to a police station with a cell on the Monday morning. We spoke with many of them, yet none thought that what was happening was in any way inappropriate – it was roughly what they would have expected to happen. In so many visits, this was one of the recurring themes – things which we would never have thought to be acceptable were considered acceptable by those who were being ill-treated, not because they thought what was happening to them was right but because they thought it was no worse, or considerably better than they had feared – or even expected – would happen to them when they were detained.

In some countries detainees expected to be beaten by the police while they were being questioned and didn't think it even worth mentioning. I recall a detainee telling me that they had been well treated, even while showing me the marks and bruises on their bodies where they had been beaten. When I asked why he thought he had been well treated given the beating he had been given, he was dismissive – what had happened was nothing compared to what he had been expecting, and he felt he had been treated well. People expected to be treated a lot worse, and he said he thought himself lucky. Although, he added, he wished it *had* been worse, as others might now wonder why he was being treated so favourably. It was difficult to know quite what to say in response, but it was clear that in this place there was an expectation that ill-treatment was inevitable and an acceptance of what we would consider to be utterly unacceptable. What we heard from others corroborated – and justified – that expectation. It was not that the detainee I was speaking with was *approving* of what had happened to him, but he was *accepting* of it. That too, is accepting the unacceptable – but it is not difficult in this instance to see why.

Sometimes, the willingness of detainees to be accepting of situations and conditions of detention which we might consider unacceptable raised difficult questions which the willingness to be accepting of physical ill-treatment does not. No detainee really *wants* to be beaten, no matter how 'grateful' they may be that the beating was not worse than it was. But when it comes to other matters, things may not be so straightforward. We visited one prison in which everything had a price: bribery and corruption was rampant, and everyone knew the price of everything. If you had a visitor, you paid: if you wanted to spend extra time with your visitor, you paid extra; holding hands carried a supplement, as did being able to hug at the end of the visit. And so on. The cell block you were housed in, the food you could have, whether your water was clean or not so clean, and on and on – everything was priced. Indeed, I was asked by a detainee how much it would cost him to speak with me, and he was bemused and confused to learn that it would be 'free'.

All the prices were transparent, fixed and well known. The system was very well organised, and, of course, actual cash did not change hands. Funds could be deposited with what is best described as the 'bribe bank', against which detainees could make 'withdrawals' in the form of crediting the person to whom the bribe was to be paid. All centrally administered and clearly efficiently run. This prompted no comment or criticism at all. Indeed, we were told, it all worked rather well. But there was almost universal outrage that when detainees, friends and family deposited money in the 'bank of bribes', the prison took a 10 per cent administration fee up front. This, we were told in no uncertain terms from numerous prisoners, was considered utterly unacceptable and a source of huge disquiet: they were being robbed! As to the rest – the endemic corruption on which the precarious existence of almost everyone depended, and the terrible consequences for those without the means to bribe – that was all considered to be fine. Normal, in fact. And in truth, in the country concerned it must be said that it was. So why was a prison going to be any different? As far as the prisoners were concerned, but for the 'dix per cent', it really was all fine. It was what they knew, and what they expected. To us, of course, it was another example of accepting the unacceptable. But why, they mused, did we have a problem with all this?

Remand detention

It is a very good question, what we do and do not 'have a problem' with. And the one thing which continues to perplex me more than most concerns remand detention. This is often referred to as 'pre-trial detention', though I now try to avoid doing so. Calling it 'pre-trial detention' presupposes that those remanded in custody are 'awaiting trial', or at least awaiting the consideration of the merits of their case in some way. Yet this is not always true. What is almost always true is that those held on remand are subjected to far worse regimes of detention than those prisoners who have been convicted and sentenced to prison. This is so well known that it really does pass without much comment or question, and tends to be accepted as being inevitable, as being just the way things are.

A moment's thought ought to be enough to say that this ought not to be so. While it is not a comparative exercise, how can it be right to treat a person who is, by definition, presumptively innocent of any wrongdoing considerably worse than a sentenced prisoner who, by definition, is not? Yet time and time again, some of the very worst conditions that I have ever seen have been in remand prisons – something which is made particularly stark and obvious when remand prisoners are held in special wings within prisons which also house sentenced offenders: you just cannot *not* observe the difference and be staggered by what you see.

At least, it might be argued, the periods for which a person can be held in remand detention are strictly limited – but that was certainly not the case in many places we visited. To meet men being held on remand for two, three, four years or more was by no means unusual, and in some verging on the normal. It was more unusual to meet women held for such long periods, but we did. And we even met children who had been too – or more accurately adults who had been children when they were first detained, years earlier. The one thing they all had in common was this: the longer they had spent in detention, the less likely it was that they would be leaving detention any time soon. I remember speaking to a 21-year-old man who was self-harming in any way he could: he had been taken into detention when he was 16, for, he said, allegedly stealing a bike which, he said, belonged to a friend who told him he could borrow it. Five years on, he was still waiting for someone to decide the truth of this.

I spoke to him while he was outside in a warm and sunny yard for the afternoon. That was unusual. We were rarely able to speak to remand detainees anywhere other than in their cells, as most of those we met were not allowed to be outside of them for more than an hour a day. Typically, family visits to remand detainees would be limited and take place under very controlled and monitored conditions since you cannot run the risk of contaminating the evidence or the fairness of the trial – even, it seems, when there does not appear to be any real likelihood or intention of taking the case to trial at all. Almost all of their day would be spent in a cell with nothing to do. Since remand detainees are to be separated from sentenced prisoners (after all, they are not prisoners!), they cannot be allowed to mix with them or, outside of their cells, with each other. So their lives are lived in cells which were often cramped, crowded, dirty and dark. Unlike sentenced prisoners, the overriding imperative of ensuring that remand detainees do not communicate with others (to ensure the integrity of the investigation process, of course) means that often any windows in their cells will be shuttered, leaving little fresh air and next to no natural light – meaning that there may be no light at all, as there would be no other source. Obviously, not all remand facilities displayed all these characteristics – but some did, and most I visited displayed some. But I remember one very well indeed.

There was a block situated within a courtyard attached to what, to be fair, was a typical and, dare I say, relatively unremarkable prison: very much what we would have expected and very much par for the course in the country concerned. Perhaps that was what made what followed such a shock. Within this courtyard, there was a block containing 16 single cells, eight on each side. Each had a solid door with a small, slatted area which would have let in air and allow you to speak through it, but not really to see. At floor level, there was a hatch which could be opened from the outside and through which food and drink might be passed. These were the remand cells. They were a little over 2 metres long and a little under 2 metres wide. A narrow, fixed bed ran down one side, from top to bottom. The door opened inwards and so required about a third of the remaining floorspace. At the 'far' end of that space by the side of the bed was an open earth-closet toilet, taking up about a third of the remaining space – and meaning of course that the head of the person lying on the bed was about 2 feet away from that fetid hole. There was virtually no light. Inside was a large man with a prosthetic leg, which he could not keep on in the cell and so was propped up in the remaining space. He had to put it on when he was allowed outside into the courtyard once a day for an hour, and during that hour twice a week was able to use the shower block just off the courtyard. He had been there a year – on remand, and legally speaking he was an innocent man.

When having spoken with him he was ushered back inside the cell and the guard turned the key in the lock, I found myself choking and gulping for air at the very thought of being in there for even a moment – not for a year. And also at the thought of turning the key, knowing that doing so consigned the person inside to a living hell. I found no record of these cells ever being mentioned in reports by any of the various monitoring bodies which had in fact visited the prison from time to time. The nature of so much that takes place in remand detention shows just how easy it is to accept the unacceptable, if it is something that you have just come to accept.

High-end security

There are obviously many real security concerns that need to be confronted and managed in places of detention, and these must not be trivialised. I vividly recall one visit to a police station where the duty police were clearly exasperated at our presence and at what they thought we might saying about the place. The atmosphere, while not hostile, was certainly rather frosty. The reason became clear when it was suggested to me that I try sitting at one of the interview desks. These had been recently installed at the insistence of human rights monitors following a previous visit, and they had no protective screens, as this was considered by the monitors to be intimidating and inappropriate. So I sat down on one side while a police officer sat on the other, and we began to talk across the open and rather narrow table that lay between us. After a couple of minutes' conversation, he suddenly leaned forward towards me and within an instant was on my side of the table and holding, no, was pressing, a sharp knife against the veins on my neck. A colleague of his had had his throat cut in that way a few weeks back, shortly after the old desks and screens had been taken away. As he put it when releasing me from his grip and easing the pressure of the knife on my neck, the police officers have rights too. They wanted their screen back – or at the very least to have much wider tables. It was a rather dramatic way of making a perfectly fair point. We can be too quick to dismiss very real security concerns.

We can also be far too quick to accept the legitimacy of some so-called security concerns too. Perhaps it may be necessary to place some even seriously unwell sentenced prisoners who have been transferred from prison hospitals to general hospitals for medical treatment in separate, locked wards – but when is it ever necessary to handcuff such seriously ill prisoners to their beds and, when out of bed, to their chairs? That would not happen in a prison. Perhaps within a prison it may be necessary to ensure that potentially violent prisoners are subject to some form of restraint when they are meeting visitors to ensure the safety of those visitors – but is it *really* necessary to have ankle and calf restraints which are anchored to the floor and which grip and immobilise the leg applied to *all* detainees when receiving extended visits from their partners and children in what is designated as a family room and is only available as a 'privilege'? And is it *really* necessary to conduct full strip and cavity searches of *all* detainees every time they move through an internal checkpoint within a prison, which simply separates off a reception area from a holding area?

In one country, we were able to view the first of a new suite of high-end maximum-security facilities which were best described (and we did describe) as tin cans: scrupulously clean, these modular units had a bed, a toilet and washing facilities and were probably about 2 by 3 metres square. There was only very limited room to move around and stretch out within them. They were certainly light and airy – but this was all controlled electronically from the outside, as there were no windows, and the doors were completely sealed – like an airlock door. Everything that took place inside was monitored (or able to be monitored) on CCTV.

In accordance with international standards, a minimum of an hour a day of 'outside exercise' was permitted: the door was opened and, escorted by two guards, the inmate stepped forward a few paces across a corridor and directly into what is best described as a metal mesh cage, cantilevered over an open courtyard below – somewhat like a fully enclosed suspended wire-basket, or a fully barred overhanging balcony. Much movement within this was impossible, and so it hardly qualified as an opportunity for outdoor 'exercise', and it was easy to understand why the person we spoke to who was being held in this way preferred not to be put in the cage at all.

Was this exceptional? At the time of our visit, 24 more such units were being installed, in a relatively small country with a relatively small prison population. Why? In a rather reflectively worded observation (doubtless intended to avoid making a direct assessment of whether this was or was not ill-treatment), the SPT mused, in a now published report, that 'it considers the use of them for any prolonged period to amount to ill-treatment and wonders whether their use under any circumstances can be other than inhuman or degrading'. If – as I believe – to detain people indefinitely in such sealed containers (for that is what they were) is unacceptable, it was clearly accepted by those responsible for bringing this about.

Conclusion

In the Introduction to this book, I said that there are many serious problems which are not even considered to be problems at all, but are just accepted as being 'the way things are'. This chapter has provided just a few examples of what I consider to be such situations which I encountered during my time working with the UN Subcommittee on Prevention of Torture (SPT). They are not necessarily the worst examples since there is no hierarchy when it comes to the unacceptable, other than the hierarchy that inevitably results from these being examples I have highlighted. There are many more besides, and every member of the SPT – every one of us – will have others. Some might contest the unacceptability of the examples I have given – and I can assure you that when we raised such examples with the states concerned, some of them did so. But what if they did? That does not matter to me: as far as I am concerned, these examples, and much else besides, were and are unacceptable – and I expect that they will be considered so by most.

The key point is that all these forms of ill-treatment were not only allowed to pass unchallenged but apparently passed unnoticed as being in any way unacceptable by those who were responsible for them. At the end of the day, they were accepted without comment or demur. The currently fashionable expression 'hidden in plain sight' might seem to sum this up: that we do not notice what is going on right in front of us; or that if we do notice, it does not concern or bother us enough to do anything about it – other than uncritically accept it for what it is. Perhaps I am being unjust here – and that those who were responsible understood the wrongness of what was occurring very well indeed, but it was easier for them to close their eyes to this rather than to try to even excuse it. Or – and in some cases I am sure this was the case – they believed (possibly correctly) that there was nothing they could really do about it and so just kept on doing it. The seemingly pleasant and helpful young chap turning the key in the lock of the remand cell I mentioned was just doing his job, just as we were doing ours. There was no evil in his eye.

There is no bright line between accepting the unacceptable and excusing the inexcusable, examples of which will be given in the following chapter. Ultimately, what – if anything – differentiates the one from the other is that there is at least an outward acknowledgement of wrong embedded in an excuse, the giving of which might provide some form of opening that can lead to change. The chief evil of unquestioning acceptance is that it does not even do that. The questioning and challenge provided by those who visit places of detention should at least achieve this, even if at times it seems to achieve little else. The need to provide excuses or justifications might not take you very far along the road of securing change and lessening the risk of torture and ill-treatment, but it is at least a start. And if National Preventive Mechanisms and the SPT are achieving this, they are achieving something of worth.

9

Excusing the Inexcusable

Introduction

The previous chapter highlighted examples of situations in which the unacceptable had become so embedded in day-to-day routines and practices that it seemed to pass almost without notice. It was 'just the way things are'. When challenged, sometimes those responsible would acknowledge the need to address the situation and seek to do so. For example, we visited a detention centre for foreign migrants considered to be in that country illegally. While this was doubtless true of some, most appeared to be migrant workers whose employers no longer wanted to pay them and who had handed them over to the authorities while retaining their documentation, thus rendering them 'illegal' and liable to detention pending expulsion. Understandably, many were agitated, angry and sometimes aggressive. Who wouldn't be, knowing that you were likely to continue to be held in one of the 12 or so large cage-like structures, each holding 20 to 30 people indeterminately, for weeks, months or longer through no fault of your own?

To help 'calm down' those in need of calming (we were told), there were a series of small, clearly visible coffin-like 'cells' in which the detainees could be placed. These were not only used for purposes of 'control', but also to 'persuade' those in the detention centre to give details of their nationality or to give their 'consent' to being returned to their country of origin or to being sent elsewhere. These 'cells' were just less than a metre square, and a little over 2 metres high. We measured them carefully. People were placed inside for periods ranging between one and 12 hours at a time, and this could happen for several days in succession. It was virtually impossible to sit down in them (I know, I tried). Apart from a small grill in the metal door at face level, there was no ventilation or light of any kind. We spoke to one man who said that having been placed in one of these containers for eight hours a day for two days in a row, and faced with being put back inside again he told the guards whatever he thought they wanted to hear. According to the definition of torture examined earlier in this book these cells amounted to tools of torture: they were being used purposively to acquire information, to intimidate and coerce in an inhuman way.

At the end of our visit, we demanded that these 'cells' be never used again and removed, since the very sight of them was intimidatory. There is good reason to believe that they were indeed taken down and taken away from that place. Of course, whether they were used again elsewhere is not something we can be sure of, although we were assured this would not happen.

The point of recounting this is twofold. First, there are times when challenging unacceptable practices can result in change. This was a good example. But the second is that, before such change happens, the demand to do so is so often met with denial and lies. In this instance, the centre Director told us that these cells had not been used for at least five years. The register of disciplinary sanctions included entries showing they had in fact been used quite regularly and had last been used a matter of days before we visited the centre (and which, by some strange coincidence, happened also to coincide with the day when our visit to the country was due to commence). Clearly, the use of these cells was considered sufficiently acceptable to be recorded, even if to our face their use was considered something to be denied – or denied by the Director, at least. Several members of staff told us, on the quiet, that they were indeed used regularly; and their personal concerns at this were evident.

In a strange sort of way, a downright lie about something is better than offering an excuse for it. As in this instance, the lie could be easily exposed for what it was, and the very fact that it was thought advisable to lie about it clearly indicated that the unacceptability of what was taking place was recognised. You do not need to lie about practices you consider to be acceptable. Perhaps oddly, I often felt that downright lies were quite helpful and in some instances a sign that we were getting somewhere: they are an admission that there is something to hide. And that can provide a platform for change.

Sometimes, 'hiding' was literally the operative word. On one occasion, we arrived at a detached suburban house that we believed was being used for unlawful detention and, as we were ringing the doorbell, sure enough three pairs of hands and arms appeared waving between some bars set high in otherwise below-ground cellars. We finally were allowed into the building about 15 minutes later after some considerable difficulty and with much complaint that it was a private property which some uniformed officers just happened to be in at the time and that no-one was being detained there. We went downstairs, and of course the cellars were empty. The three men were now in a cupboard in an upstairs room, gagged. On another occasion, we visited some large rooms in an administrative building where we believed detainees were likely to be found, although no-one was meant to be held there at all. The rooms were all deserted, but they did contain bunkbeds and there were signs of recent occupancy and of rapid movement – such as still glowing cigarette butts on the floor. Looking around the offices more generally, there was a scattering of unkempt and strangely dressed workers sitting in front of desks trying to look as if they were doing something on computers which were not even switched on. Every worker in that office must have known what was going on in that building – and so did we.

What I found far more dispiriting than the lies and attempted deceptions that we so frequently encountered but which were so easily identified were the endless excuses for treating people in ways which just could not be excused and were often devoid of any form of credibility, or which at best were only superficially so. Some of these excuses were, in truth, tantamount to a refusal to accept the legitimacy of our criticisms and, to be blunt, amounted to little more than 'taking the p★★★'.

Buckets

The wilful acceptance of the unacceptable was exemplified in the previous chapter by an account of the routine recording of the utterly outrageous conditions in which people were being held in police detention as being 'calm and normal', the benchmark of normality being sub-human. There is a short coda to this account which now needs to be added. We could hardly leave what we saw without raising it immediately with the staff on duty and demanding that something be done about it. It ought not take much to convince the staff that leaving 15 to 20 or more men surrounded by their own excrement for prolonged periods was utterly wrong. They did not disagree – and pointed out that from time to time the entire area was hosed down (while the men were still in the cell). We did not discuss what happened to the run-off water. Even if this ameliorated the situation in some way from time to time, it hardly addressed it. When we saw it, it was what it was.

Obviously, one partial solution would be for the cell not to be used for holding large numbers for prolonged periods, but we did understand that this was not something that the staff could themselves bring about. They had to hold whoever was taken there, and saying that the cell was full made no difference to the number of people who were brought to them. It was also true that there was nowhere else in the police station that could be used as a holding cell. These were matters over which they had no control and which needed to be taken up elsewhere – as we did at the end of our visit when we spoke with the national authorities and again in our written report. Be that as it may, whatever might or might not have been possible concerning the introduction of proper (or even half proper) sanitation at some point in the future was not going to do anything in the here and now, and it was here and now that some form of solution – no matter how inadequate – was needed. One obvious possibility immediately sprang to mind: some of the detainees had been given water in plastic bottles which they had then 'repurposed' and which were sitting in a corner (still full of urine). There were not many of them. Could not more be provided? No: water in bottles cost money, and they were only authorised to provide water from a tap (which did not actually seem to be working – but that's another matter). And, it seems, water was only available at all if the detainee paid for it. So if the bottles were used to hold urine, then they could not be used to hold water – so it was their choice what they wanted. And the guards preferred to sell them the water, naturally.

OK – so that was not an answer. And in any case, it could not have addressed the full scale of the problem. So we made an alternative suggestion: how about putting some plastic buckets in the cell? I was already anticipating the obvious answers … we have no buckets, there is no budget for a bucket. What I was not expecting was the excuse that we in fact received: which was that this could not be done because the detainees would use the buckets to escape. How? By hiding in them if they were taken away to be emptied? I did not bother to ask. There really was not any point in doing so.

Other police stations which we had visited in that country were not dissimilar, but most did at least provide buckets. It could be done and was being done elsewhere. There really was no reason why that could not be done here, and all we received were the most pathetic of excuses that simply magnified the enormity of what was going on.

When we met with the national authorities at the end of the visit, this was one of the by now very long list of such concerns that we raised. It prompted looks of surprise and concern, perhaps even of consternation, and there was swift agreement that something needed to be done about it. But what? It was suggested to us by the national authorities that we might like to suggest sources of funding so that the staff in that police station could be sent on a course to receive appropriate human rights training. I muttered in reply that it might be better to send them on a course to be trained in how to use a bucket and a mop …

The simple truth was that those in charge just could not be bothered to try to do anything about it, and those in charge of them either did not know or did not care. Once it becomes clear that something is to be bothered about, simple solutions can often be found which, while hardly perfect, can make a big difference. Without our being there to prompt such change – would it ever happen? I should like to say that this particular problem was addressed because of our intervention. But I cannot. I just do not know. Even if I had been told it had been, how *could* I know? There was no practical way of going back to find out – not for years and years by the UN Subcommittee on Prevention of Torture (SPT) anyway (and this was in country that had not set up its own National Preventive Mechanism, as it ought to have). Was this a failure then? Perhaps. But sometimes, not knowing means exactly that: you just don't know. And raising these concerns is not nothing, it is at least doing something to try to prevent ill-treatment: and doing something is better than doing nothing.

Padlocks

Another prison, another problem. As we walked around, we were struck by quite how many empty cells there were. The official figures which we had been shown suggested that the prison, while not overcrowded, was approaching its maximum occupancy level, and so we expected to see most cells in use. In addition, it was all rather quiet – there few signs of detainees being out of their cells or involved in other activities. That said, it would have surprised us somewhat if we had seen such signs of life, since this had not been much in evidence in other prisons we had visited in that country.

A reason why it was so peaceable became apparent when we entered one of the cell blocks. The cells within it were all relatively clean and of a decent size and easily capable of holding two, three or in some cases even four detainees without being overcrowded. There were no toilets inside the cells, but at the end of the corridor there were a few toilets and showers that were in good working order, and the prisoners appeared to have frequent and easy access to them. There were beds, mattresses and blankets in each cell, and there were books to read, board games to play, food and drinks to hand and, all in all, it was one of the better places we had seen during our visit. Moreover, by no means all of the cells were full, and we then entered another cell block where things were very different indeed.

The cells were quite small – somewhat less than 3 by 2 metres square. They also contained an open toilet and a shower head, though whether that was usable we never did find out. It is unlikely that it was, and, for once, that might have been for the best. Clearly, these had been intended as single-person cells and even as such would have been cramped and unpleasant given the open toilet which took up a considerable space. There were no beds, but it was just about possible for one person to lie down on the floor. The problem was that they all contained two people, and it was impossible for them both to do so. As a result, makeshift hammocks had been hung up inside, meaning that the person on the floor had another person in a hammock immediately – a couple of feet – above them all the time. This in itself was completely unacceptable, but what made this all the more difficult to accept was that nearly half of the cells in the block were standing empty.

The number of detainees held in the block was not that great – perhaps about 20 or so. Had they all been taken out and distributed around the cells in the block we had just been in, with its comparatively spacious conditions and decent sanitation, then things would have been very much improved for them, though doubtless this might have been unwelcome to the inmates currently housed in the (relative) comfort of that other block. But even if this was not done, why not use *all* the cells in the block that they were in? Why leave so many empty? Bad as they were, it would have been better to have had only one prisoner in each cell, surely? But the reason was obvious, and we had been idiots not to have realised it at once. When we asked why this could not be done, it was pointed out to us that all these empty cells did not have padlocks on them: the doors closed well enough, but there were just not enough padlocks to go around, and so they could not be locked. Of course! What were we thinking of!

Clearly, we were not thinking of a similar situation that we have encountered elsewhere, but this time involving a medium-sized cell which was really badly overcrowded, and once again not everyone could lie down at the same time. However, the cell next to this was completely empty, and so we had asked why it was not being used to relieve the pressure on the chronically overcrowded cell. Patiently, it had been explained to us that there was only one padlock. OK, we thought … well, no, we did not think it was OK, but let's assume that just for now that it was OK. OK, we thought … so our next suggestion was that they might like to move everyone in the overcrowded cell into the empty cell next to it, which was about 50 per cent bigger, and then move the padlock that they did have to the other door.

While hardly a great solution, it was something that could easily be done, and done quickly. Surely it would be something of an improvement, as it would mean at the very least that everyone could lie down at night. It is strange how something that is so easy, basic and obvious can suddenly appear to be a really ambitious goal and its achievement such a triumph. Were we on the brink of something big, or a major success? Alas – no. We were still overlooking something crucial: "It's the padlock for the smaller cell: not the one for the bigger cell", we were told. So that was that then.

As we drove back to our hotel, we passed an endless number of roadside shops and stalls selling all sorts of things. Including padlocks.

Overcrowding

Many prisons and police station cells are chronically overcrowded, and what we found in that prison was by no means unusual. We have found police holding cells designed to hold five or six people for a few hours being used to house 15 or 20 for days at a time. We have found large prison cells designed to hold 20 prisoners holding 50 or more detainees; we have found cells so small that holding even one person in them would be improper holding three, four, five or more. I could spend page after page setting out example after example, and the net effect would be to anaesthetise against what I am writing. There is no doubt that we became anaesthetised against much of what we saw. Not in the sense of accepting what we saw as normal, or by in some way excusing what we saw, but in the sense of the numbing feeling of 'here we go again'. In a way, I think we had to be, in order to be able to cope with what we ran into, and after having been a member of the SPT for a while I really thought I had lost the capacity to be shocked by what we might find. But that was not true. There was always something new to surprise and shock. And it was not always the levels of overcrowding that we encountered which was the most shocking aspect of what we found. In some cases, what shocked the most was that it was not only completely unnecessary but was in fact entirely deliberate.

We visited one place which had held large numbers of migrants and asylum seekers. It comprised around four or five quite sizable units, some of solid construction, while others were very large and rigid canvass tent-like structures which had been subdivided into living zones, both for individuals and families. At the time of our visit, only a couple of these were still in use, as the numbers being held in the centre had declined. Within the tent-like units we visited, there was a constant problem with mildew getting into the possessions of those housed there and a real problem with the lack of privacy, which was particularly acute for families with young children living cheek by jowl with each other. Their overall situation was generally poor and, while certainly not impossible, exacerbated the difficulties which they faced. This is hardly unusual. What was unusual was that this was deliberate.

As the numbers held decreased, the size of the camp was likewise decreased, with units withdrawn from use so as – it seemed – to ensure that those who remained were unable to benefit from the additional space which would otherwise have become available. It was difficult to avoid the impression that this place was being run to ensure it was only ever just on just about the right side of humane – which in its own way seemed to me to make it one of the most inhumane places I had ever seen. There was absolutely nothing that those held there could do about it. The entire point of the exercise, it seemed, was for it to be as bad as it could 'legitimately' be – irrespective of the effect this was having on those who were already there. Small wonder self-harming was rife.

That, of course, is not always the case. Sometimes whether a detainee was being held in overcrowded cells or not came down to their ability to pay, or their willingness to bribe. 'Bribe', however, is not quite the right word, since it connotes a degree of secrecy, and often there was absolutely nothing clandestine about what was going on. There was plenty of evidence to suggest that in some prisons we visited newly admitted prisoners were placed in the very worst conditions until they found the money to be moved to better facilities; and if they couldn't, then they weren't. And in some prisons, cells with carpets on the floor, TVs, fridges, beds, chairs and copious quantities of food and much else besides were to be found in close proximity to cells with thin, urine-soaked mattresses on floors and not much else. Some were able to leave their cells at will, others hardly at all.

None of this will come as any surprise to anyone familiar with the realities of prison life in many parts of the world, though the extent of what might be acquired, and the unashamedly open nature of the transactions involved, might take some by surprise and can still shock. I cannot say that I know it was the case, but in one prison in which juveniles and adults were both held in separate wings there were good reasons to suspect that adult men paid the guards to bring them juvenile boys. There was no doubt that boys *were* taken to certain adult cells and left there overnight as a punishment for alleged infractions of prison rules, the nature of which were entirely unclear to all concerned, while the nature of the punishment was absolutely clear to everyone. I am not sure why I am including this in a chapter about attempts to excuse the inexcusable. We neither asked nor were offered any excuse for this, for there could be none. That said, had we asked, I am sure that there would have been some pathetic attempts to give us some. But frankly, it is sometimes better not even to ask. Some things are so wrong they do not merit discussion with those responsible and can only be taken up with others elsewhere – and quickly.

Watching and waiting

Cruelty is not always obvious. Indeed, things which at first sight might appear quite benign can turn out to have a cruelty to them which defies explanation or excuse. After the really quite terrible things we had just seen in the adult male section of a large prison complex on which I still do not wish to dwell, a number of us went into an adjoining women's prison. This was much smaller, and its various cell blocks – all relatively small and in some ways looking like large bungalows – were arranged around a large pleasant rectangular garden. Was there a small fountain in its centre? I cannot quite remember that detail, but if there wasn't, there could easily have been. It was that sort of space. Unlike the men's prison, these living units (they could not really be properly described as cells) were not overcrowded and were quite well furnished. It was by now late afternoon, and in the pleasant, weakening sunshine it felt a world apart from the hell of we knew was to be found just a couple of hundred yards away.

The contrast appeared ridiculous, and it seemed almost rude to intrude upon the female prisoners as they went about their business. In the garden, a small group were moving around tending to some plants, while on the narrow veranda of one of the bungalows a group of three of four women were sitting quietly on a bench, in the shade of the evening surveying the scene. We chatted with those in the garden first, and they told us of their daily routines and the problems and concerns they had. We then went to speak to the women on the veranda. We introduced ourselves, they smiled – but said nothing, which seemed strange. After a while, one of them told us "we are not allowed to talk here". This puzzled us, as the group down in the garden had no such inhibitions. We went and spoke with a guard, who then came to tell them that they were free to speak with us if they wished, and a very long conversation ensued.

They were life prisoners, housed together in the same building. When their rooms were unlocked, which they were for at least six or seven hours each day, they were permitted to sit on the bench on the veranda, but not to speak with each other or with anyone else: they were certainly not permitted to step off the veranda under any circumstances. As a result, the sum total of what they were permitted to do during a day was to sit in silence watching other people, yards away from them who were free to move, to meet and to talk – and to do so day in, day out, year in, year out. It was a very deliberate form of cruelty. Of course, we later challenged this and asked why it was so. Life-sentenced prisoners were not allowed to mix with others, we were told. This is often the case. But that did not explain why they were never allowed to move from the bench on the veranda, or to speak even with each other while they were there.

The best that can be said is that at least they were outside, surveying scenes of life and the lives of others. And that is something. So many serving life sentences are held in the most barbaric of conditions, locked up for most of the day – or more likely for days or weeks on end – in small cells which are in effect punishment blocks, and sometimes worse. Cells in which the only form of seating is the fixed metal bed hinged to the wall on which a thin mattress may be placed in the evening when the guard comes in to lower the bed, and which is taken away in the morning when the bed is folded away and locked up against the wall, so that there is nowhere to sit other than the floor – and of course with nothing to do and no hope of this ever changing.

There is an old expression that 'hope dies last', but for many life prisoners that is certainly not the case. Hope died long ago, and many just wish they had too. I cannot forget a conversation with a rather well-known man whose death-sentence had been commuted to life imprisonment following a case that was something of a legal cause célèbre in the campaign to abolish the death penalty. Politely apologising for what he was about to say as he knew I was a lawyer, he observed that his lawyers had built very successful careers on what they had done for him, but that once they had 'won' his case, after a short while he had never heard from them again, and that while they might have felt that his case was a victory, years later he was wondering whether he had been a 'winner' at all. What did I think, I who had come to prevent ill-treatment, he asked? Who had ill-treated whom; who was now ill-treating whom? This was a more difficult conversation than I was expecting to have that day – made somewhat easier by the graciousness of my interlocutor in the face of my discomfort. There are of course extremely good reasons why lawyers usually sever connections with clients at the end of a case – or are these excuses too? This man was devoting the rest of his life to reflecting on that question.

Water

Some things are so utterly and irremediably fundamental to life itself – literally – that the wilful failure to provide them to those whom you deny the ability to access them for themselves must surely be an inhuman thing to do. We might debate what might be on such lists, but one of the very first things just has to be water. We can survive for weeks without food, but most studies suggest we can on average only survive without water for about three or four days. So why was it that in some countries we found no water was provided to those taken into police custody, when police custody could legitimately last for up to 48 hours in theory and could last considerably longer than that in practice? Detainees might be locked up in cells with no access to water throughout all that time – unless of course they were able to pay for it, when a bottle of water would doubtless be able to be found. I never heard of that not being possible. But what if you could not pay? What if you had no money with you when you were detained, or no longer had any at your disposal by the time you are placed in the cell? You might have friends or family who will come and provide you with water, or more likely pay the guards to get you some. But you might not be so lucky, or you might not be able to contact them to let them know where you are. That also can cost. Those in your cell might share their water with you, if they have any – and that was certainly not uncommon. Nor, however, was it uncommon for them not to: in some countries, this would be contingent on new arrivals paying a 'cell fee' of something like $5 to the others being held – and failure to pay the cell fee was a serious matter which had other, and immediate, negative consequences too.

We did meet guards who would provide water themselves, going out to buy bottles of water with their own money when there was no clean water available to distribute, since they understood that something really had to be done about it. The excuse in virtually all such cases was the same – no official budget. It is extraordinary that there can be budgets for all sorts of things when a person is taken into police custody, including (at least in theory) the provision of state-funded legal and medical assistance – but not water. Really? Oh yes, really. Except, of course, so often this is just not true, and it is just a part of the corrupt money-making circus which can characterise so much of the exercise of official authority over the most vulnerable of detainees. I never saw a wealthy person in want of water in a police station anywhere. But then, I rarely saw a wealthy person being held in a police cell in countries where access to drinking water was ever an issue. There is no need to labour the point which is obvious enough, I think. To recall Thucydides and the 'Melian Dialogue' of 2,500 years ago, the powerful do what they can while the weak suffer what they must. This remains a pretty accurate description of a considerable number of so-called criminal justice and custodial systems in the world today.

Conclusion

There is nothing quite like a plausible justification to make one feel better about not doing anything about something that you know something needs to be done about, but which you either cannot or will not do. The problem might be written off as being just too difficult to deal with, or that it is someone else's fault, someone else's problem or someone else's responsibility. And it's often easier not to try. As a result, ill-treatment is often allowed to continue simply because no-one really wants to deal with it or feels the need to deal with it. These are the problems which are seen and recognised for what they are, but which are ignored or side-lined. When challenged, one is presented with so-called reasons which are not really reasons at all. There is a difference between a reason and an excuse. And in the face of torture and ill-treatment, excuses are just not good enough. And there are no acceptable reasons.

10

Prescribing the Inappropriate

Introduction

One of the easiest things in the world is to say that 'something should be done' about the sorts of situations that the UN Subcommittee on Prevention of Torture (SPT) encounters. However, it is often surprisingly difficult to know what to do and *who* should do it. International human rights lawyers and international human rights treaty bodies tend not to think too much about this because, generally speaking, they do not have to. They are addressing the state, and frequently it is sufficient for them to determine whether the state has been responsible for a breach of its international obligations and to require that this be remedied, usually by providing financial compensation, changes in primary legislation, the amendment of administrative rules, guidance or practices. Often there is not much scope for nuance regarding to whom those recommendations need to be made: they are made to the state, and it is expected that the state will implement them. Precisely whose job it is to do that is not really the concern of the international body. As a result, many international bodies can legitimately skate over the question of who it is that should be taking action to bring about the changes that are necessary by addressing their recommendations to 'the state', and to its 'relevant authorities'.

The SPT often addressed the 'relevant authorities' in its recommendations too, and often it was perfectly appropriate to do so since, once again, it could sensibly be left to the state to determine how the recommendation in question might best be implemented. On other occasions, however, I would wince at the sight of the expression, since it was really being used to avoid the difficult truth that we just did not know who was going to be able to do anything about the problem which we had identified and wanted to see solved, let alone how. It was the equivalent of throwing one's hands in the air and saying "someone should do something" – and then leaving it to others – to the 'relevant authorities' – to sort it all out. Yet more often than not, the entire problem was that the 'relevant authorities' were *not* sorting it out, being either blind to the problem, ignoring the problem or too busy offering excuses to seek solutions. Sometimes, the 'relevant authorities' had tried to act but just found themselves unable to deal with the situation; a prison's management cannot itself authorise the building of a new prison or additional accommodation; the police cannot change the code of criminal procedure.

To make headway, you may need to know what the cause of a problem *really* is and who has the ability to do something about it. And that is often a lot less obvious than it might seem and rarely comes down to something that a single decision-maker can do something about. You need to raise the matter at the right level to be able to make a difference. But, as we have seen, raising a concern with the state at the end of a visit or making a rather generic recommendation without specifying who or what should be done might itself not be of very much help since the national authorities might not know the answers to those questions either, being too far removed from the day-to-day operational management of a situation to be able to understand what would really make a difference. You have to be able to suggest what the answer to a problem might be if you are to be listened to and make a difference. Yet knowing the right answer is not always straightforward.

For example, if a police officer has beaten a suspect to make them confess to a crime and that person has been wrongly convicted because of that confession, then there are a whole host of possible responses that might be called for. It might be that this is a single incident involving a single officer, in which case disciplinary action would be required and prosecution considered. This would require a response by their superior officer and the investigating and prosecuting authorities. But what if it is not a disciplinary offence to have done so? This might require changes to the disciplinary codes of conduct, which might require action by a completely different body. Are there statutory defences applicable to the police, shielding them from prosecution? If so, then this may require a change in primary legislation, requiring governmental as well as administrative action. Similarly, confession evidence acquired through torture should be inadmissible in court proceedings, so why was that able to happen? Perhaps it was not considered by the prosecutor's office or raised by the defence lawyer or raised or accepted by the judge. Do any, or all, of these failings provide a ground of appeal or do they not? Is there a need for better training, or amendments to codes of conduct or to Judges' Rules? Or perhaps such evidence *is* admissible in court, in which case legislative change might be required. Prevention calls for all these responses – and others – to be addressed, and many different actors and agencies may need to be involved to bring them about.

Even calling for a person who is directly responsible for an act of torture to be 'held to account' – what does this mean? Is torture a discrete offence that can be separately charged, and are the penalties attaching to it sufficiently serious? There are numerous cases in which law enforcement officers have been prosecuted for lesser offences, such as common assault or misfeasance in public office, and although they have been found guilty the sentence available in respect of that offence can be inappropriately lenient, such as a suspended sentence or a fine. Even where prison sentences are available and have been given, they might be for comparatively short periods which under the domestic law of the country concerned can be converted into monetary fines and swiftly paid by others on their behalf, and the officer in question is not only soon back at their job but is then swiftly promoted. This is the very antithesis of prevention – it is tantamount to exonerating and even rewarding those responsible for torture and ill-treatment. The SPT encountered plenty of such examples – but it encountered relatively few examples of those responsible for routine acts of torture and of ill-treatment being held to account in an appropriate way.

Even if the person responsible is held to account and appropriately punished, has that really addressed the matter properly from a preventive perspective? Almost certainly not. Why was this person in the position that they were? What training had they been given? What safeguards were in place around the questioning process? What other tools of investigation – other than brutality – were open to the officer? What pressure might the officer have been under to 'get a result'? What had been the reaction to any similar incidents in the past? Was there a culture of tacit acceptance of ill-treatment, and so on, and on and on …

This is not meant to be a pathology of policing. The purpose is simply to highlight the 'ripple' that extends from the identification of the problem that needs to be addressed, the many different potential dimensions that it might have and the myriad of preventive possibilities that may need to be explored. Whether, how and by whom each of these might been to be examined, appropriate action identified, authorised and undertaken will vary greatly and is likely to require a combination of intervention at multiple levels if they are to be successful. Simply leaving this to 'the relevant authorities' without at least some indication of the range of 'authorities' that are potentially relevant can be a high-risk strategy.

If simply telling the 'relevant authorities' to take 'appropriate action' was one of my bugbears, another was asking them to do things which appeared to be the 'right' thing to recommend but which, given the circumstances, were probably not. What is the point of recommending the doing of something that you can see for yourself just cannot be done, or, even if it were done, would not really make very much of a difference at all? This was a problem we frequently ran into. And what if a possible solution to a problem might appear to be rather unorthodox or not the sort of thing that is usually recommended in such situations? We ran into that problem too. As a result, we ended up making some quite unusual suggestions and recommendations from time to time, and which are not generally found in sets of UN or other human rights standards.

But prevention is not limited by standards – and, as has already been seen in earlier chapters, the SPT has not followed others in contribution to formal standard setting. Rather, when it decided to place its focus on setting out its understanding of the 'concept' of prevention, and producing a number of documents outlining its 'approaches' prevention as previously mentioned, the SPT was already reflecting its early realisation of this: and when it said in its document on the 'Concept of Prevention', there is no logical limit to the range of things which can have a preventive effect, this was intended to free itself from the shackles which prescriptive standards can provide. As a result, there is also no logical limit to what the SPT can recommend, or to whom. The only thing that really matters is whether a recommendation makes a meaningful contribution to the prevention of torture or ill-treatment in the context in which it is being made. It really ought not to matter whether the recommendation would be appropriate in other places or at other times: what matters is whether it is appropriate in *this* place, now.

As a result, there have indeed been times when the SPT has made some rather unorthodox suggestions in response to situations which it has encountered. This was because in those situations recommending the orthodox would have been quite inappropriate – either because recommending the orthodox simply would not have worked, because it was not the right solution to the problem, or even because doing the 'right thing' could well have been the wrong thing to do.

Write on

One of the most fundamental of preventive safeguards is that no-one should be held incommunicado: a detained person should be able to inform a third party of what has happened to them (or indicate whom the detaining authorities should inform of this), and the fact of their detention should be promptly and properly recorded in custody registers. In essence, no-one should be detained without this being known and without this being recorded. One of the very first things the SPT would do on arrival at a police station was to ask for the custody register in order to see how many people were currently being detained, when exactly their detention commenced and whether it has been subject to judicial scrutiny within the legally prescribed time limits – and to see whether people were being kept in police custody for longer than the law allows. It often turns out that there are more people being held than are recorded in the registers – and sometimes there are less. Both are problematic. Checking whether these records are accurate and up to date is part of the 'stock-in trade' of the custody monitor, and rightly so. They provide essential baseline information which can be checked relatively easily, and their accuracy or otherwise can be confirmed by speaking with those who are to be found in the police cells, at least in theory.

In practice, none of this is necessarily quite as simple as it sounds. Police stations tend to hold more detainees late at night and first thing in the morning, as their cases are being dealt with during the working day. These are times when the SPT is not always able to visit, and although it does do so when it can, this is not straightforward. For example, you need the help of the interpreters and drivers, and they cannot be required to work a 16-hour day – though in practice, they often were very happy to do so. But none of us is superhuman, and when you are getting back after a night visit in the early hours of the morning and need to be on the road by 7 am the next day, then it can all become just too much and counterproductive.

When visiting police stations during the course of the working day in countries where things were all reasonably efficient, there were often relatively few detainees to be found in police cells. If custody limits were generally respected, people were only being held for a few hours or so before being taken to court, released on police bail and the like – and you really do not want to be responsible for holding things up. Moreover, many detainees in police custody did not really want to talk with you anyway, as they had other things on their minds than our questions. Some, inevitably, would be asleep, others intoxicated, some violent and most angry or upset, and particularly so at night.

This means that the paperwork available was often far more than just a 'baseline': it could sometimes be almost all that there was on which to build an understanding of the way in which the police station was run, and, perhaps, how detainees were treated. Of course, the conditions of even empty cells were often eloquence itself, and when combined with the information available from the registers concerning the numbers that had been held in those cells in recent days, and for how long, revealed quite enough to let us know what we needed to know about the way detainees were being treated, even if we could not corroborate this through first-hand accounts. Indeed, in many countries those in police detention are far too intimidated or wary to be prepared to say very much at all to strangers, and this is entirely understandable. As a result, the most revealing accounts concerning treatment in police custody often come from those held in remand prisons. We would often draw on what we heard from remand detainees when deciding what police stations to visit, and what to look for when we did.

All this shows just how important it was for us to be able to consult the record books in police stations. In many places I have visited, they could be located relatively easily. Sometimes they were locked away, but given how frequently entries needed to be made, this was not very often the case. They needed to be accessible, and we generally had good access to them. A look down the largely chronological entries listing the times of commencement and termination of custody was often quick and easy to do, and gaps and inconsistences easy to spot and thus to question. Sometimes, however, the records were very badly kept, and it was clear that some officers did not bother to make any entries at all when they were on shift, as others filled in gaps in other handwriting later.

Interestingly, most of the handbooks on monitoring places of detention still seem to assume that registers are handwritten when in many countries increasingly they are not, and electronic record keeping had been introduced. To be honest, this may have many advantages for the detaining authorities, but they were the 'speedy monitor's nightmare': do you have the ability to print off reports covering the periods you want and to interrogate the electronic system, not to mention having access to the relevant passwords and so on? It takes much longer to consult computer records, which often fail to let you see at a glance what you are looking for. When you can access the relevant systems, it was not uncommon for these also to be not very well kept either, with gaps and inconsistencies.

The standard response and recommendation to such serious failings in basic record keeping concerning who is being detained would be to insist on better record keeping and better training. The need for the latter was particularly obvious in some countries which had introduced electronic systems: I recall an instance where I ended up showing a junior police officer how to operate their own system in a small police station, having learnt how to do it myself through practice at several others. But there could be other problems. On one visit, the systems were fine, and the staff knew how to operate them. However, the electricity supply was erratic, and when it was down it could not be used. Apart from reverting to the written records, the only solution was to get a generator – which would of course be needed for all other purposes anyway. But it was an unusual solution to the problem of failing to keep accurate and up to date custody registers. In another country in which the pages in the handwritten books were just not being completed by some officers, it turned out that this was because they could not read or write. Most UN standards tend to assume a basic level of literacy. A completely different form of training, and of recruitment, was going to be required if that problem was to be solved ...

Taken to court

In retrospect, it was obvious that there was going to be a problem, but, strangely, it had never entered our heads that this might be so. We were wanting to visit some prisons, police stations and border guard facilities that were situated at quite some distance from the capital city in which we were based for the duration of our visit, but this was not easy. We had already got used to spending a couple of hours each day travelling slowly, at first across very congested areas of the city and then with painstaking care along difficult roads and tracks to reach our destinations, sometimes feeling quite unwell from the never-ending jolting along the way. How families and others managed to visit these places is a question in itself. But where we now wished to get to this time raised problems of an entirely different order. Most unusually, we were able to have use of a helicopter which flew us for 90 minutes or so to a landing place where we were met by two cars and after another quite lengthy drive arrived at a prison. Shortly afterwards, two of us left in one of the two four by fours to reach the police station and border area we were also wanting to reach.

Suffice to say the road was, at times, little more than a track through densely wooded areas, and jolting over tree roots and sliding down some muddy inclines was much the norm. In retrospect, undertaking the journey at all was seriously questionable from a personal safety perspective, but at the time we were more concerned about how long it was taking to get to our destination. I cannot now be entirely sure about the length of the journey, but it was at least an hour and felt considerably longer. It was certainly longer than we had expected, and we needed to get back to the helicopter by a given time, or else it would leave without us as it had to be back at its base before a curfew commenced. Time was of the essence.

When we arrived, we were able to access the police station without difficulty, check the records, talk with the handful of detainees and also with the police officers. It was all very relaxed, as well as revealing. One of the things we discovered was that, according to the records we saw (and we had no reason to doubt them), most were detained on a Friday evening and were released, usually without charge, at some point on the following Monday or Tuesday. There was absolutely no evidence of those detained being taken before a judicial authority to authorise their detention for such a period. So we asked about this – and received blank looks from all concerned.

The nearest court was in the small town we had set off from, where the prison was to be found. It had taken us well over an hour, or longer, to travel from there in a four by four able to grip what road there was. What transport was available at the police station to take a detainee to a court? There was a scooter. Except that there was no suitable fuel available for it, so it did not really work. The policeman said he tended to use a bicycle locally – and indeed there was one propped up to hand. I don't suppose it is terribly easy to take a detainee to a courtroom 20 or 30 miles or more away when they are sitting behind you on a scooter, and even less so again on a bike. I am sure that better transportation must have been available from time to time, but it was fairly obvious that this would have been the exception rather than the rule.

There is not a lot of point in getting to the court at all if when you get there no-one has the authority to exercise judicial authority. And it turned out that this was quite likely to be the case. There were, in theory, local magistrates, but for various reasons they had not been re-affirmed in their official positions and no others had been appointed, and so it was not at all clear who was able to exercise 'judicial authority' over such cases at all. At various points in the year, a judge would be dispatched from the central court in the capital to hear cases, but when the judge would be there was unpredictable, to say the least. It had taken us nearly two hours in a helicopter: the judge would have to come by road, and, we were told, it would take a day or two. It was not a salubrious posting, and we already knew that this meant judicial visits were infrequent across the year, with those assigned to do so often finding reasons to delay, postpone or cancel.

This was one reason why so many detainees in the local prisons were in pre-trial detention: trials could be few and far between (and thus quite perfunctory on the occasions when they did occur as there were a lot to get through). On the other hand, judges were only expected to be sitting in Court for less than half of the year. So might it not be reasonable to suggest that they worked for a bit longer? That might have a real impact on a pre-trial detention rate which was, frankly, astonishingly high – and it was very common for the sentences of those ultimately convicted to be mere fractions of the several years they had already spent in custody. And given that there was no real limit to the length of pre-trial detention in practice, being convicted was the only way they were ever likely to be freed ... In short: change your plea to guilty and go free; maintain your innocence and remain in prison indefinitely. What sort of justice system is that?

We had plenty of time to think about this on our long journey back to the capital. If it had been so difficult, demanding and time consuming for us to get there, with all the resources that the UN had at its disposal to assist – including helicopters and state of the art vehicles – how on earth was a local police officer to take a person to a courtroom within 48 hours of their being detained as generally required in the interests of prevention of ill-treatment or incommunicado detention? And what was the point if no-one was going to be there anyway? No recommendation that we, or anyone else on the face of the planet, might make was going to change the realities of geography and topography. We could recommend better transport facilities be provided, but new roads too?

This is an extreme example, and it is notable that in some other rural and isolated parts of the country the 48-hour rule was generally adhered to, while in the capital where it should have been much easier to do so this did not seem to be the case – and a multiplicity of factors were at play here.

The same can be said of another 'fundamental safeguard' for those taken into custody: that all detainees have access to legal assistance. In country after country which I visited, even where the law provides that some form of legal assistance is to be provided to detainees from the outset of their detention, this was the exception not the rule, and it was a comparative rarity to come across detainees in police custody who had received legal assistance promptly in many parts of some countries. When public defence lawyers are all located in the major population centres of large and sparsely populated countries, it is difficult for this to be otherwise. For the SPT to simply repeat in parrot-like fashion the requirement that all those in police custody be taken before a judicial authority within the legally specified period was unlikely to achieve anything. Everyone knew all this already, and everyone also knew that the reasons why this varied so greatly from place to place. Why offer a single solution for a very common problem but which came about for very different reasons? You need to recommend solutions, not outcomes.

Unusual answers to unusual problems

Finding the right solution to a problem is not always as difficult as it seems. Sometimes it is staring you right in the face, but it can seem so odd a thing to recommend that it can feel almost uncomfortable to do so. Shorn of context, some recommendations might seem not only inappropriate but completely bizarre. If detention staff are taking bribes from prisoners, or extorting money from them – should we perhaps recommend that they be better paid? We have encountered situations in which corruption was so rife that almost everyone in a superior position of authority seemed to be syphoning money off those on the next rung below, and those on the bottom rung had no-one else left to exploit other than the detainees. Unless or until the guards were able to receive what in theory they were earning, simply telling them to stop financially exploiting the detainees, or insisting that their corrupt superiors take action, was not likely to have much effect. The problem was endemic and systemic – and so even paying the staff rather than exploiting detainees could only ever be one small part of a much larger set of answers that needed to be found to a complex problem that went well beyond the reach of our mandate.

Similarly, if you do not pay detention staff appropriately, then you will have trouble recruiting the sort of staff you want. In one country, many members of prison staff were actually police officers who were serving disciplinary sanctions: unsurprisingly, there was a considerable amount of brutality and not a lot of professionalism on display. A better-educated, trained, and paid professional staff is an excellent recommendation to make since ensuring that this is so can address many problems – but it can also easily be misrepresented as 'rewarding' rights-violators. This does not mean it is not the right thing to do though, however, counterintuitive it may seem.

Without doubt, the most counterintuitive advice I think I have ever given concerned a terrible situation in which the occupants of a number of barracks-like cell blocks had not been allowed any outdoor exercise for weeks and weeks. They were now riotous and, as a result, dangerous to both themselves and others. The insides of the blocks, which were badly over-crowded, were unspeakable. Some of the men were losing their eyesight and suffering terrible skin problems. They were desperate to be allowed out. The prison staff were desperate to let them out too, but they just could not. There were only a handful of prison staff on duty, no more than four or six at any one time – a hopelessly inadequate number. The blocks were all surrounded by a single perimeter wall. The gates of the prison were in that perimeter wall – or they should have been. One of the main gates had fallen off its hinges … If any prisoner was let out of their block, there was absolutely nothing to stop them walking right out of the prison. The only way to let the detainees outside of their blocks was either to put extra fences around them or – more realistically perhaps – to repair the main gate. These are not usual responses to the problem of prisoners being locked up for too long and not let out of their cells. But it was just about impossible to see what else realistically could have been done to allow that to happen.

Conclusion

You cannot expect people to fill in written registers if they cannot read or write; or to take people in vehicles they do not have, along roads that do not exist to attend courts that are not open; or to lock gates that are not there. Many more examples could be given, but I hope these three brief vignettes will suffice. In all these situations, prevention required thinking beyond the recitation of what should be achieved. It required making practical recommendations setting out what might usefully be done about the situation as we found it. Sometimes that might indeed involve making a standard, generic and high-level recommendation which was of general application. On other occasions, however, it meant being localised, focused and specific, even if this might at times mean that there was a degree of inconsistency (or even downright contradiction) with what has been recommended at another time and in another place where the underlying causes of the problem to be addressed were very different.

Inconsistency and contradiction need not matter. What matters is being honest with yourself and with everyone else about what can and cannot be done. This involves the discomfort of sometimes having to accept, in the short term at least, that what ought to be done just cannot be done, in which case you must focus on the next best thing. Suggesting what can be done is better than suggesting what cannot, even if it is not necessarily ideal. But sometimes, lateral thinking can come up with ideas which can produce at least partial mitigations, and that is a start, and it is preventive, and that,

I would suggest, is what really counts. Even if you cannot make things right, perhaps you can help make things better. The thing which bothered me the most, perhaps, was that some thought this approach was controversial. Departing from the orthodox in the human rights world is greatly frowned on – even if all you are doing is stating the blindingly obvious.

11

Working with Fictions

Introduction

We all tend to see what we expect to see and understand things in the way that we expect them to be understood. When those expectations are in fact very far from reality, it is quite possible to spend a great deal of time and energy visiting a place of detention while not really seeing or understanding what is in front of you at all. If things look familiar, you assume that they will be what you expect them to be and respond to them accordingly. But as we saw in the previous chapter, this is sometimes not true at all. Things are not at all what we expect them to be, but nevertheless we still project our assumptions and our expectations into our evaluations and into our recommendations.

Sometimes this simply renders those evaluations and recommendations perplexing to those who receive them and leaves you looking a little foolish because you have just not 'got it'. That can be embarrassing, but it is not the end of the world. What is far more serious is when you have become so blinded by your expectations that you end up working with a fictional, parallel universe. There is then a real danger that what you say might not only be inappropriate, but can even be harmful, and the standards and expectations you demand others comply with may not only be useless or unhelpful but, in some extreme examples, might even put people at greater risk of suffering the very things you are seeking to protect them from.

Twenty years ago, I was involved on behalf of the Association for the Prevention of Torture (APT) in a project with the African Commission on Human and Peoples' Rights that resulted in the adoption of the Robben Island Guidelines on Torture Prevention in Africa in October 2002 (for the background to, and text of which, see APT, 2003), which some years later provided the springboard for the establishment by the African Commission of the Committee for the Prohibition and Prevention of Torture in Africa.[1] I was a member of the seven-person drafting committee and one of the two 'core drafters' of the final document. It is now largely forgotten that one of the purposes of those Guidelines was to build support for the adoption of the Optional Protocol to the United Nations Convention against Torture (OPCAT) by African states during the period when it was being considered at the UN (Long and Murray, 2012, p 316), and the Guidelines do indeed call for such support and were very helpful in that respect.

In addition, the Guidelines also set out fundamental standards to be adhered to within the detention process, and these closely mirror those reflected in the work of the European Committee for the Prevention of Torture (CPT) – which is hardly surprising as some members of that Committee, as well as myself and the APT who were steeped in its work, were very heavily engaged in the drafting process. One of those standards, in paragraph 31 of the Robben Island Guidelines, provides that during the pre-trial process 'all persons deprived of their liberty have access to legal and medical services and assistance and have the right to be visited by and correspond with family members'. Some of our European CPT colleagues jumped on this, pointing out that it could be completely inappropriate to allow visits and correspond with family members in all circumstances – what if this risked prejudicing an investigation, for example? Our African colleagues pointed out that not ensuring this risked the person not being visited starving – as it was family members who usually provided detainees with food and drink. The standard was duly changed to reflect this.

The UN Subcommittee on Prevention of Torture (SPT) has had plenty of opportunity on its numerous visits to recognise the overwhelming importance of ensuring that family members know that their relatives have been detained and of ensuring that they can visit them. This is probably the most important of all the preventive safeguards for those in pre-trial detention in some of the countries we visited. To prevent such visits would be disastrous. As this suggests, transposing expectations and concerns relevant in one context into others where they are not appropriate can be extremely serious indeed. This chapter provides some salutary examples of situations in which insisting on what is generally expected can turn out to be the wrong thing to do, because it is *your* world that is the fictional one, while *theirs* is for real. Doubtless it should not be that way – but it is.

What's really going on?

The previous chapter highlighted the importance of properly registering everyone who is taken into custody, to ensure that there is transparency around the detention process and to avoid the dangers associated with incommunicado detention. Once a person is registered, it is then possible to trace what happens to them and to follow their pathway through the criminal justice system, checking that their rights have been respected and preventive safeguards adhered to.

For example, you can check if a third party has been notified of their detention. We once visited a relatively small prison to which was attached a police station – an unusual arrangement but which given the overall country context was entirely understandable and sensible enough. We asked whether the families of the two or three men in the police cells had been informed of their detention and were met with blank stares. Why would they need to tell the families? We explained about the importance of this as a preventive safeguard, and so on. The uncomprehending stares remained; it seemed as if we were talking past each other, and indeed we were.

We had made the fundamental mistake of assuming that just because it was a police station and that there were people locked up inside police cells that this had something to do with the exercise of police powers. It didn't. What happened was that if someone either came home drunk or otherwise worse for wear, then it was quite normal in that small community for the family members to bring them to the police station, where they would be locked up overnight until sober and then collected and taken home. Of course, they had not needed to tell the family about these men being in the police cells – it was the men's families and not the police who had put them there.

This was not quite as unusual as it sounds, but also not always quite so benign. In another place, we were struck by the sheer numbers of people we found in police custody who were drunk, or who were sleeping off being drunk. It's fair to say that attempting to conduct interviews with them was a bit of a lost cause too. In that country, the police had power themselves to detain individuals who were intoxicated, and, if it was then certified that their blood alcohol levels were over a certain threshold, they could be taken directly before a judge who would authorise their being taken to a centre where they could be held for up to two weeks to be 're-educated' about the dangers of alcoholism. These centres were not necessarily problematic places in themselves – but the net effect of these laws was that a person could, for being, or for being reported to be, drunk, find themselves subject to summary detention for a significant period of time. And evidence suggested that neighbours might often report each other to the police, and alcohol tests could always be administered in ways to ensure that they showed a person to be just over the threshold ... And sometimes they might (at a cost) be just under the threshold ... But there was little point in appealing to the judge, since the proceedings were administrative, conducted on the basis of paperwork and seemed always to result in the same outcome, detention. Obviously, the potential for mischief was considerable. Suddenly, a very different type of problem, and form of potential abuse and ill-treatment, became apparent.

At least these men would be released after 14 days. Elsewhere, this might not have been so. In another, relatively remote, place it was entirely common (even if entirely wrong) for neighbours, rivals, enemies and the like to settle disputes between themselves and seek to execute punishment by taking the loser in the argument to the local police station to be locked up for a few days. If after two or three days no further complaints were made – and enough being enough – the police would simply let them go, and that would be the end of the matter. Nevertheless, in the meantime they were properly recorded by the police as being in police custody, as strictly speaking they were – and all those in police custody were meant to be taken before a judicial authority within 48 hours.

From a preventive point of view, of course this should have happened. Except that if it had, then they would have been remanded in custody and taken to a remand prison many miles away – because this is what happened to almost everyone who appeared before a judicial authority in that country, irrespective of whether they should have been. Had this happened, then, what had started out as a few days of inappropriate 'private punishment' would suddenly have turned into potentially years of inappropriate pre-trial detention–though 'pre-trial' is something of a misnomer as there was never any real possibility of there being a trial at all, as there was no case to answer. And as there was no system of effective review or limits on the length of pre-trial detention, this could last indefinitely. In short, the very worst thing that could possibly have happened to the people we met in that police cell was that they should be taken before a magistrate within 48 hours. Give it a couple more hours and they would be free – as they should have been from the start. The implementation of that preventive safeguard would not have been a safeguard for them: it would have been the equivalent of a protracted prison sentence.

A final but very different situation also comes to mind. I spoke with a group of four mid-teenage boys in a police cell in a relatively busy area of a city one afternoon. They said they had been there for a couple of hours, but they were all quite relaxed about it. They said they had been out that morning when a group of police rounded them up and brought them to the police station in a van. Immediately on arrival they were told to inform their parents, which they did by calling them on their mobile phones (which they still had with them in the cells). They expected their parents to be there very soon, and that their parents would pay some money to the police and then they would then be free to go. It had happened to them before, they said, and it was not a lot of money. Unsurprisingly, the boys were not listed in the custody register, unlike all the adults in the police station. All the indications were that the boys were right – it was a money-making exercise and, if the modest sums requested were paid out quickly, then that would be the end of it.

The point of all this is simple, but difficult too. We tend to assume that police stations operate as police stations. That is not always true. There might well be a lot more going on there than we think, and you have to be alert to this if you are going to be able to make sense of what is happening and make appropriate recommendations. And avoid making inappropriate ones.

Who's really in charge?

There is a similar problem when it comes to prisons – that we make assumptions which are simply not justified. What strikes me most about this is that unlike, perhaps, in policing, we *know* that the assumptions we are making are not justified, but we carry on making them anyway. The biggest of these 'false assumptions' concerns to whom we address our recommendations – the 'relevant authorities' discussed earlier. In the context of prisons, this is sometimes a nice way of glossing over what no-one really wants to admit, which is that the 'relevant authorities' are sometimes the prisoners themselves and the so-called authorities are not really that 'relevant' at all on a day-to-day basis.

The extent to which prisoners and prison gangs can dominate life in some prisons is well known and well documented. But this is usually projected as a matter of concern and something to be addressed. Doubtless naïvely, I was surprised to discover the extent to which in so many prison settings in so many different countries, powerful prisoners were in effect co-opted into the day-to-day running of facilities by the prison authorities themselves. To all intents and purposes, those prisoners became the gaolers, with the single and sole exception that at the end of each day, when all else had been dealt with, they would turn their keys (and they had the keys) on themselves.

It could be the cell leaders (recognised as such by the prison administration) who might determine, in large and overcrowded cells, who would sleep where; often with fees attached which reflected the relative desirability of the available options. Cell leaders would be expected to organise access to toilets, the distribution of food, to identify those in need of medical attention, to deal with any 'internal' disagreements or tensions within the cell, and much else besides. Cell leaders might have their own designated areas within large cells – literally screened off from others, with TVs, fridges, food and the like freely available for the leaders and their henchmen, who lived in their 'compounds' within the cells and in which there could be beds, tables, chairs, TVs and the like, while everyone else lay in cramped conditions the other side of the makeshift partitions.

A society within a society, such systems that we saw – it has to be said – seemed to work well, delivering a degree of order and control which would otherwise not have been remotely possible given the staffing levels within those prisons. And although obviously completely inequitable, frequently these systems were generally accepted by those who were subjected to them, and even valued by some who felt they provided them with a degree of support and safety that they would not otherwise have had. In some cases, it was difficult to disagree.

Not all such examples were like this. Some cell leaders were violent, brutal and exploitative, and the prison staff afraid to intervene. From an SPT visiting point of view, the 'rule book' has a lot to say about ensuring that interviews take place out of the sight and hearing of the staff of a detention facility, but it says nothing about doing so out of the sight and hearing of other detainees. This was often far more important, with the detainees being much more worried about speaking up in front of their cellmates than in front of the prison staff. Time and time again, we would enter a cell and find that only one person would speak to us and would limit themselves to saying that everything was fine. And if anyone else in the cell gave the merest hint of demurring, there would be an obvious stare, or kick from someone to remind them to keep quiet. It was not their place to speak to us. And if we sought to speak to anyone in private then no-one would be willing to do so, except, of course, the cell leaders.

Being alert to the risks of detainees suffering at the hands of their fellow detainees was at least as great a concern to us as was the risk of their suffering some form of reprisal from the staff for having spoken to us. Yet the many guides to visiting produced to support the work of the SPT and National Preventive Mechanisms (NPMs) rarely if ever allude to this. It is not a comfortable truth that some of the worst physical ill-treatment that a detainee may ever receive may well be at the hands of fellow prisoners. Sometimes this is because the staff just cannot control the cell leaders – and sometimes it is because they are used by the staff as a means of control. But the source of the danger remains the same. What is odd, if perhaps also inevitable, is that when so much of the risk of inhuman and degrading treatment takes the form of ill-treatment at the hands of other detainees, all the recommendations concerning how to protect detainees from ill-treatment are directed solely at the state authorities, who so often are in no position to do very much about it. Of course, they *ought* to be. But that is the fiction. They simply are not.

The professionalism of the professionals

As has already been said, from its very beginnings, the theory of prevention has stressed the importance of three fundamental safeguards: that on being taken into custody a person must be able to inform a third party; that they must be able to have access to a lawyer, state funded when necessary; and be medically examined. To this can be added the need to ensure that those in detention are either charged or brought before a judicial authority promptly. There are detailed glosses to all of these which need not detain us here. We have already chronicled numerous instances when it can be almost impossible for detainees to have swift access to lawyers and doctors once they are taken into custody, no matter what the law says. Obviously, if there are none to be had then they cannot be accessed. However, while improving access and extending the scope of the provision of free legal assistance frequently is the subject of recommendations, the quality of the services legal or medical professionals provided is not generally commented on and it is rarely the subject of much scrutiny at all. It is as if the preventive nature of the safeguard lies in there being access to such services, rather than the quality of the service that results from their being accessed.

While very many lawyers, medical professionals and judges – the majority, I expect – fulfil their roles within the criminal justice system diligently, many do not. One of the most common refrains from remand prisoners was that although they were entitled to legal assistance, they often only met their lawyer for the first time shortly before a hearing and those lawyers were often barely acquainted with the facts of their case. Indeed, in one prison where, commendably, a temporary courtroom had been established in order to hear cases without the need to transport them to court in an effort to speed up proceedings and reduce the levels of pre-trial detention, we were able to witness for ourselves a lawyer apologising to the judge for talking about the wrong one. At least he realised and admitted it.

Sometimes the hearings took place in the absence of the defendant: we saw documentary evidence of cases in which the defence lawyer did not object to orders of continued detention, but the defendant did not know that this had happened and still expected to be released. We heard lists of names of defendants simply being read out in court and continued detention – beyond maximum statutory periods – being confirmed by judges without reasons being asked for or given, other than that the extension was requested. We spoke with some defence lawyers who admitted that they were paid so little by the state to represent detainees, even those charged with very serious offences, that they did not usually acquaint themselves with the facts of the case but simply advised most clients to plead guilty and said would offer up some plea in mitigation when it came to sentencing if they did.

We encountered very impressive medical facilities in some prisons which were clearly very busy. The doctors and nurses working there appeared able, concerned and seemed to run an efficient, effective and popular service with those we met within those facilities. Yet strangely few of the prisoners seemed ever to be taken there despite frequent requests for medical assistance, the need for which in some cases was perfectly obvious to even the most untrained medical eye (such as festering open wounds, sores, skin diseases, chronic pain and difficulties with mobility). Others told us that for almost every ailment the same tablets were routinely dispensed, being largely ineffective painkillers. Checking the medical records confirmed this. It seems that the well-trained, pleasant and affable staff were spending the bulk of their time treating family and friends on the prison budget, and treating them to a level of care that few prisoners could ever hope to experience.

Returning for a moment to police detention and initial custody, we found, for example, medical forms certifying that a person taken into custody was fit and in good health, despite it being blindingly obvious that their general health was not that way at all, the person concerned having easily visible cuts and bruises that must have pre-dated the cursory medical 'all clear' that had been given only a few hours earlier. And enough has already been said of judges who rubber stamp whatever the detaining authorities request of them with barely a question being asked. As one judge told me, "I see the prosecutors every week, and I have no reason not to do what they ask."

On many visits, we met with representatives of local Bar and Medical Associations, to better understand their role and their knowledge relating to effective safeguards against torture and ill-treatment, including the extent to which medical practitioners were aware of the Istanbul Protocol concerning the effective documentation of torture by medical professionals (for which, see Iacopico, 2020) and whether it was adhered to in practice. In such conversations, the difficulties under which they often laboured became all too apparent. The numbers of lawyers and medical practitioners available to service the needs of the criminal justice system were often vanishingly few, and that they achieved so little could hardly come as a surprise; it could hardly be otherwise.

Nevertheless, the toxic combination of weak legal frameworks, minimal resourcing, hopelessly inadequate numbers of professionals available and an appalling lack of professionalism by some of those who were, simply *has* to call into question the practical effectiveness of even these most fundamental of preventive safeguards. Yet we continued to insist on them all the same, despite knowing that the safeguards that they were able to offer were largely fictional. But what was also rarely mentioned was that the purported professionalism of too many of the so-called professionals was also frequently fictional and offered no meaningful protection against torture and ill-treatment at all. And in such cases the usefulness of recommending these safeguards became our little fiction too.

The relevance of the law

In some police stations, what takes place is not policing as we know it. In some prisons, the prisoners exercise at least as much internal authority over the lives of detainees on a day-to-day basis as do the prison officials. We cannot always rely on the professionals on whom we place so much reliance to behave as they ought. None of this is revelatory and is well known to just about everyone who has anything to do with these subjects, even if these truths can be too awkward to acknowledge when it comes to the issuing of recommendations by human rights bodies which pretend that things are other than they are because this is what we want and expect them to be: orthodoxy demands this of us. But there is an even bigger, and even more problematic fiction.

Just about everything that the SPT and NPMs do presupposes one thing, which is adherence to some version of the rule of law. If you advocate for legal safeguards and legal protections for those taken into detention on the basis of public authority, or even on the basis of acquiescence or acceptance by public authorities, you are at least assuming that systems of detention are governed or informed, or at least influenced, by the rule of law, and that it is accepted that they should be, even if they are not working as they ought. All our recommendations were ultimately directed at that end, and even when rather inchoately directed at the various unspecified 'relevant authorities' it was at least assumed that there would be official, or quasi-official, relevant authorities to direct them at. Even in prisons where self-governance regimes operate, there usually is a degree of official 'acceptance' of this, even if at times this is in the sense of accepting the unacceptable, rather than in the sense of toleration or tacit approval. However, even this is not always the case.

It would be wrong of me to go too far here, but I suspect it does not take much imagination to hypothesise that the reason why the SPT has not yet visited at least some of its states parties is because it does not think there is much point in doing so, even if this were practically possible. It has visited plenty of countries where there are real and pressing security issues: in its early years, a coup took place while it was visiting a country; it has been in countries where there have been serious civil disturbances or armed conflicts of varying natures taking place. As mentioned, in 2016 we were in Eastern Ukraine, witnessing at first hand the situation in the Donbas and undertaking our work throughout the internationally recognised territory of our state party, irrespective of who was exercising de facto control over parts of it. Nevertheless, there are some countries – which I deliberately do not name – where it is simply implausible to believe that the structures of governance do anything other than trace the contours of the rule of law and that the practice related to detention within the country – either in part or in whole – is such as to make it simply not worthwhile visiting with the purpose of issuing recommendations to a governmental authority which is palpably unable to act as such. Since the SPT is a body focused on the prevention of torture and ill-treatment this always pained me, but it reflects the realities of the SPT's mandate, and importantly, the UN has other tools in its toolbox which are better equipped to work in such situations. At the end of the day, a confidential report to a dysfunctional or ineffectual state apparatus is not going to protect anyone from anything or prevent anything that ought not to be happening from happening.

And therein lies the fiction that needs to be recognised: that this is the situation in far more states than we (or at least I) imagined.

As an international lawyer, I have to assume the sovereignty of the state: it is the foundation stone on which the entire conception of the international political and legal order is built. Contemporary international law makes little sense without it – and contemporary approaches to the international protection of human rights through law absolutely depend on it. In the international arena, states demand that their sovereignty is not only protected but that it is respected, and routinely this is the case – with all the privileges and dignities of statehood that this accords to each by each other and the status, dignity and power that then follows. It is akin to absolutist medieval monarchs creating and awarding each other ever more grandiose titles and offices. But at least those medieval monarchs understood that these trappings of power were only to be taken seriously for as long as they should be taken seriously. In the modern world, statehood and the trappings of statehood are treated as if, like diamonds, they are forever. Not only that, but the sovereign *equality* of states is similarly reified – the great fiction that all states are endowed with the same potency in the international arena and entitled to equal levels of respect, deference and authority. This is nonsense of course, but these are the rules of the game, and there are reasons for those rules.

As an international lawyer, knowing that at the international level the sovereign equality of states is little more than pious rhetoric (or impious rhetoric, perhaps), honoured symbolically but routinely flouted, should have made me realise that the same would be true within the territories of the sovereign polities we visited. Nevertheless, the writ of law ran far less extensively in far more states than I ever would have expected.

At a fairly trivial level, it was often the case that the credentials signed by senior governmental officials or ministers carried surprisingly little weight on the ground: what mattered was not the stamp of officialdom, but the voice of their immediate superior. Some might take note of our official credentials, but others would simply pass our requests for access to a place of detention up their chain of local command until a response was received. And if it was negative, then our credentials themselves counted for nothing, making it clear that in that organisation the ministry's authorisation carried little practical weight. At best, their instructions on this might be something to consider, not something which was to be done. Most incidents of this nature were usually solved amicably, but they certainly indicated that some sectors of the detaining authorities felt themselves unconstrained by the usual channels of officialdom.

Such issues were not always so easy to solve, however. Indeed, I encountered some cases where the ministries themselves appeared genuinely surprised to discover how little effect their instructions had 'on the ground', though there were others in which I was left with the impression that they would have been more surprised if that had been of use. Real authority seemed to lie elsewhere, and it was not uncommon to find that those operating detention systems within some sectors, such as military or special security services, simply did not accept the authority of civilian governance over them at all.

We also ran into situations where entire local administrative regions paid no heed at all to instructions from central authorities. We even ran into situations where the national authorities themselves admitted that there were 'islands of autonomy' within the country – in truth, their authority barely extended to the limits of the capital. And within many countries, while some ministries carried weight, others didn't. In this, we were sometimes hampered by having to work through the ministries of foreign affairs, who seemed – and despite the deference shown to them in international fora – incapable of securing even the passing attention of domestic ministries. I recall mentioning this to a local diplomat in one country who burst out laughing, saying "you were asking them to do what? They haven't got the authority to order a cup of tea, let alone fix up a meeting." Doubtless this was an exaggeration, but it was clear that the underlying point was correct.

All such examples represent failures of governance and meant that the 'relevant authorities' with whom we, as an international body, were bound to meet with and to whom our recommendations were directed might be largely incapable of doing much about them. Another problem was that we tended to address ourselves to the government; but legislative change requires the assent of legislatures and this opens up very different issues, and indeed potentially useful avenues through which to make progress. Unusually for a body such as ours, we increasingly turned to meetings with parliamentarians and parliamentary committees (on a non-partisan basis) as this often was a more powerful point of pressure for change than speaking with the government, which had little reason to do what we asked and which often could not really have done so without such support anyway.

These realities of governance are so often overlooked by international mechanisms, yet they are an essential component of bringing about change. Haranguing states and officialdom about their failures to swiftly achieve legislative outcomes that cannot easily be achieved because of the constraints of systems of representative democracy, good governance and the rule of law which we ourselves wish them to adhere to is not a particularly good look. Of course, where such changes could be easily achieved but were just not being pursued – that was another matter. What mattered most was responding appropriately to what you found, not necessarily responding consistently in all cases, and this sense of realism and pragmatism about what was achievable helped win around some national authorities who were not expecting such an approach from an international body. Trying to see the challenges of changing ingrained practices 'from their side' can help greatly to make recommendations that can make a difference by being achievable.

As has been said before, there is little point in recommending what cannot be done.

Nevertheless, the problem that we did run into that was almost completely intractable concerned the existence of parallel justice systems, sitting alongside the official systems but very different from them. Sometimes these might be versions of alternative dispute resolution or community-based settlement, in which the national authorities co-opted the assistance of respected figures within the communities to work with them, or under their delegated authority, to address crimes or disputes outside of the formal parameters of the criminal justice system. These might sometimes be hybrid in nature, the national authorities being involved in convening meetings between disputing parties, holding individuals until such meetings or informal hearings took place and following up on the outcome of such processes; but those processes themselves were often opaque and certainly did not respect preventive safeguards as we would understand them. Sometimes, however, the informal systems were entirely free-standing of the apparatus of the official justice system and it might be just a matter of preference, or chance, as to which was employed.

Sometimes these might involve forms of traditional justice, including means of questioning, testing the veracity of claims, which could appear to be little more than 'trial by ordeal' or variants thereon, and even of punishments, some of which, while described as restorative in nature, could involve physical punishments or rituals which might easily be considered inhuman or degrading. Once over, matters were considered settled, and everyone involved was expected to put it all behind them and 'move on'.

It is easy to be dismissive and censorious of this. Yet it was clear that in some, rare, cases, such approaches carried at least as much legitimacy within the communities as the 'official justice' systems, and sometimes considerably more – particularly in cases where the rule of law was generally fragile, or was badly run, administered and generally dysfunctional. As we were once told:

> You international people always come and tell us that what we do is wrong – but where was the rule of law when the government collapsed and there was anarchy? Nowhere. This is how we kept order then, and it worked – and now you come back and tell us to abandon it for systems that end up putting people in prisons waiting for trials for years and which you yourself says does not deliver justice.

This was from a senior official with responsibility for justice affairs. Stepping back and reflecting on this, although we were hardly going to agree, it was difficult not to see where he was coming from.

I do not intend to debate the rights and wrongs of these starkly contrasting views. The simple point I want to make is this: we assume that the justice systems we look at are the justice systems which matter, and that the people we talk with about them are the people that matter. This is because we think they should be. Sometimes, however, this is just not true, and we are deluding ourselves. We are discussing fictions with fantasists, but we carry on because no-one can really afford to accept the truth of this. The result, inevitably, is that the entire exercise can become a complete waste of time.

Conclusion

Much is said about the need for transparency when it comes to the prevention of torture and ill-treatment; indeed, the entire premise of the OPCAT is that opening places to scrutiny can permit better means of prevention to be put in place and so reduce the chance of its occurring. But it seems to me that not enough is said about being honest about what one finds. Not for a moment would I wish to suggest that when there is torture, ill-treatment and failings identified within the systems and structures of the justice systems that these are ignored, side-lined or covered up by the SPT and other international human rights bodies and mechanisms. Most manifestly, they are not. However, there *is* a reluctance to accept that things really are the way they are, when that is not the way we think they ought to be. We have a tendency to invest states and systems of top-level governance with a greater capacity to effect change than is sometimes warranted. These are the rules of our game – and some of those rules turn out to be fictions too.

But there is one final fiction that needs to be mentioned. Once a state has ratified a treaty or has voted for the adoption of sets of standards concerning the treatment of detainees – of which there are many – one might reasonably expect them to at least try to achieve what they have undertaken to do. In so many cases, however, it is perfectly and painfully obvious that the state does not have the slightest intention of doing anything of the kind – and their promises and protestations to the contrary need to be accepted for what they are, just another fiction.

Note
[1] ACHPR Res 61 (XXXII) 02 Resolution on Guidelines and Measures for the Prohibition and Prevention of Torture, Cruel, Inhuman or Degrading Treatment or Punishment in Africa (Robben Island Guidelines) 2008, https://www.achpr.org/instruments/robben-island-guidelines-2008/

12

Thinking Positively
about Prevention

Introduction

If some of the last few chapters seem unremittingly bleak it is because they are. They seek to sketch the outlines of just some of the realities encountered by the UN Subcommittee on Prevention of Torture (SPT) in its pursuit of the prevention of torture and ill-treatment. Each merits further detail and explanation, and there are many others that could also have been highlighted as well. Taken collectively, they convey an impression of the problems that prevention needs to confront, including the need to challenge some deeply embedded assumptions about the causes of torture and ill-treatment and how we respond to it.

Those who have read this far might have spotted what may appear to be a significant disjuncture in my presentation of prevention. Much of the discussion in the earlier chapters focused on torture and how this related to inhuman and degrading treatment, but little was said about inhuman and degrading treatment itself. Yet the later chapters of this book have largely raised matters concerning the treatment of detainees and the application of the criminal justice process. Does this mean that the two halves of the book do not join up? Is 'torture prevention' just another fiction, and although we say we are 'tackling torture', in fact we are not? We might be doing something of importance, but is it what we say it is?

When the European Convention on the Prevention of Torture (CPT) was being drafted, it was made clear that the purpose of the Convention was to prevent torture, and it was not about the conditions in which people were detained. Yet that is precisely what much of the work of the CPT and the UN Subcommittee on Prevention of Torture (SPT) and National Preventive Mechanisms (NPMs) is in fact all about. Is this a contradiction? I do not think it is – although that does not mean there is not a lot more that could be done to make the SPT and NPMs better at preventing torture too. This concluding chapter seeks to explain why, and how.

Revisiting 'what is torture?'

There is an 'easy' answer to all this, which is that these preventive bodies were set up to tackle not only torture but also to tackle inhuman and degrading treatment as well, and so they are only doing what they were always intended to do. While that is quite true, I do not think it is quite good enough. If there is indeed a 'special stigma' attached to torture, then concentrating on those aspects of the mandate to which that 'special stigma' does not attach seems at best to be a failure to properly prioritise and, at worst, a failure to fulfil the mandate appropriately. To understand why this is not so, it is necessary to revisit our understanding of what torture is, where it takes place and what brings it about.

The opening chapters of this book introduced the current approach to these questions and highlighted the difficulty, if not the impossibility, of distinguishing between torture and inhuman or degrading treatment on the basis of thresholds derived from the degrees of pain or suffering that it causes. It was argued that it was the deliberate and purposive use of inhuman means that forms the essence of torture: that is, the deliberate infliction of cruelty for a particular purpose. The question we now must ask ourselves is which of the incidents and the examples that I have touched upon in the previous chapters amount to such behaviours? Some of them clearly do – for example, the evidence of the use of electric shocks on tethered detainees; of bloodied batons and of plastic bags used to asphyxiate; of locking people up in coffin-like cells to make them 'volunteer' to be removed from the country. It is easy to accept that such forms of ill-treatment amount to torture since they fall into the popular imagery of what torture is. When such things are found, it is right and proper to call them out for what they are, and the legitimacy of doing so is rarely, if ever, contested. Who would dare? They are forms of torture.

But was it torture to simply keep a man with a prosthetic leg in a tiny cell for 23 hours a day for months and months on end? The purpose of doing so was not to get a confession or to extract information, so perhaps it wasn't really torture, strictly speaking? Purpose defines and does not excuse torture. Nevertheless, in some ways, and this needs to be said carefully, the very purposelessness of this man's treatment was itself a part of what was so shocking about it. He could not even agree to do or say something to get himself released. You can never, ever, hold a torture victim responsible for their own torture by suggesting that all the victim needs to do is 'talk' and the torture will stop. This is what torturers say to their victims all the time. But for a pre-trial detainee suffering the most appalling of conditions for no other reason than that they are a pre-trial detainee who is waiting and waiting and waiting for a trial that may or may not ever happen, is that not at least as bad in its own way, but just different? Does not treating people as a matter of course in ways which are so shocking, and which cause so much pain and suffering, demand to be called out in the same way as torture too? And if it does not, might that be because of how we have become conditioned to think about torture?

Surely the difference cannot depend on the application of some form of matrix, weighing the size of the cell against the length of detention against the reason for detention, such as whether it was for a very particular and illegitimate purpose, such as coercing a person or extracting information, rather than a more general and potentially legitimate purpose, such as holding a person in pre-trial detention? Yet such reasoning already takes place when, for example, it is said that a small police holding cell may be suitable for holding a person for up to 24 hours but not for longer, or that a cell holding three or four people is acceptable if the detainees are confined within it for only a limited part of the day. Such approaches – often based on standard formulae of square meterage per person – can help distinguish the acceptable from the unacceptable and provide some objective benchmarks against which to do so. Ultimately, however, this can never only be a question of mathematics and is more often a matter of overall perception – is this OK or is it not OK? – and, perhaps surprisingly, this is generally not a particularly difficult question to answer. The real problem is knowing how to describe what you perceive to be wrong, not determining the rights or wrongs of it.

In circumstances such as these, the SPT would usually 'fudge' the issue by describing something as being 'torturous in nature', or of being 'akin to torture', or some other such linguistic near-neighbour, while avoiding the precise label of 'torture' itself. This often felt weak and something of a sell-out given what you thought about what you had seen, but sometimes it was the best you could do.

As a result, I have come to question the entire idea of there being a 'special stigma' attached to torture: not in the sense of torture being 'not as bad' as it is said to be, but because it can have the effect of meaning other things are not considered 'not as bad as they really are' because they do not fulfil the definitional requirements of torture. As the example I have just been using illustrates – and this is the classic approach of lawyers – the temptation is always to highlight something that is generally accepted to be a form of torture, and then to argue that what you now have in front of you is so similar, or sufficiently similar, that there is no justification for not also including it within that 'category'. In essence, you increase the size of the envelope. So, as in the *Costello-Roberts* case discussed in Chapter 2, is hitting a seven-year-old three times with a shoe to be equated with hitting a teenager three times with a cane? Or in the cases looked at in this chapter, what if you are in a cell in which you cannot sit down for eight hours, as opposed to being in a cell in which you can sit but not lie down for eight days? And so on …

Perhaps these are inevitable debates which just have to be had. But sometimes there is just difference, and there is no real possibility of shoehorning what you see into an existing category. What about when we saw a prison block holding over 100 prisoners – sentenced for life – living four or five in a cell designed for one – and the only 'toilet', other than buckets in each cell, being a crack in the concrete above a sewer that ran through the exercise yard to which there was access for a few hours each day? Was living like this for the rest of your life a form of torture – a real, not a 'rhetorical' torture? I have no idea. And I am not sure that it matters all that much. Perhaps there is a good reason why the absolute prohibition is of 'torture and inhuman or degrading treatment or punishment'. The problem is that we too often forget that this is so, or think that things 'falling short of torture', as we understand it, are somehow not so bad. They are *not* 'not so bad': they are just different – bad in a different way – and are just as prohibited.

This changes the entire understanding and dynamic of the preventive approach to tackling torture and ill-treatment. The vast bulk of violations of the prohibition of torture and ill-treatment take place in the day-to-day routine practices of detention systems, the 'acceptance of the unacceptable', as it was characterised earlier. When challenged, this so often prompts what I have described as the excusing of the inexcusable. As I have already acknowledged, there is no bright line between the unacceptable and the inexcusable. The difference is not so much in what they are but in the responses we see to them. Neither is there a bright line between the varying forms that ill-treatment can take, nor indeed when such ill-treatment can rightly be considered as 'torturous'. The entire point of prevention is to try to roll back ill-treatment wherever it is found to a point as close as possible to its elimination, and to erect barriers that seek to ensure that it does not roll back the other way and return. Rather than focus exclusively on the 'apex' which might be represented by the cruelty and barbarity of stigma-bearing purposive torture, there is every reason to focus heavily on the routine, mundane and often shockingly purposeless ill-treatment that characterises the experience of so many of those taken into detention but which, because their suffering is of a different order, tends not to attract the same levels of interest, attention or concern. This is where the preventive system can make its greatest contribution. But does it?

Working towards prevention with the UN: the art of the possible

One of the criticisms which is so often made of the UN in general, and its Human Rights Council in particular, is that it is too political in what it does. I have never really understood that criticism, since the UN, and the UN Human Rights Council, are political bodies. The members of the Council are states and it is the representatives of those states who, through their decision-making, determine what the organs and agencies and those whose work is directly supported by the UN can and cannot do. It is states that through the UN adopt declarations and treaties, establish the mandates of various human rights bodies and procedures and, through Universal Periodic Review, engage in their own direct scrutiny and evaluation of each other's human rights record (Freedman, 2020). Quite why we should not expect a system of this nature to be heavily influenced by political factors is difficult to fathom.

If anything, it is the relatively limited degree to which the UN's human rights work is overtly politicised that is one of its more remarkable features. Another is that it takes place at all. That states should set up and support such systems, the main function of which is to probe the extent to which they honour their international commitments regarding the way they treat people over whom they exercise authority, is quite remarkable and something which we probably take far too much for granted. When that system fails to do so, or fails to do so as well as it might, then this should simply serve to remind us how precarious the entire edifice of international human rights protection is and to be grateful for what it is able to achieve, despite the odds against it. This is not a 'glass half full, not half empty' approach: it is more of a 'there is a glass, and it is already half full' approach. Indeed, the baseline realities of the political nature of the UN play out less in terms of the overt politicisation of the human rights system as a whole but in more subtle and less visible ways which affect the ability of the bodies that are established by that system to protect human rights to undertake their work as efficiently and effectively as they might.

Various examples have been given already. Quite why it is necessary for all officially published SPT documentation to be made available in Mandarin Chinese and in Russian is, for example, questionable to say the least. Neither China nor Russia is a state party and neither has ever been one of its working languages. No SPT visit has ever been conducted in Chinese or in Russian, and it is highly improbable that it will be any time soon – if ever. So why do it? Because they are two of the six official UN languages (the others being Arabic, English, French and Spanish). While doubtless it is comforting to think that Mandarin Chinese and Russian speakers will be able to read any of the published reports relating to other countries and official general SPT documentation, this is likely to be a minority pastime among the population at large. It would certainly be far more beneficial for SPT reports to be available in, say, Portuguese, which is the language of several states parties and several hundreds of millions of people who fall within the Optional Protocol to the United Nations Convention against Torture (OPCAT) system. But that, of course, is completely out of the question.

This might just sound like 'nit-picking', until the actual costs of making these translations is taken into account. They soak up staggering amounts of the UN budget. Some years ago now, the official figure that we were given was that it cost US$2,000 to translate a single 500-word page of documentation[1] – that's $4 a word, or $40,000 for a standard SPT report, which are about 10,000 words. This can be roughly the cost of the visit to the country – or even more than the cost of some visits. Written summary records used to be made of the Plenary meetings of the SPT which might only appear years afterwards and which were rarely consulted. There were in addition verbatim records taken. Quite why it was necessary to produce the summary records as well, years after the event, was never clear. But it absorbed much time, effort – and money.

The 'standard package' of conference support for the Plenary meetings of the SPT held in Geneva was superb – but that standard package did not extend to supporting break-out groups or sub-committees meeting outside of the main committee room, or the fixed hours of 10.00–1.00 and 3.00–6.00 each day. Everything was geared towards the delivery of that standard operational model – and operating outside of it could be problematic. 'Reactive' and 'nimble' the system was not (and though many went to great lengths to try to be as flexible as possible, this was like watching a strong-man trying to bend an iron-bar). This is hardly unique to the UN, but the sheer scale of the UN magnified the difficulties and locked you into working practices which were not necessarily well suited for what you needed to achieve, and sometimes made it extremely difficult to do so.

It was the unexpected consequences of seemingly trivial things that irked the most. Perhaps one of the more irritating examples was that SPT documentation had initially been given a Committee against Torture reference number: our documents were styled 'CAT/OP/ ...'. So what? Well, this meant that the SPT Annual Report could not be published as a stand-alone document but only as an annex to the CAT Report. And as a UN Committee could only present one report to the General Assembly, this meant that the SPT Annual Report, although it was a completely separate report from a completely separate body, could not be made available in the meeting room for members of the UN 3rd Committee as it would have meant there were two Annual Reports under a CAT reference number – and that would never do. Doubtless members of the 3rd Committee could never have coped with such chaos and confusion! Of course, as Chair, I was able to go to New York to present that report to them orally, to take questions on that report from members of the Committee, but they could not have a hard copy of the report that I was talking about ... and so on, and on, and on ...

Yet all this must be put into perspective. If the SPT had not been operating within the UN framework, it is, in my view, inconceivable that it could have achieved what it has achieved. As I have already said, the power of the UN imprimatur is, in most countries, most of the time, simply astonishing. It opened doors that would otherwise have remained permanently closed to us (literally). It enabled meetings with high-level officials which otherwise would never have happened. It allowed us to draw on the entire apparatus of the various UN agencies, field missions and programmes operating in so many of the countries in which we visited places of detention, and which were a vital source of information, advice and practical support. Above all else, it enabled us to be serviced by a series of professional and often exceptionally talented and dedicated UN Secretariat members, many of whose commitment to their work in support of us defied all limits of reason and rationality. As a Committee, we, and certainly I, as Chair, were very fortunate indeed to be as well supported by our Secretariat as we were, even if I am absolutely sure that we failed to make our gratitude sufficiently clear at the time.

At the end of the day, the real problem in delivering the SPT mandate was what it was always going to be: money, or the lack of it. All these other issues of a largely bureaucratic nature would have been nothing more than minor irritations or inconveniences had there been a sufficiency of general resources to allow us to go about our work as we would have wished and as the OPCAT itself required. But there never was. Indeed, there was never anything approaching it.

There are three main elements to the SPT's preventive work: visits, supporting the establishment and operation of NPMs and contributing to the work of other bodies working in the area of torture prevention. As was explained in earlier chapters, the number of visits that the SPT conducted, but for a couple of years when it averaged about ten per year, has been inadequate. It reduced to almost zero in 2020–21 due to the COVID-19 pandemic – unlike the CPT in Europe, which was still able to carry out a reduced programme of international visiting. This is now recovering and on the cusp of improving, as the SPT was able to conduct eight visits in 2022,[2] the first full year of post-pandemic visiting, and another eight visits have so far been confirmed for 2023.[3] This could increase further, and that would be encouraging.

However, the SPT still does not have sufficient capacity to engage in direct discussions with states once its visit has ended, this usually being limited to rather formalistic and largely sterile exchanges of official documentation, sometimes supplemented by online meetings during Plenary sessions or unofficial contacts which lack the 'clout' of a more formal and official discussion regarding the implementation of recommendations. More worrying, it remains that case that most states do not really buy into the need for ongoing discussions between visits at all.

In addition, there is still no routine funding to support and develop the work of the SPT in relation to the establishment and functioning of NPMs, despite the near universal recognition that this is the single most important element of the OPCAT framework. This still tends to be seen as being more a matter of technical assistance which is best provided directly through the Office of the High Commissioner for Human Rights itself rather than being a job for the members of the SPT themselves, though some helpful collaborative work has taken place that has resulted in excellent guides[4] and some in-country assistance. Useful as this has been, it is still dabbling on the margins of what should be a discrete strand of work directly supported by the SPT Secretariat – something which its size and funding currently makes impossible.

As is the case when working within any organisational framework, there are operational constraints, and the UN being by far and away the single most important global inter-governmental organisation, tasked with ensuring the most ambitious set of goals ever given to any such body, it is unsurprising that there are constraints aplenty. However, all of this is easily outweighed by the authority that is invested in the SPT as a human rights body operating within the framework of the United Nations – and through the OPCAT this authority is extended to the NPMs established and operating within each OPCAT state party. This, I believe, is unique to the OPCAT system of torture prevention and its importance cannot be overstated. The frustrations that arise when working for prevention within the UN framework are largely the frustrations of not being able to do even more than is currently done to release the potential of that system. There is indeed so much more than can and should be done, and done better – but there always is and always will be.

What might be done next?

The most obvious thing that might be done is to increase the amount of money available to support the SPT's work, allowing it to undertake more visits and to be more thorough and systematic in how it is able structure meaningful dialogues with states concerning the implementation of its recommendations. There are very real practical limits to the number of SPT visits that can be undertaken each year, and I suspect that that figure is probably about ten. This may not be an adequate number, but if supplemented by other forms of operational change, then it is probably sufficient. A visit by the SPT should be an element of an ongoing relationship with each state party, conducted not according to some rather generalised cyclical approach, but undertaken when it makes sense to do it; when it can make a positive impact – or is necessary to try to force the pace of change. But this can only work if there is a sufficient 'density' of ongoing activity with each and every state party, as without this the decision to conduct a visit can be more a matter of guesswork than of intelligence. Good decisions need to be based on reliable information, and the SPT should be able to acquire more of this information for itself.

As a starting point, every newly ratifying state could receive a short visit, lasting no more than a day or so, from a member of the SPT accompanied by a member of the Secretariat, to introduce themselves and to establish contact with a senior national official who would be designated as a national OPCAT 'point of contact'. A national 'focal point' is currently appointed once a visit is announced and lasts for the duration of the visit, including its planning and preparation, but there is no reason why this could not be made into an ongoing and standard expectation for all ratifying states. In addition, an introductory visit of such a nature would provide an early opportunity to understand how the process of establishing the NPM was proceeding, and what, if any, input into that process it would be useful for the SPT to provide, and how this might best be done.

None of this would be particularly expensive and would have many benefits, the most important of which would be the clear demonstration that becoming a party to the OPCAT has consequences. But it would also show that the relationship between the SPT and the state party is meant to be, and should be, cooperative and collaborative, not combative and oppositional. It would set that relationship on a better footing than is currently the case, where initial introductions are made by letter and perhaps a short virtual discussion in the margins of a busy Plenary. It would show commitment to the process by both sides.

Similarly, after a visit has occurred, enabling a discussion to take place back in the country with those directly responsible for implementing the SPT's recommendations would be a very positive development. Currently, this sometimes happens on an ad hoc basis, but to build this into the standard working practices of the SPT would be very beneficial and, again, not necessarily particularly costly. A single such meeting might be all that is required to move that process forward.

The SPT has recently expressed the view that, if it were to have more meeting time in Geneva, it could have 'cyclical dialogues' with states concerning their implementation of recommendations.[5] This could be a very beneficial development, but it should supplement, and not supplant, in-country meetings. Switching to a more diplomatically driven, Geneva-based exercise might blur the difference between the SPT and the reporting process of other treaty bodies and diminish the effectiveness and distinctiveness of its work. It might be cheaper than holding in-country dialogues, but it carries other costs for the OPCAT system. Much better to work towards enhanced in-country talks with the in-country officials: that's where the problems are, and that is where the solutions must be found – not in the diplomatic bubble on the shores of Lake Geneva. It is all very well to acknowledge – as the SPT does – that this is not the best approach, and that it should be seen as a stopgap until it has the necessary support to enable it to take this work to the field.[6] But once things get established *in* Geneva, it is very difficult to get them *out* of Geneva – and stopgaps become full stops …

Once an NPM is established, it is vital that it feels that it has a place within the overall OPCAT system and is in regular contact with the SPT. Regular does not need to be frequent if there is no need for this, and the presentation of the NPM's annual report to the SPT presents an ideal opportunity for this. Many NPMs give copies of their annual reports to the SPT which are meant to be read by the country rapporteurs, and then discussed in the SPT's regional teams, to help inform their understanding of the work of the NPM and the situation within the country. However, this was not always done, or not always done thoroughly enough. Once again, developing a more effective and better-supported process around the relationship between the SPT and the NPMs would be to the benefit of both.

However, none of this can be done without increasing the size of the SPT Secretariat considerably, and this one of the most intractable problems of all. The SPT has said that it needs six professional staff and associated general staff in its Secretariat to support its latest proposals, accepting that these proposals in many ways fall short of what is called for.[7] In truth, this assessment – though doubtless at the outer edge of what might plausibly be sought – is laughable; frankly, it is ridiculous. Such a number would still only be about a third or less of the size of the European CPT's Secretariat which numbers in excess of 20. The current number of professional staff on the UN SPT's Secretariat oscillates between three and four at best. Six is indeed aspirational! However, unless and until the entire levels of staffing, and thus spending, in support of the entire UN human rights treaty bodies increases exponentially, even this modest increase is unlikely to happen in the regular run of things.

This is not an accident. It need to be said loud and clear that one of the ways in which states use their political muscle is to neuter the effectiveness of human rights bodies such as the SPT by keeping their metaphorical fingers firmly pressed on the fiscal jugular, allowing through a sufficient flow of funds to sustain life, but not to allow for very much more: it is all very carefully calibrated to allow for just 'enough' activity to be able to maintain the impression that the system is alive – but not enough to allow it to be 'alive and kicking'; after all, it is they who are the ones who would be kicked. This, I strongly suspect, is not going to change any time soon if states have their way. And in the UN, which is ultimately an inter-governmental organisation, they usually do.

As a result, further innovation is called for. Some UN special procedures mandate holders receive significant levels of support from external institutions, as do some of the other human rights treaty bodies. So should the SPT. This already happens in modest ways[8] but, welcome as this is, it does not stand comparison with the help given to some other UN Committees by others, who routinely organise events to follow up on their recommendations and work to secure they are implemented. Perhaps the difficulty is that while the concluding observations and recommendations of other treaty bodies are public, those of the SPT, at least at first, are not. There is, then, seemingly little incentive for NGOs and National Human Rights Institutions to organise events in which they cannot participate. This, perhaps, is a failing of their imagination – they do not have to be 'in the room' in order to be of assistance. I have sometimes suspected that the difficulty is that unless they *can* be in the room they generally do not really want to be. Nevertheless, it is genuinely difficult to expect others to support the implementation of recommendations which they simply do not know about because they are confidential: after all, you might not even agree with their content. I would be reluctant to do so myself, and so it is hardly fair to be critical of others who may have similar reservations.

Even confidential SPT reports can, however, be shared with the national NPM in confidence. It would be an excellent idea if, following the issuance of a report, and if it were appropriate to share it with that NPM, a 'tri-lateral' meeting could take place, comprising the state representatives, the SPT and the NPM, to consider the implementation of the recommendations. This would also allow the NPM to follow up with the state itself – after all, the SPT cannot be everywhere all the time. Such a meeting could help kick-start such a process. Although NPMs have occasionally been invited to the final meeting at the end of an SPT visit when the SPT presents to the state authorities its initial thoughts on what it has found, to the best of my knowledge no such joint meetings have ever taken place following the issuing of a report. Why not? And at the very least, if the SPT's proposal for holding cyclical dialogues in Geneva comes to pass, there seems to be no reason why the NPM could not be invited to them.

One could go further. Why limit such meetings to the delivery of visit reports? Might it not be possible for the SPT and NPM to meet with the state to discuss issues and concerns anyway? Why not? In Europe, an even more ambitious idea was once floated – that such meetings might take place including the European CPT as well; national prevention 'roundtables', with the NPM, CPT, SPT and national authorities in the room. A real alphabet soup, admittedly, but a potentially very powerful way of drawing together a series of essential but separate conservations into one place, rather than their being dispersed and potentially pulling in different directions.

Issues of confidentially can be overcome: indeed, the CPT and SPT have both agreed in principle to the mutual sharing of reports, in confidence, with the consent of the state[9] – though to the best of my knowledge, this have never actually happened. This simply highlights the extent to which there really are possibilities for coordinated action which could greatly enhance the overall impact of preventive endeavours but which, possibly for the want of imagination or simply of follow-through, has never come about. Gaining agreement to ambitious ideas is sometimes so taxing and time consuming that there is never any energy left to implement them, and things are left to carry on in the same old grooves, as if that energy and effort had never been expended.

Conclusion

It might have been nice to finish with some headline-grabbing major and transformative proposals that would change the face of torture prevention and set out new and ambitious agendas which, if only they were adopted, would tackle torture once and for all. But I cannot do so because there are none. Torture does not happen in ways that permit of this, nor are the causes of torture and ill-treatment such as to allow this. They are insidious temptations which lurk beneath the surface of all societies, and which can surface anywhere from time to time if we do not exercise continued vigilance against them. As was seen in earlier chapters, it is all too easy to believe that torture is a thing of the past, and not to acknowledge how easy it can be to resort to torture when we want to. Perhaps the absolute legal and moral opprobrium which we attach to torture suggests that we understand this all too well, and in its own way it is yet another 'tool of prevention'? But perhaps too our reluctance to condemn those that do resort to torture also reflects a realisation of this – and perhaps a desire to 'hedge our bets': what if *we* find ourselves wanting to do what *they* do? Is it too trite to suggest that torture is a reflection of a dark side of human nature, no more, and no less – and all the more intractable for that?

There are more ambitious ideas that could be pursued which might certainly help tackle torture and improve the international protection of human rights through the UN more generally. For example, I have come to believe that there is a pressing need to undertake a fundamental reappraisal of the structure of the UN Office of the High Commissioner. As currently conceived and structured, it is ill-suited to servicing the needs of the treaty body system because it is also the chief executive arm of the Human Rights Council, the membership of which comprises the very states with which the treaty bodies have to critically engage. There is a clear conflict of interests here. There is also a case to be made for transforming the entire way in which the UN's human rights work, and in particular the work of the independent and expert human rights treaty bodies, are funded, in order to lessen the insidious political control which is exercised by those who can control the cash. A better alternative might be a global human rights trust fund, managed by an independent board of trustees and solely focused on achieving human rights outcomes.

This is not the place to dwell on such schemes, desirable as they may be. This is partly because, if the root causes of torture are what I suggest they might be, then even these more 'ambitious' proposals cannot really begin to touch them either. And while it is probably true that changes of a fundamental nature such as these would help release the full preventive potential of the OPCAT, of the SPT and of the NPMs, such changes are unlikely to occur any time soon. No matter how desirable they might be, sweeping and dramatic solutions take a long time to come about and usually bring other problems in their wake. There are more pressing and practical things that can be done, and it is on these that our focus should fall, and they need not be put on hold while more visionary solutions are canvassed. The seemingly less ambitious and more technically focused ideas presented earlier are all capable of being achieved within existing systems and structures, and it is approaches such as these which offer the most realistic means of bringing about real improvements in torture prevention, and of doing so quickly.

As was said at the outset of this book, torture is the subject of more legal prohibitions than just about anything else, and this book has not attempted even to scratch the surface of the astonishing array of legal, practical and policy tools that now exist to try to make that prohibition a practical reality. Yet whether we are prepared to admit it or not, there always has been torture and ill-treatment and there always will be. To say this is not to be defeatist. Many things are illegal and considered morally and ethically abhorrent – yet they still happen. This does not make those practices acceptable or right. Nor does it mean that such practices must be tolerated. They remain wrong and they remain prohibited.

You cannot demonstrate that someone would not have been tortured or ill-treated if a particular preventive measure had been in place, or that a particular person has not been tortured or ill-treated because it was. Despite the constant calls for illustrations of successful prevention of this nature, it is almost impossible to do so. This is not because there are none, but because they are virtually impossible to give. What you can do is show that preventive measures have been put in place which should reduce the risk of torture or ill-treatment happening – even if they sometimes fail to do so. The very existence of the SPT and of the NPMs, their work, their now countless visits, interviews and recommendations and the changes to law and practice that have resulted from them are all examples of successful prevention, even if they cannot offer a guarantee of success.

Understood in this way, everything that has been described in this book is an example of successful prevention in action, as it is all the product of preventive intervention. However imperfect, even the very worst, the most unacceptable and the most shocking of the situations recounted, have all now been the subject of observation, comment and recommendation. They are known to those whose primary task is to seek to prevent them from happening in a way that simply was not known before, and this has set the preventive ball rolling, even if in too many cases it still has some way to roll.

Moreover, it has never been suggested that prevention will always prevent: the claim has always been that it will make torture less likely, and there *is* statistical evidence which supports this claim and thus that the possibility of preventing torture through the introduction of preventive safeguards is therefore real (Carver and Handley, 2016). This means that the tools that have been developed and which are embodied in the OPCAT do indeed have within them the potential to provide effective means of preventing and tackling torture and ill-treatment.

Deployed properly, I firmly believe that the OPCAT system has the potential to make a dramatic impact on the incidence of torture and ill-treatment, to have a transformational effect on the lives of those who are in detention and, it is important to add, on the lives of the many others who are touched by the fates and fortunes of those who are. I genuinely believe that such transformations have already begun to happen, as more and more NPMs are established and go about their work.

Changes to codes of criminal procedure, the introduction of preventive safeguards, to systems of legal aid, to medical services, to disciplinary regulations, to prison rules, to recruitment and training, to rules of evidence and the like all can make a major difference in practice, and this is why the SPT and NPMs so often make recommendations concerning such matters in response to what they see. There is also the need to deploy imagination and innovation to identify workable solutions to what are often deep-seated systemic problems. At times, all that is required is making sure that people are told to do their jobs properly. But far more difficult and fundamental shifts and changes in societal attitudes may also be required.

This is particularly true of attitudes towards the poor, the vulnerable and the marginalised within our societies, who, already being its victims, can find themselves at the mercy of those who can exercise power over them, and who so often abuse their power simply because they can. Then, torture prevention simply comes down to keeping on trying to do whatever you can to make sure that they can't. And if this is all that all of this achieves, then even if what is done is not enough, it is enough that it is done at all to make all this worthwhile.

Notes

1   In a report on the strengthening of the UN treaty body system in 2012, the then High Commissioner for Human Rights records that translating a 300-page document into five other UN official languages cost in the region of $560,000, based on an average full cost of translation, editing, referencing and quality control of between $1,900 and $2,000 per page (Pillay, 2012, p 54). Report by the UN High Commissioner for Human Rights, Navanethem Pillay, 'Strengthening the United Nations Human Rights Treaty Body System' (Geneva, Office of the High Commissioner of Human Rights, 2012).

2   These, in date order, were to Brazil, Tunisia, Argentina, Lebanon, Turkey, Ecuador, Australia, Bosnia–Herzegovina. See https://tbinternet.ohchr.org/_layouts/15/TreatyB odyExternal/CountryVisits.aspx?SortOrder=Chronological

3   The SPT announced on 30 June 2022 that in the first half of 2023 it was planning to visit Croatia, Madagascar, Nicaragua, and the State of Palestine (https://www.ohchr.org/en/press-releases/2022/06/un-torture-prevention-body-announces-visits-2023). It is worth pointing out that this means that it will finally have completed the backlog of visits which it had previously announced it was intending to conduct in 2019, and which were postponed for financial reasons, and in 2020, which were postponed due to COVID-19 restrictions. It will, then, have been over three years since the SPT has added substantial numbers of countries to its visiting programme. It is, then, not yet able to 'catch up' for the lost years, and probably never will. In November 2022, it added the names of a further six countries to that plan, these being Georgia, Guatemala, Kazakhstan, Mauritius, South Africa and Philippines – but at the same time announced it was unable to proceed with its plans to visit Nicaragua due to the failure of that state to cooperate, the first time such an admission has been made (https://www.ohchr.org/en/press-releases/2022/11/un-torture-prevention-body-announces-upcoming-visits-2023). At the same session, the OPCAT Article 16(4) procedure was used for the first time in relation to Nicaragua (see chapter 5). https://www.ohchr.org/en/statements/2022/11/nicaragua-two-un-rights-committees-deplore-refusal-cooperate-and-lack), underlining the gravity of the problem faced.

4   An excellent example being 'Preventing Torture: The Role of National Preventive Mechanisms; A Practical Guide', UN OHCHR Professional Training Series no 21 (2018).

5   'Statement of the Subcommittee on Prevention of Torture and Other Cruel, Inhuman or Degrading Treatment or Punishment on the 2020 Review of the Process of Strengthening the Human Rights Treaty Body System', 25th Annual Report of the Subcommittee on Prevention of Torture and Other Cruel, Inhuman or Degrading Treatment or Punishment, CAT/C/73/2, annex, paras 12–13.

6   'Statement of the Subcommittee on Prevention of Torture and Other Cruel, Inhuman or Degrading Treatment or Punishment on the 2020 Review of the Process of Strengthening the Human Rights Treaty Body System', 15th Annual Report of the Subcommittee on Prevention of Torture and Other Cruel, Inhuman or Degrading Treatment or Punishment, CAT/C/73/2, annex, para 11 makes it clear that it is advancing this proposal 'in the current context where post-visit on-site dialogues and/or follow-up visits are not feasible owing to the lack of appropriate financial and human resources'.

7   'Statement of the Subcommittee on Prevention of Torture and Other Cruel, Inhuman or Degrading Treatment or Punishment on the 2020 Review of the Process of Strengthening the Human Rights Treaty Body System', 15th Annual Report of the Subcommittee on Prevention of Torture and Other Cruel, Inhuman or Degrading Treatment or Punishment, CAT/C/73/2, annex, para 17.

8   For example, the Human Rights Implementation Centre at the University of Bristol for years helped by producing background briefs from open-source material for the SPT in advance of its visits, as have others.

9   As has been seen earlier, OPCAT Article 31 enjoins the SPT to cooperate with regional bodies with a similar mandate to its own. There is only one such body, the CPT, and in the summer of 2018 the CPT and SPT adopted mutually reflective positions on cooperative arrangements which were reflected in a public joint statement by their respective Chairs. This proposal was one of them. See 'United Nations and Council of Europe Torture Prevention Bodies to Strengthen Cooperation', Joint statement of 26 July 2018, available from: https://www.coe.int/en/web/cpt/-/united-nations-and-council-of-europe-torture-prevention-bodies-to-strengthen-cooperation

References

Alleg, H. (1958) *La Question*, Paris: Editions de Minuit.

APT (2003) *Preventing Torture in Africa: Proceedings of a Joint APT– ACHPR Workshop, Robben Island, South Africa 12–14 February 2002*, Geneva: Association for the Prevention of Torture.

Başoğlu, M. (2017) *Torture and Its Definition in International Law*, Oxford: Oxford University Press.

Bicknell, C., Evans, M.D. and Morgan, R. (2018) *Preventing Torture in Europe*, Strasbourg: Council of Europe Publishing.

Burgers, J.H. and Danelius, H. (1988) *The UN Convention against Torture: A Handbook to the Convention against Torture and Other Cruel, Inhuman or Degrading Treatment or Punishment*, Dordrecht: Martinus Nijhoff.

Carver, R. and Handley, L. (2016) *Does Torture Prevention Work?*, Liverpool: Liverpool University Press.

Cassese, A. (1989) 'A New approach to Human Rights: The European Convention for the Prevention of Torture', *American Journal of International Law*, 83(1): 128–53.

Cassese, A. (1996) *Inhuman States: Imprisonment, Detention and Torture in Europe Today*, Cambridge: Polity Press.

Corbain, I. (2012) *Cruel Britannia: A Secret History of Torture*, London: Portobello Books.

Cryer, R. (2020) 'International Law, Crime and Torture', in M.D. Evans and J. Modvig (eds) *Research Handbook on Torture: Legal and Medical Perspectives on Prohibition and Prevention*, Cheltenham: Edward Elgar, pp 288–313.

Daems, T. and Robert, L. (eds) (2017) *Europe in Prisons: Assessing the Impact of European Institutions on National Prison Systems*, London: Palgrave Macmillan.

Danner, M. (2004) *Torture and Truth: America, Abu Ghraib and the War on Terror*, London: Granta.

Dershowitz, A. (2002) *Why Terrorism Works: Understanding the Threat, Responding to the Challenge*, New Haven, CT: Yale University Press.

Evans, M.D. (2002) 'Getting to Grips with Torture', *International and Comparative Law Quarterly*, 51(2): 365–83.

Evans, M.D. (2020) 'The Prevention of Torture', in M.D. Evans and J. Modvig (eds) *Research Handbook on Torture: Legal and Medical Perspectives on Prohibition and Prevention*, Cheltenham: Edward Elgar, pp 258–87.

Evans, M.D. (2021) 'The United Nations and Human Rights: Reform through Review?', in J. Hartmann and U. Khaliq (eds) *The Achievements of International Law: Essays in Honour of Robin Churchill*, Oxford: Hart Publishing, pp 85–120.

Evans, M.D. and Morgan, R. (1998) *Preventing Torture: A Study of the European Convention for the Prevention of Torture and Inhuman or Degrading Treatment of Punishment*, Oxford: Clarendon Press.

Evans, M.D. and Haenni-Dale, C. (2004) 'Preventing Torture? The Development of the Optional Protocol to the UN Convention against Torture', *Human Rights Law Review*, 4(1): 19–55.

Farrell, M. (2020) 'The Ticking Bomb Scenario: Evaluating Torture as an Interrogation Method', in M.D. Evans and J. Modvig (eds) *Research Handbook on Torture: Legal and Medical Perspectives on Prohibition and Prevention*, Cheltenham: Edward Elgar, pp 10–41.

Freedman, R. (2020) 'The Human Rights Council', in F. Mégret and P. Alston (eds) *The United Nations and Human Rights: A Critical Appraisal* (2nd edn), Oxford: Oxford University Press, pp 181–238.

Gautier, J.-J. (1980) 'Torture: How to Make the International Convention Effective', Geneva: International Commission of Jurists/Swiss Committee against Torture.

Ginbar, Y. (2008) *Why Not Torture Terrorists? Moral, Practical and Legal Aspects of the 'Ticking Bomb' Justification for Torture*, Oxford: Oxford University Press.

Ginbar, Y. (2017) 'Making Human Rights Sense of the Definition of Torture', in M. Başoğlu (ed) *Torture and Its Definition in International Law*, Oxford: Oxford University Press, pp 273–314.

Greenberg, K. (ed) (2006) *The Torture Debate in America*, Cambridge: Cambridge University Press.

Haenni, C. (1007) *20 Ans Consacrés à la realisation d'une Idée*, Geneva: Association for the Prevention of Torture.

Heyns, C., Rueda, C. and du Plessis, D. (2020) 'Torture and Ill Treatment: The United Nations Human Rights Committee', in M.D. Evans and J. Modvig (eds) *Research Handbook on Torture: Legal and Medical Perspectives on Prohibition and Prevention*, Cheltenham: Edward Elgar, pp 106–27.

Iacopico, V (2020) 'Medico-legal Documentation of Torture and Ill Treatment', in M.D. Evans and J. Modvig (eds) *Research Handbook on Torture: Legal and Medical Perspectives on Prohibition and Prevention*, Cheltenham: Edward Elgar, pp 455–77.

Kittichaisaree, K. (2018) *The Obligation to Extradite or Prosecute*, Oxford: Oxford University Press.

Langbein, J.H. (1977) *Torture and the Law of Proof*, Chicago: Chicago University Press.

Lauterpacht, H. (2013 [1945]) *An International Bill of Rights of Man*, Oxford: Oxford University Press.

Levinson, S. (ed) (2006) *Torture: A Collection*, Oxford: Oxford University Press.

Long, D. and Murray, R. (2012) 'Ten Years of the Robben Island Guidelines and Prevention of Torture in Africa: For What Purpose?', *African Human Rights Law Journal*, 12(2): 311–47.

McGlynn, C. (2009) 'Rape, Torture and the European Convention on Human Rights', *International and Comparative Law Quarterly*, 58(3): 565–95.

Mégret, F. and Alston, P. (eds) (2020) *The United Nations and Human Rights: A Critical Appraisal* (2nd edn), Oxford: Oxford University Press.

Méndez, J. and Nicolescu, A. (2020) 'The Mandate of the Special Rapporteur on Torture: Role, Contributions, and Impact', in M.D. Evans and J. Modvig (eds) *Research Handbook on Torture: Legal and Medical Perspectives on Prohibition and Prevention*, Cheltenham: Edward Elgar, pp 154–76.

Modvig, J. and Quiroga, J. (2020) 'Torture Methods and Their Health Impacts', in M.D. Evans and J. Modvig (eds) *Research Handbook on Torture: Legal and Medical Perspectives on Prohibition and Prevention*, Cheltenham: Edward Elgar, pp 410–31.

Morgan, R. and Evans, M.D. (eds) (1999) *Protecting Prisoners: The Standards of the European Committee for the Prevention of Torture in Context*, Oxford: Oxford University Press.

Morgan, R. and Evans, M.D. (2001) *Combatting Torture in Europe*, Strasbourg: Council of Europe Publishing.

Murray, R. (2008) 'National Preventive Mechanisms under the Optional Protocol to the Torture Convention: One Size Does Not Fit All', *Netherlands Quarterly of Human Rights*, 26(4): 485–516.

Murray, R., Steinerte, E., Evans, M.D. and Hallo de Wolf, A. (2011) *The Optional Protocol to the UN Convention against Torture*, Oxford: Oxford University Press.

Mute, L. (2020) 'Ensuring Freedom from Torture under the African Human Rights System', in M.D. Evans and J. Modvig (eds) *Research Handbook on Torture: Legal and Medical Perspectives on Prohibition and Prevention*, Cheltenham: Edward Elgar, pp 227–57.

Nowak, M. (2018) *Torture: An Expert's Confrontation with an Everyday Evil*, Philadelphia: Pennsylvania University Press.

Nowak, M., Birk, M. and Monina, G. (2019) *The United Nations Convention against Torture: A Commentary* (2nd edn), Oxford: Oxford University Press.

Office of the High Commissioner for Human Rights (2018) 'Preventing Torture: The Role of National Preventive Mechanisms; A Practical Guide', Professional Training Series no 21, Geneva: OHCHR.

Pérez-Sales, P. (2017) *Psychological Torture: Definition, Evaluation and Measurement*, London: Routledge.

Pérez-Sales, P. (2020) 'Psychological Torture', in M.D. Evans and J. Modvig (eds) *Research Handbook on Torture: Legal and Medical Perspectives on Prohibition and Prevention*, Cheltenham: Edward Elgar, pp 432–54.

Peters, E. (1996) *Torture*, Philadelphia: Pennsylvania University Press.

Pillay, N. (2012) 'Report by the UN High Commissioner for Human Rights, Navanethem Pillay, Strengthening the United Nations Human Rights Treaty Body System', Geneva: Office of the High Commissioner of Human Rights.

Rejali, D. (2007) *Torture and Democracy*, Princeton: Princeton University Press.

Rodley, N.S. (2002) 'The Definition(s) of Torture in International Law', *Current Legal Problems*, 55(1): 467–93.

Rodley, N.S. (2006) 'The Prohibition of Torture: Absolute Means Absolute', *Denver Journal of International Law & Policy*, 34(1): 145–60.

Rodley, N.S. (2009) 'Reflections on Working for the Prevention of Torture', *Essex Human Rights Law Review*, 6(1): 21–30.

Rodley, N.S. and Pollard, M. (2009) *The Treatment of Prisoners under International Law* (2nd edn), Oxford: Oxford University Press.

Rodríguez-Pinzón, D. (2020) 'The Prohibition of Torture and Cruel, Inhuman or Degrading Treatment or Punishment in the Inter-American Human Rights System: Systems, Methods and Recent Trends', in M.D. Evans and J. Modvig (eds) *Research Handbook on Torture: Legal and Medical Perspectives on Prohibition and Prevention*, Cheltenham: Edward Elgar, pp 203–26.

Scarry, E (1985) *The Body in Pain*, Oxford: Oxford University Press.

Steinerte, E. (2014) 'The Jewel in the Crown and Its Three Guardians: Independence of National Preventive Mechanisms under the Optional Protocol to the UN Torture Convention', *Human Rights Law Review*, 41(1): 1–29.

Waldron, J. (2010) *Torture, Terror and Trade-Offs: Philosophy for the White House*, Oxford: Oxford University Press.

Index

References to endnotes show both the page number and the note number (231n3).

Printed in the USA
CPSIA information can be obtained
at www.ICGtesting.com
CBHW052101161023
1371CB00007B/325

9 781529 225693